Cambridge English
First for Schools

FIRST CERTIFICATE IN ENGLISH FOR SCHOOLS FCE

Teacher's Book 2nd Edition

T0346201

CENGAGE
Learning·

Australia • Brazil • Japan • Korea • Mexico • Singapore • Spain • United Kingdom • United States

CENGAGE
Learning®

Cambridge English First for Schools Practice Tests Teacher's Book Second Edition

Publisher: Sharon Jervis

Content Project Manager: Jon Ricketts

Cover Designer: Ken Vail Graphic Design Ltd

Compositor: Cenveo Publisher Services

Acknowledgements

Thanks to signature manuscripts for their help with the production of this title

Edited by Carole Hughes

Audio produced by Liz Hammond

Recorded at GFS-PRO Studio and Motivation Sound Studios.

Mixed at GFS-PRO Studio by George Flamouridis.

ISBN: 978-1-4080-9601-7

National Geographic Learning
Cheriton House, North Way, Andover, Hampshire, SP10 5BE United Kingdom

Cengage Learning is a leading provider of customized learning solutions with office locations around the globe, including Singapore, the United Kingdom, Australia, Mexico, Brazil and Japan. Locate our local office at **international.cengage.com/region**

Cengage Learning products are represented in Canada by Nelson Education Ltd.

Visit National Geographic Learning online at **ngl.cengage.com**
Visit our corporate website at **cengage.com**

Photo Credits

The publishers would like to thank Shutterstock for permission to reprint the majority of photos in this book. Further acknowledgment goes to:

p. 40: Shutterstock (for photo of Ashley Tisdale by Paul Smith); **p. 42:** Shutterstock (for photo of flash mob by Eugenio Marongiu); **p. 89:** Corbis (for photo of Leaning Tower of Suurhusen, Germany); **p. 89:** Shutterstock (for photo of Capital Gate in Abu Dhabi by hainaultphoto); **p. 111:** ALAMY (for photo of Aye-Aye Lemur); **p. 143:** Shutterstock (for photo of Concord by Keith Naylor); **p. 182:** Shutterstock (for photo of Mona Lisa by kai hecker); **p.182:** Shutterstock (for photo of Kolkata ICT conference by arindambanerjee); **p. 182:** Shutterstock (for photo of Milan sculpture gallery by Adriano Castelli); **p. 196:** Shutterstock (for photo of stilt dancers by Kamira).

Illustrations

Kate Rochester c/o Pickled ink

Contents

Introduction

Cambridge English: First for Schools Exam Overview

Cambridge English: First for Schools, which is also known as *First Certificate in English (FCE) for Schools*, and is produced by University of Cambridge ESOL Examinations, is an internationally recognised exam for students at Level B2 of the Common European Framework of Reference for Languages.

The *First for Schools* exam has 4 papers: Paper 1 Reading and Use of English, Paper 2 Writing, Paper 3 Listening, and Paper 4 Speaking. Papers 1 – 3 are administered in one session. Paper 4 Speaking is administered in a separate session, usually on a different day, with two examiners and two candidates. The papers are structured as follows:

Paper 1 Reading and Use of English

Timing	Task	Task focus	Scoring
1 hour 15 minutes	**Part 1** A modified cloze test, consisting of a text with 8 gaps followed by 8 4-option multiple-choice items	Lexical, lexico-grammatical	1 mark each
	Part 2 A modified open cloze test, consisting of a text with 8 gaps	Grammatical, lexico-grammatical	1 mark each
	Part 3 A text with 8 gaps, where each gap corresponds to a word The stems of the missing words are given beside the text and must be changed to form the missing word	Lexical, lexico-grammatical	1 mark each
	Part 4 6 separate questions, each with a lead-in sentence and a gapped second sentence to be completed in 2-5 words, one of which is a given key word	Lexical, grammatical	2 marks each
	Part 5 A text followed by 6 4-option multiple-choice questions	Understanding detail, opinion, gist, attitude, purpose, main ideas, meaning from context, text organisation features (comparison, reference, implication, etc)	2 marks each
	Part 6 A text from which 6 sentences have been removed and placed after it in a jumbled order, together with an extra sentence	Understanding text structure, cohesion and coherence	2 marks each
	Part 7 A text or several short texts preceded by 10 multiple-matching questions	Understanding specific information, detail, opinion, attitude	1 mark each

Paper 2 Writing

Timing	Task	Task focus	Scoring
1 hour 20 minutes	**Part 1** One compulsory task of 140 – 190 words Task type: essay	Agreeing or disagreeing with a statement, giving information, giving an opinion, giving reasons, comparing and contrasting ideas and opinions, drawing a conclusion	Each part carries equal marks (see below for marking criteria)
	Part 2 One task of 140 – 190 words from 4 choices Questions 2 – 4: Possible task types: article, letter/email, review, story Question 5: Two options based on a set text Possible task types: article, essay, letter, review	Advising, comparing, describing, explaining, expressing opinions, justifying, recommending	

Paper 3 Listening

Timing	Task	Task focus	Scoring
40 minutes approx. (each part is heard twice)	**Part 1** 8 short unrelated extracts from monologues or conversations with 1 3-option multiple-choice question for each extract	Understanding genre, identifying speaker feeling, attitude, topic, opinion, purpose, agreement between speakers, gist and detail	1 mark each
	Part 2 A monologue with 10 sentence completion questions	Understanding detail, specific information, stated opinion	
	Part 3 5 short related monologues with 5 multiple-matching questions	Understanding gist, detail, function, purpose, attitude, opinion, relationship, topic, place, situation, genre, agreement	
	Part 4 A monologue or conversation with 7 3-option multiple-choice questions	Understanding opinion, attitude, gist, main ideas, specific information	

Introduction

Paper 4 Speaking

Timing*	Task	Task focus	Scoring
2 minutes	**Part 1 Interview** A conversation between the examiner and each candidate (spoken questions)	Ability to use social and interactional English and give basic personal information (about school, leisure time, future plans, etc)	(see below for marking criteria)
4 minutes	**Part 2 Long Turn** An individual 1-minute long turn comparing two photographs for each candidate, with a brief 30-second response from the second candidate (visual and written prompts, with spoken questions)	Ability to organise a larger unit of discourse; comparing, describing and expressing opinions	
4 minutes	**Part 3 Collaborative task** A two-way conversation between the candidates (written prompts, with spoken questions)	Ability to sustain an interaction, exchanging ideas, expressing and justifying opinions, agreeing and/or disagreeing, suggesting, speculating, evaluating, reaching a decision through negotiation, etc	
4 minutes	**Part 4 Discussion** A discussion related to the topic of Part 3 (spoken questions)	Ability to engage in an in-depth discussion (expressing and justifying opinions, agreeing and/or disagreeing and speculating)	

* This assumes two examiners (one interlocutor who speaks with the candidates, and one who silently assesses) and two candidates. In cases where there is an uneven number of candidates at an exam centre, the final Speaking test of the session is taken by three candidates together, with a total time of twenty minutes rather than fourteen.

Marking and scoring

Each paper is worth 40 marks, so the overall total is out of 200. Each paper is graded A – E, with a C grade being satisfactory. However, it is not necessary for a candidate to gain a satisfactory level in each paper to get the 60% needed to pass the whole exam.

The standardised scores are given out of 100.

Grade A = 80 – 100   Grade B = 75 – 79   Grade C = 60 – 74   Grade D = 55 – 59   Grade E = 54 or below

Certificates are issued to candidates gaining a passing grade (A, B or C). Certificates are not issued to candidates awarded a failing grade (D and E).

Marking criteria for Writing

Each piece of writing is assessed with reference to two mark schemes: one based on the examiner's overall impression (The General Impression Mark Scheme), the other on the requirements of the particular task (The Task Specific Mark Scheme). A band from 0 – 5 is awarded depending on how well the candidate performs in terms of content, organisation and cohesion, range of structures and vocabulary, register and format, and target reader indicated in the task.

Marking criteria for Speaking

The interlocutor awards an impression mark for Global Achievement.
The Assessor awards candidates a band from 0 – 5 depending on how well they perform over the whole test in terms of four criteria:

• Grammar and vocabulary – How accurate and appropriate is the candidate's range of grammatical forms and vocabulary?

• Discourse management – How well are the candidate's utterances linked to form coherent, relevant, logical speech, without too much hesitation?

• Pronunciation – How well does the candidate produce sounds and use stress and intonation to make what they say understandable?

• Interactive communication – How well does the candidate participate in and develop interactions?

Contents of the book

This book contains eight full practice tests for the *Cambridge English: First for Schools* exam. There is also a section-by-section introduction to the test which explains what candidates need to do in each section and what the focus of each section is. The first three tests in the book also contain useful guidance and tips for candidates.

Guidance for candidates

These sections are designed to help you achieve the best possible results by giving you an overview of the different parts of the exam and what is expected from you in each one. There is valuable information on the exam format and length, type of questions and the skills that you need in order to do well.

Tips

These sections focus more closely on the types of questions you will face in each part of the exam. The tips break down the structure of individual questions and show you how the questions actually work. They show you what you need to look for and be careful of. They remind you of the most important things to think about in each part of the exam. They explain why certain answers are correct and why others may look right but are in fact wrong. You can use these tips to become familiar with each part of the exam and so complete the tasks with more confidence.

Glossary

There is a glossary at the back of the book giving definitions of some words and phrases you may not know, including phrasal verbs and expressions.

You will often find that you can answer a question even if you don't know the meaning of a particular word or phrase. Maybe you can guess the meaning from the context or the question may not require you to actually know the meaning. Try to answer the questions in these practice tests before you look up the meanings of any unknown items in the glossary.

The words and phrases in the glossary are in the order you will meet them in the book.

Audio CDs

The CDs that come with this book have recordings which are just like the ones in the actual exam and give you valuable practice for the listening paper. Remember the listening paper has the same marks as the other four parts of the exam.

Cambridge English: First for Schools

The *Cambridge English: First for Schools* exam tests the practical language skills you need when using English as an international system of communication for travel, work or study in an English-speaking environment. Each exam covers all four language skills: listening, reading, writing and speaking, and you have to complete tasks which reflect real life. There is also the Use of English part of the Reading and Use of English paper which tests your ability to use structures and language systems. It tests your knowledge of vocabulary, word formation, grammar, syntax, punctuation and discourse structure – the way texts hang together and are meaningful.

The topics in the tests are selected to be interesting to you, and the practice you will get will be useful to you even if you are not actually going to take the exam.

Successful candidates in the exam will be at least at an upper-intermediate level, able to use English independently in a variety of situations. These practice tests, together with the guidance, tips and glossary sections, will help you develop your confidence in English and be ready to show what you can do.

Practice Test 1

READING AND USE OF ENGLISH PART 1

For questions **1 – 8**, read the text below and decide which answer (**A, B, C** or **D**) best fits each gap. There is an example at the beginning (**0**).

Example:

0 A displayed   **B** shown   **C** presented   **D** known

0	A	B	C	D

Social media in schools

Good news for students! New research has **(0)** _____ that there are benefits to allowing students to access Internet-based social media, such as blogs, websites and student-friendly social networking sites, while at school. Students who do so complete more assignments, get better marks and **(1)** _____ classes more often. Because students are **(2)** _____ to them in their free time, social media sites and apps can **(3)** _____ a great way for them to learn.

One of the many positive aspects of the Internet is the **(4)** _____ variety of educational content available online. As well as encyclopaedias and dictionaries, there are websites which students can access for virtually every subject they study. Content **(5)** _____ from technology and literature to fashion and the arts. Teachers can also encourage students to read particular news websites and write reports **(6)** _____ on what they've read.

Of course, there are risks **(7)** _____ with Internet access, particularly in terms of restricting inappropriate content. Having said that, there are safe, free social media apps and programs available, many of which are specifically **(8)** _____ for doing assignments and other schoolwork. If social media applications in schools are used properly, the benefits seem to be far greater than the drawbacks.

1	**A** visit	**B** contribute	**C** participate	**D** attend
2	**A** joined	**B** entertained	**C** attracted	**D** called
3	**A** include	**B** provide	**C** donate	**D** contain
4	**A** long	**B** open	**C** wide	**D** high
5	**A** ranges	**B** points	**C** applies	**D** reaches
6	**A** set	**B** concerning	**C** regarding	**D** based
7	**A** associated	**B** put	**C** named	**D** placed
8	**A** drawn	**B** designed	**C** done	**D** planned

GUIDANCE FOR CANDIDATES

There are seven parts to the Reading and Use of English paper. You have 1 hour and 15 minutes for this paper. To do well, you need to have a good feel for the language. When you write an answer, say to yourself silently: *Does that sound right in my head?* The way you're going to get a feel for natural sounding English is by reading English, listening to it and using it yourself.

When you're learning words, always note them down with any words or forms that go with them, eg *interested in (+ ing), keen on (+ ing), avoid (+ ing), manage to do, work hard.*

Try and learn the difference between words with similar meanings, eg *hit, punch, slap* and *tap.* Also, learn words in lexical sets, eg words for ways of looking such as *stare, glare* and *gaze,* or words for the weather such as *cloudy, misty* and *foggy.*

Many words have a base form and can be changed in different ways, eg *load* can be a noun and a verb and from this stem we can have *upload, download, overload, loading, loaded* and *unload.* Note down such words with the way they can be changed. When you learn expressions, group them with other ways of saying the same thing, eg *on my own* and *by myself.* This will be useful for Part 4.

Remember you've got 1 hour and 15 minutes to complete the seven sections of the Reading and Use of English paper and transfer your answers to the answer sheet. A correct answer in Parts 1, 2, 3 and 7 gets one mark. A correct answer in Part 4 gets one or two marks (one mark if you get half of it right, two marks if you get it completely right) and a correct answer in Parts 5 and 6 gets two marks.

All the texts in the Reading and Use of English paper have got titles. They are there to give you the main theme of the text. Each part has an example (0) to show you what to do. Do not write the example answer on the answer sheet.

It's a good idea to read through each text in the Reading and Use of English paper to get an idea of what each is about before you start answering the questions.

Remember to write your answers to Parts 2, 3 and 4 in pencil and in CAPITAL LETTERS. There may be more than one correct answer to a question in Parts 2 and 4, eg *that* or *which,* but you must only write one answer. Correct spelling and clear handwriting is important. For Parts 1, 5, 6 and 7, where you have to mark a lozenge, use a pencil and shade in the lozenge completely. Make sure you put your answers next to the correct number on the answer sheet. Be especially careful if you don't answer a particular question. If you write an answer and then change your mind and want to write a different answer, rub out the first answer and write the new one.

Part 1 consists of a text with eight gaps followed by eight, four-option multiple-choice items (plus an example). For each gap you have to decide which of the four words or phrases is correct. Each correct answer gets one mark.

This part tests your knowledge of individual words and also words with the prepositions, adverbs and verb forms that follow them. Your knowledge of phrasal verbs is often tested in this part. Option choices may also be words with similar meanings, eg *total, amount, number* and *lot* or similar functions, eg *Since, Although, Despite* and *However.*

It's not enough to know the meanings of words; you have to know how they are used, so learn words in phrases and remember what grammar and which other words go with them.

Quickly read the text through first – ignoring the gaps – to get a general idea of what it's about.

Read the words that come before and after each gap. Sometimes the preposition or adverb following a gap determines the correct option. For example, in question 6 here, only one of the four options is followed by the preposition *on.*

A good thing about Part 1 is that you don't have to come up with your own answers. The answer is given to you; you just need to find it. As with all multiple-choice tests, always put an answer even if you're just guessing – you may be lucky.

Practice Test 1

READING AND USE OF ENGLISH PART 2

For questions **9 – 16**, read the text below and think of the word which best fits each gap. Use only **one** word in each gap. There is an example at the beginning (**0**).

Write your answers **IN CAPITAL LETTERS**.

Example: | **0** | *B* | *E* |

It smells like heaven!

They can **(0)** _*BE*_ sold in many different kinds of bottles. Some smell nice, others smell too strong; some are made from flowers and others consist **(9)** _*OF*_ spices and oils. But when did people actually start using perfumes?

In ancient times, the Egyptians were famous **(10)** _*FOR*_ their scents and used them primarily in religious rituals. They believed the gods would be kinder when people smelled nice and that going to heaven depended on **(11)** _*HOW*_ strong the perfume was. When archaeologists opened Tutankhamun's tomb in the early 1920s, there was still a trace of the strong fragrance from the aromatic oils surrounding the body - **(12)** _*EVEN*_ after more than 3,000 years!

The Egyptian art of perfumery was passed down to the western world by the Greeks and Romans. Although it prospered in many European countries, it was France **(13)** _*THAT/WHICH*_ became the capital of cosmetics manufacture between the 16th and 17th centuries. **(14)** _*ONE*_ of the reasons perfumes became so popular in those days was that rich people didn't wash often, and had unpleasant body odours to hide.

Today, most of the better-known fashion houses sell a wide variety of perfumes in fancy packaging and **(15)** _*AT/FOR*_ quite high prices. **(16)** _*DESPITE*_ the fact that 100ml of perfume by Calvin Klein, for instance, costs at least €50, many young people consider it a must-have.

GUIDANCE FOR CANDIDATES

In Part 2 you also have a text with eight gaps (plus an example), but here you have to think of a word that will fill each gap correctly. Each correct answer gets one mark.

In this part, all the gaps can be filled with short, simple words such as prepositions – *on, at;* articles – *the, an;* linkers – *which, so;* auxiliaries – *must, did* and verb forms – *going, went.* A gap might need completing with a word in a collocation or set phrase, eg *Have a nice day.*

Quickly read the text through first – ignoring the gaps – to get a general idea of what it's about. Remember to read the title, too.

If you're not sure of the answer, ask yourself: *What are they testing here?* The example (0) in this Part 2, is testing whether the candidate knows that modals such as *can* are followed by the bare infinitive, and that here the bare infinitive is *be* because this is part of the verb *to sell* in the passive.

Remember that if you're completing a gap with a verb, it should agree with its subject, eg *We work (not works) hard every day.*

Don't write abbreviations such as *sthg* for *something* and remember that contractions such as *don't* and *won't* count as two words, so you can't use them. (The exception is *can't = cannot,* which counts as one word.)

If you're really not sure of an answer, make a guess – don't leave any gaps blank. Remember that you don't lose marks for incorrect answers.

For some gaps, there may be more than one possible correct word, but you can only write one word as your answer.

Once you've filled all the gaps, read the text through again inserting the correct word in each gap. For each gap, ask yourself: *Does the word I've chosen make sense logically, and does it make sense grammatically?*

READING AND USE OF ENGLISH `PART 3`

For questions **17 – 24**, read the text below. Use the word given in capitals at the end of some of the lines to form a word that fits in the gap **in the same line**. There is an example at the beginning (0).

Write your answers **IN CAPITAL LETTERS**.

Example: | 0 | P | R | O | F | E | S | S | I | O | N | A | L | L | Y | | | | | |

Computer safety

People use computers everywhere these days – in schools, offices and at home. But whether it is used **(0)** _PROFESSIONALLY_ or for entertainment or education, a computer needs the best **(17)** _PROTECTION_ against hackers and infections, as there is always the danger that a virus will attack your PC. In addition to the wide range of software you can buy, there are also many free Internet **(18)** _SECURITY_ programs available to **(19)** _DOWNLOAD_ which are just as good. However, all virus software must be constantly updated and occasionally the updates themselves can cause the very problem they are supposed to prevent.

PROFESSION
PROTECT

SECURE
LOAD

The effects of a virus can be extremely dramatic. A quiet computer can become very **(20)** _NOISY_, and a fast computer can start running very slowly. At this point, the computer must be **(21)** _DISCONNECTED_ from the Internet as quickly as possible, unless the screen has **(22)** _FROZEN_, in which case the only thing to do is unplug it from the **(23)** _ELECTRICITY/ELECTRICAL_ supply. An infected computer should be taken to a qualified technician, who will be able to assess the damage. **(24)** _UNFORTUNATELY_, some viruses can cause the loss of all the information on a computer, which is why it is so important to guard against them.

NOISE
CONNECT

FREEZE
ELECTRIC

FORTUNE

GUIDANCE FOR CANDIDATES

In Part 3 there are eight gaps in a text and eight words in capital letters at the end of some of the lines (plus an example). Where there is a gap in the text you have to change the form of the word in capitals to fill in the gap in that line. Each correct answer gets one mark.

Quickly read the text through first – ignoring the gaps – to get a general idea of what it's about. Remember to read the title, too.

For each gap, always read the text before and after the gap to get the meaning and context before you decide how to change the word in capitals so it fits. For example, in question 24 here, we can only work out if *FORTUNATELY* or *UNFORTUNATELY* fits by reading on to see if it's talking about something positive or negative.

If you're not sure of the answer, ask yourself if the missing word should be a verb, a noun, an adjective or an adverb. Does it need to be in the negative or the plural?

Often you will have to change the word by putting a prefix, eg *DIS-, UN-* or *IM-*, or a suffix, eg *-LESS, -ABLE* or *-FUL*, but sometimes an adjective such as STRONG needs to be changed to a noun such as *STRENGTH*.

For some gaps, there may be more than one possible correct word, but you can only write one word as your answer.

If you're really not sure of an answer, make a guess – don't leave any gaps blank. Remember that you don't lose marks for incorrect answers.

Be very careful with your spelling in this part, and remember to write your answers in capital letters.

Once you've filled all the gaps, read the text through again inserting the correct word in each gap. For each gap, ask yourself: *Does the word I've chosen make sense logically, and does it make sense grammatically?*

READING AND USE OF ENGLISH `PART 4`

For questions **25 – 30**, complete the second sentence so that it has a similar meaning to the first sentence, using the word given. **Do not change the word given.** You must use between **two** and **five** words, including the word given. Here is an example (**0**).

Example:

0   Mary's mother made her tidy her room before she went out.

   WAS

   Mary ___*WAS MADE TO TIDY*___ her room by her mother before she went out.

The gap can be filled by the words 'was made to tidy', so you write:

Example: | **0** | | *WAS MADE TO TIDY* |

Write **only** the missing words **IN CAPITAL LETTERS**.

---

25   Nigel wanted to know if I resembled my mother or my father.
   LOOK
   'Who ___*DO YOU LOOK LIKE*___, your mother or your father?' asked Nigel.

26   My dad's car is being repaired by a local mechanic.
   HAVING
   My dad ___*IS/'S HAVING HIS CAR REPAIRED*___ by a local mechanic.

27   That was the funniest film I've ever seen!
   NEVER
   I ___*HAVE/'VE NEVER SEEN A FUNNIER*___ film!

28   The weather was so terrible that we didn't go out.
   SUCH
   It ___*WAS SUCH TERRIBLE WEATHER (THAT)*___ we stayed in.

29   Can you please turn the music down a bit?
   MIND
   Would ___*YOU MIND TURNING*___ the music down a bit?

30   I saw Carol and Diane sitting by themselves in the café.
   OWN
   I saw Carol and Diane sitting ___*ON THEIR OWN*___ in the café.

GUIDANCE FOR CANDIDATES

In Part 4, there are six sentences with a key word and a second gapped sentence (plus an example). You have to use the key word without changing it in any way to complete the gap in the second sentence. You can only fill the gap with between two and five words including the key word. Each correct answer gets two marks, but it's possible to get one mark if your answer is partly correct.

This part tests how well you can express the same meaning in two different ways. What you have to do here is to paraphrase – put things in other words, eg

I regret doing it. **WISH**
I wish I hadn't done it.

You may have to change something from active to passive, direct to reported speech or use a phrasal verb instead of a one-word verb in the answer, but the meaning of the second sentence must always be the same as the first. Make sure all the information in the first sentence appears in the second sentence. If it doesn't, you've done something wrong.

Although the instructions say write between two and five words, it's very unusual for an answer to be only two words. Answers are almost always at least three words. In your answer, only write the two to five words needed to complete the gap. Don't write the whole sentence.

Remember that contractions such as *don't* count as two words, but *can't (cannot)* counts as one word. If you write more than five words, your answer is marked as wrong.

If you're not sure of an answer, ask yourself: *What are they testing here?* Usually, they're testing two things. In the example sentence (0) here, the first thing they're testing is whether you're able to take an active verb and make it passive. The second thing they're testing is the knowledge that there's something unusual about the verb *make*, in that in the active it's *make someone **do** something* but in the passive it's *be made **to do** something*.

If you're really not sure of an answer, make a guess – don't leave any gaps blank. Remember that you don't lose marks for incorrect answers, and that you can get one mark for getting part of the answer right.

READING AND USE OF ENGLISH PART 5

Questions 31 – 36

You are going to read a magazine article about bags. For questions **31 – 36**, choose the answer (**A, B, C or D**) which you think fits best according to the text.

Paper or plastic?

There was a time when a trip to the supermarket in the United States often ended with a seemingly simple question from the cashier: 'Paper or plastic?' It was a question customers expected and one they'd already prepared an answer for, perhaps when asking themselves the more general question: 'What can I do to help the environment?'

Now it seems that the bag providers of the world have sat down with the same question and decided to answer it for us. At least on high streets in many European cities, paper bags are in abundance and plastic ones have disappeared. But has the right decision been made? New studies show that perhaps we may have to start from scratch in terms of thinking about which type of bag is better for the environment. As it turns out, paper is not quite as eco-friendly as we might think.

While all types of bags have some impact on the environment, it has long been supposed that paper is kinder. After all, plastic bags can kill dolphins, and anything that harms those adorable creatures must be terrible, mustn't it? But it seems that while paper bags are made from a renewable source, degrade naturally, burn without emitting harmful fumes and can be recycled, the manufacturing and transport process behind paper bags
line 14 consumes lots more energy than that of plastic ones. How can this be?

Studies show that paper bag production requires four times as much energy as plastic bag production – that energy being from fossil fuels. And if that's not enough to give you pause, consider that the amount of water used to make them is twenty times higher. Additionally, the impact on forests is enormous. It takes approximately fourteen million trees to produce ten billion paper bags, which happens to be roughly the number of bags used in the United States yearly. In terms of recycling, the idea that paper bags are more environmentally-friendly than plastic ones can be quickly discarded. Research shows it requires about 98% LESS energy to recycle plastic than it does paper.

Despite the surprising news that paper bags might be more harmful than plastic, plastic still seems to be perceived by governments as the more harmful of the two. In Ireland, for example, a tax has been introduced to discourage the use of plastic bags. Consumers are charged 22 cents for every plastic bag, and as a result, their use has dropped significantly. There's no doubt it makes more sense to reuse existing bags. However, we don't seem to be doing that at present. Statistics show that plastic and paper bags are very rarely reused, if ever. That may be because they tend to fall apart quickly, or because people just throw them under the sink and forget about them. Cloth bags are a better option in terms of reusability, but still, their production also has a negative impact on the environment.

So what's the solution? How should we answer our original question of 'Paper or plastic?' It seems we need a new question, perhaps along the lines of, 'Did you bring your own bag or do you want to pay for another one?' Only then may we see ourselves grabbing an old bag from under the kitchen sink and reusing it.

GUIDANCE **FOR CANDIDATES**

Part 5 consists of a text followed by six, four-option multiple-choice questions. Each correct answer gets two marks.

This part tests how well you can understand main ideas, implication, details, opinions and attitudes expressed in a text of general interest. It may also test your understanding of the organisation of the text, for example by asking what a word in a certain line refers to. You may have to work out the meaning of words or phrases, or state why the text was written.

The questions are presented in the same order as the information appears in the text. The last question, however, may ask you to give an answer relating to the whole text.

Quickly read the text first before you read the questions to get a general idea of what it's about. Underline key words and phrases in the questions so that you know what you need to look back for in the text. The correct option either answers a question or completes a sentence correctly based on the information in the text. The wrong options may, for example, use words taken directly from the text but will not answer the question, or they may be partly but not completely true. If you're unsure of an answer, cross out the option or options that are obviously wrong first. This will leave you with fewer choices.

Underline in the text where you find the answers to questions. This will help you check your answers at the end.

Answer all the questions, even if you aren't sure. Marks are not taken off for incorrect answers.

31 In the first paragraph, what does the writer say about the customers' choice of bag?
   A Customers never connected it to environmental issues.
   B Some customers knew it might affect the environment.
   C Many customers frequently made an on-the-spot decision.
   D Most customers needed a long time to think about the issues.

32 In the second paragraph, what does the writer suggest?
   A Our beliefs about paper bags are basically correct.
   B We often still have to decide between bag materials.
   C Bag manufacturers don't want to be involved in the issue.
   D Most people think paper is a better choice of material.

33 What does 'that' refer to in line 14?
   A making and transporting
   B consumption of energy
   C the recycling process
   D the amount of fumes given off

34 In the fourth paragraph, the phrase 'if that's not enough to give you pause' is used to show that the writer
   A is not sure we will believe the facts we're told.
   B thinks certain facts will shock or surprise us.
   C is asking us to continue reading the article.
   D wants us to stop reading for a short while.

35 What do governments believe today, according to the writer?
   A that they were wrong that plastic bags do more damage
   B that all shopping bags should be made of paper
   C that paper bags do less damage than plastic ones
   D that taxes probably need to be increased further

36 In the last paragraph, what solution does the writer suggest?
   A We should carry out more research.
   B We should find alternative materials for bags.
   C People should be charged for bags in shops.
   D People should be more careful which bags they reuse.

READING AND USE OF ENGLISH PART 6

Questions 37 – 42

You are going to read a magazine article about football referees. Six sentences have been removed from the article. Choose from the sentences **A – G** the one which fits each gap (**37 – 42**). There is one extra sentence which you do not need to use.

THE MEN IN BLACK

Football is undoubtedly the most popular sport in the world today. Matches on television between the most successful teams attract millions of viewers, the star players are paid movie-star wages, and everyone wants to know what sports journalists and the coaches and managers are saying about the big game. **37** G As a result, the life of a referee can be very difficult.

In order to become a professional referee, you have to take a number of courses and pass several exams. It isn't easy and, apart from a lot of training in the gym

to prove you're fit enough to run around for 90 minutes, you have to know all of the many rules intimately and be prepared for anything that could happen during a game. **38** C Well, that's the idea, at least. Your first time refereeing in a competitive match might be a very different thing.

Martin Geiger has seen everything in his 25 years as a professional referee but he still remembers his first game. He says the most shocking thing was the behaviour of some of the players and their attitude towards the referee. 'Whenever I blew the whistle, they would question my decision, which I never expected,' he says. **39** B

One of the things that trainee referees learn about on their courses is match control. **40** E When the game restarted, he says, they were much better behaved as a result of their little chat, and the rest of the game was easier for him to control.

But sometimes a warning is not enough. Helena Gow was one of the first female professional referees in the country, and has had some very difficult moments.

41 F In one game, for instance, a player grabbed hold of another player's shirt and pulled him to the ground. 'I had no choice but to send him off the pitch, which, of course, his teammates didn't like.'

A little later in the game, the opposing team scored a goal. The player who'd scored took off his shirt in celebration, which is not allowed according to the rules, so she had to show him a yellow card as a warning. This made her unpopular with the other team, too.

So the next time you watch a football game and the referee makes a decision which causes an argument, put yourself in their shoes. Referees are only human, and they can make mistakes just like anyone else. Technology these days allows us to watch the same moment again and again, in slow-motion replay and from many different angles, so we have a clearer view of what happened to help us make up our mind. **42** D Remember that if they don't get everything right all the time. Referees have a job to do, and they do it the best they can, and because they love the game, just like you.

A The coaches gave a final talk to their teams as I checked the goals and made sure I had my whistle, a red and a yellow card, and a pen and notebook.

B When a referee is faced with such a situation, his training can be very useful.

C If you prepare properly, nothing should go wrong during the match.

D Referees only have a split second to make a decision and they only see what happened once.

E 'At the half-time break,' Martin continues, 'I decided to have a talk with the players.'

F She doesn't necessarily think it's because she's a woman, but she does say she sometimes finds the situation extremely difficult.

G But sometimes the person who gets the most attention is the one in the middle, the one who has to make all the decisions.

GUIDANCE **FOR CANDIDATES**

Part 6 consists of a text from which six sentences have been removed and put in jumbled order after the text. There's also an extra sentence which doesn't fit any of the gaps. You have to decide where the missing sentences fit in the text. Each correct answer gets two marks.

Part 6 tests how well you can understand text organisation – how information is presented logically and sticks together. You should be able to follow the development of ideas in a text.

Read the text with the gaps in it before you look at the missing sentences so you get a general idea of the structure of the text and the development of the writer's ideas.

When you're deciding on which sentence goes where, it's really important to concentrate on what comes both before and after the gap. If you select a particular sentence for a gap, ask yourself if that sentence makes logical sense when you read it through with the sentence before and after it in the text.

You need to be able to recognise the sorts of words and phrases that show how ideas are connected in texts – words and phrases such as *However, This shows that, What's more, Before that, In other words, Without him, So,* and so on.

The little words such as *it* and *this* in the missing sentences refer to something mentioned in the sentence that comes earlier or later in the text, so when you're selecting an answer, make sure you can match them with what they refer to. Also always check that the grammar fits. If, for example, a missing sentence is in the past perfect, it is not likely to fit in a gap between two sentences in a future tense.

When you've chosen a sentence for a gap, put a line through its letter (A – G) so you don't consider using it again by mistake.

When you've filled all the gaps, quickly read the text through again, inserting the correct sentences. For each one, ask yourself: *Does the text make sense with this sentence here?*

READING AND USE OF ENGLISH PART 7

Questions 43 – 52

You are going to read a magazine article about some young businesspeople. For questions **43 – 52**, choose from the people (**A – D**). The people may be chosen more than once.

Which person says

they can use other people's money?	**43**	A
they learnt the basics from a member of their family?	**44**	B
they follow in their family's footsteps?	**45**	C
they started by giving out presents?	**46**	C
they started by making alterations to existing things?	**47**	B
they can meet famous people at work?	**48**	D
they drew inspiration from others?	**49**	B
they were discovered by accident?	**50**	A
they spent hours doing something because they were asked to?	**51**	D
they weren't happy with what was already available to buy?	**52**	C

⌐GUIDANCE FOR CANDIDATES⌐

In Part 7 there are ten questions before one long text or, more usually, a number of short texts. You have to find the information in the text(s) that matches the idea expressed in each question. Each correct answer gets one mark.

Usually in this part different people give their views on a particular subject, or there may be several different advertisements etc and the task begins with the words: *Which person/advertisement says ...?*

This part tests how well you can quickly find specific information and detail. You'll also have to be able to recognise opinion and attitude.

The reason the questions come before the text in this part is because sometimes when you read something you already have questions in your mind that you want the text to give you answers to. You look through the text quickly to find the information you need.

Read all the questions first and underline the key words and phrases in each one so you know what you are looking for. Try and keep as many of the underlined words or phrases in your mind as you read the texts. Don't worry about individual words you may not know. Remember you're looking for phrases that mean something like the idea in the question, not the actual words repeated. Let's look at an example from Test 1. The first question asks: *Which person says they can use other people's money?* Daria (A) says: ... My job involves ... purchasing and stocking products at the best prices I can get. I get to spend money ..., so A is the correct answer.

Remember that speed is important here. If you read the text very slowly and carefully from start to finish to find the answer to each question, you'll run out of time. For each question, you have to scan the text. In other words, you run through the text as quickly as you can looking for the information you need.

Fab jobs!

Worried about the future? Read about some young people and get inspiration from their stories!

A Daria, 21
fashion buyer

I've been into fashion since my teens and some of my friends at school even called me a fashion victim. I always dressed up in the latest styles to stand out and I spent all my money and time on clothes. People began to worry. But then, quite by chance, I got noticed by a scout because of my trendy outfits and my unique style and I was approached by a popular clothes retailer. They wanted me to choose new fashions and create styles for teenagers. And it was a success, so I've been working for the firm ever since and I totally love it! My job involves looking at samples and deciding what the customers will want, and purchasing and stocking products at the best prices I can get. I get to spend money and I've turned my hobby and passion into a well-paid job. I couldn't have done better even if I'd tried!

B Damien, 17
apps designer

You know how everybody our age worries about choosing a job? This hasn't been the case for me! When I was ten, my dad gave me his old computer and showed me some basic things about how to use it. I took to it immediately and started looking for ways to change the programs, personalising them and making them do different things. A little later I started creating my own programs and games from scratch and, as I grew up, I started designing programs for my classmates. I came to realise there was a whole market for stuff like that – my classmates provided me with inspiration – so I started producing mobile phone apps and computer programs for students. I knew then that this was what I really wanted to do, so I've just set up my own company!

C Maggie, 20
jewellery maker

Both my parents are artists and my older brothers work in creative jobs, too, so I wanted to be like them. I actually started off producing metal sculptures. I experimented with various materials and techniques, but I didn't seem to have any real inspiration. At the same time, I was making my own jewellery, because I didn't like anything that was in the shops, and some of my friends started asking me to make things for them, too. So, little by little I started designing and producing jewellery, which I originally gave to my friends for free. But demand grew, so I started producing more and more until it crossed my mind that I could make money from it. So now that's what I do. I design and market my own line of jewellery for young people. I use various techniques and different kinds of materials, ranging from precious metals to wool and paper. In the last couple of years it's really taken off. It's amazing!

D Justin, 19
animal trainer

I can't remember any period in my life when we didn't have pets at home. My parents both have office jobs, and are out of the house for long hours every day, so they think pets are good company for kids. Because of this, I grew up understanding what animals feel and how they should be treated. I took an active interest in animal training when I was about eleven. My parents had brought a new parrot home and asked me to train him and look after him. He was the first pet I was completely responsible for and I spent hours teaching him to talk and do tricks! Later, I trained other animals. It started as a hobby, but I soon realised that I could make good money out of it, so now I specialise in training animals that perform in advertisements and films. I think it's a fabulous job because I work with animals, which is such great fun, but also because I'm sometimes introduced to movie stars and other celebrities when we're filming!

WRITING PART 1

You **must** answer this question. Write your answer in **140 – 190** words in an appropriate style.

1 In your English class you have been talking about using the Internet to make new friends. Now your teacher has asked you to write an essay for homework.

Write your essay using **all** the notes and giving reasons for your point of view.

Some people use the Internet to meet new people.

Is this a good or bad way to make new friends?

Notes

Write about:

1 finding others with similar interests

2 meeting dishonest people

3 .... (your own idea)

Students' own answers

GUIDANCE FOR CANDIDATES

You need to do a lot of writing practice before the exam so you are familiar with the types of tasks and topics that come up and are confident that you can write to the required length in the time allowed. There are two parts to the Writing Paper. Each has the same number of marks. You have 1 hour 20 minutes to do two pieces of writing.

You don't have to make a plan before you write, but it is a good idea and the exam is designed to give you enough time to do so. When you make a plan you can organise your thoughts about what you want to include in short note form and write down any useful words and phrases to use. There are blank pages at the back of the booklet for you to use for this purpose. If you don't make a plan, you may run out of ideas half way through or find you are not answering the question properly. Don't worry about how messy your notes are – they won't be marked.

Don't try to write out the whole composition on the blank pages and then copy it to the lined answer space. You probably won't have time. As you're writing your answer, or when you read it through at the end, you may want to make corrections or change some things. That's fine, but remember that you can't use correction fluid. Just cross out the part you want to change and write it again. As long as the examiner can read what you write, it doesn't matter if it looks a bit messy.

You need to show that you can use more than very simple language when you write and that you can join ideas together so the reader can easily follow what you're saying. Try and use a range of complex language – longer sentences, interesting, varied vocabulary and linking words. Take a few risks! The examiner wants to see how well you can use a range of English – even if you make some minor errors doing it.

You can write with joined up letters or not; in UPPER CASE or lower case. You cannot use a dictionary in the exam. Always give yourself time to re-read what you have written to make any changes and check grammar, spelling and punctuation. Don't waste time counting the exact number of words – if you've practised enough, you should have an idea of the correct length.

There's only one question in Part 1 and you must answer it. It asks you to write an essay and the input that you will have to deal with may be up to 190 words, including the rubric. The rubric will set the scene and give you the topic for the essay.

The essay may take the form of a direct question or statement and you will have to give your opinions on it. The essay in Part 1 will have two given prompts which supply ideas clearly linked to the question or statement. You must address both prompts and also introduce a third distinct idea of your own. This third idea is in addition to any overall conclusions.

You need to ensure that all the content of your essay is clear and easy to follow. Good organisation and cohesion are important elements of a successful essay. You will be required to use a range of structures to communicate your ideas and opinions, along with the use of appropriate vocabulary.

WRITING PART 2

Write an answer to **one** of the questions **2 – 5** in this part. Write your answer in **140 – 190** words in an appropriate style.

---

2   You have seen this announcement in your favourite technology magazine for teens.

> *Texting vs. Emailing: Which do teens prefer and why?*
> The best article wins a brand new mobile phone!

Write your **article**.

3   You have seen a competition on an English-language website for the best short story and you decide to enter. Your story must begin with this sentence:

Sam was packed and ready to go, and was sure it was going to be the best weekend of his life.

Your story must include:

* an exciting destination

* an unusual event

Write your **story**.

4   You have seen this notice in your school newspaper.

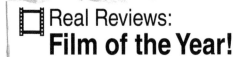

Real Reviews:
Film of the Year!

Tell us about a fantastic film you've seen this year and see your review printed in next month's issue!

Write your **review**.

5   Question 5 always consists of a question on the set text. Only answer question 5 if you have studied the set text. Here is an example of the kind of question you might be asked:

Your English class has had a discussion about the different characters in the book. Now your English teacher has asked you to write an essay about your favourite character for homework. You should describe the character and his or her part in the story and explain why he or she is your favourite.

Write your **essay**.

Students' own answers

GUIDANCE FOR CANDIDATES

In Part 2 you have a choice of four questions (or three if you haven't read the set text). You should write 140 – 190 words. You should read each question carefully before deciding which one to write. If the review or article question is on a subject that doesn't interest you or that you have never thought about before, you may have difficulty getting your ideas together and in that case it's best to avoid this question. If you have a good imagination, you might prefer to answer the question on the story or letter/email. If you choose the set text, you should make sure you've read the book well (and seen the film if possible), have discussed it in class and have practised writing about it.

Letter/Email

The letter/email you write will be in response to the situation outlined in the question. Letters and emails in the Writing paper will require a response from you which is consistently appropriate in register and tone for the specified target reader. You can expect to be asked to write letters or emails to an English-speaking friend or colleague, a potential employer, a university principal or a magazine editor, for example.

Article

The article will usually be for a teen or school magazine and will be on a topic of interest for your age group. You may be given a title or a question to respond to. For example, *Which three things would you take to a desert island and why?* If you're not given a title, you should give your article a good, short title. The point of the article is that it should be something that someone like you would want to read, so make it interesting. You can be funny, use direct and indirect questions – whatever makes the article lively and keeps the reader's attention.

Reading English language teen magazine articles or blogs on the Internet will help you prepare for this type of writing task.

Review

When you write a review, you are writing for a magazine, newspaper or website and you are expressing your personal opinion about something you have experienced. It may be a film, a book, a holiday, a website, a product, a TV programme, etc. You should say what it is like, give your opinion and make recommendations. Try and use interesting adjectives and give explanations for your views. Write about something you have actually seen or done – don't make it up.

Reading real reviews of films or books on the Internet in English is really useful preparation.

Story

It was a dark and stormy night and we were all alone in the old house. This is an example of the prompt sentence you will get in the story question. You will also have to use the two prompts provided, for example, *Your story must include a ghost and a surprise.* It's totally up to you how you develop the story, but remember you are writing it for a teen magazine or website, so it has to be interesting for someone like you. You can make the story as strange as you want – vampires, ghosts and werewolves are quite acceptable here. The important thing is to try and give the story a beginning, a middle and an end. Use interesting adjectives, adverbs, expressions and time phrases. Try to include some direct speech and some reported speech. Use some description, but keep the action going. The reader wants to know what happened next and most importantly what happened at the end.

A useful activity is to write stories from a starter sentence and two prompts in pairs or groups in class and then read them to the whole class. You can all vote on the best.

Set text

Many of the set texts have been made into films and are available on DVD, YouTube or on other media. Watch them as well as reading the book. The question on the set text will be quite general and you should feel confident that you can answer it because it will be about the main characters or story/plot. You don't have to memorise quotes, though if you can support your opinion with a short quote, this is fine.

Make sure you read the question carefully. Does it ask you to write an article, essay, letter or review? You need to use language to advise, describe, compare, explain and give opinions in this task.

Class discussions on the characters, their relationships, the main events and themes of the book will be useful to you in preparing for this task.

LISTENING PART 1

Questions 1 – 8

You will hear people talking in eight different situations. For questions **1 – 8**, choose the best answer (**A**, **B** or **C**).

1   You hear two girls having a conversation.
    What are they trying to do?
    A   decide where they should go that day
    B   confirm their plans for the evening
    C   make travel arrangements

2   You hear a boy talking about a pop concert.
    How does he feel about his experience?
    A   He enjoyed the music but resented paying so much for tickets.
    B   He was disappointed that he couldn't see the musicians.
    C   He had a good time even though things didn't go as planned.

3   You hear a woman leaving a voicemail message for her son.
    What is she most concerned about?
    A   that her son hasn't done his homework for weeks
    B   that her son didn't attend his class that day
    C   that her son failed his exam that week

4   You overhear a conversation between two friends.
    What is the boy doing?
    A   describing a recent event
    B   inviting someone to an upcoming event
    C   complaining about the weekend

5   You hear a woman speaking to a group of students.
    What is she saying?
    A   that the students must be aware of other people
    B   that the students should respect the establishment's rules
    C   that the students should appreciate their surroundings

6   You overhear two boys talking about a cinema.
    What do they both like about it?
    A   that it uses the latest technology
    B   that the décor is stylish and up-to-date
    C   that it is bigger than other cinemas in the area

7   You hear a girl and her brother talking.
    What is the girl trying to do?
    A   persuade her brother to do something
    B   help her brother to do something
    C   give information to her brother

8   You hear a caller on a phone-in radio show talking about sport.
    What does the man think?
    A   Schools should only offer traditional sports.
    B   A lot of sports are too dangerous for teenagers.
    C   Teenagers are given more opportunities these days.

GUIDANCE FOR CANDIDATES

You probably listen to quite a lot of material in English. You see films, hear songs and watch English language TV programmes. You've listened to your teacher and classmates speaking English and you have had listening practice with CDs in class. You are already well-prepared for this part of the test.

What you will hear in the four parts of the Listening paper is either one person speaking alone or two or more people speaking together. The questions test how well you understand not only the information they pass on in what they say, but also the way they feel about something or somebody, where they are and why they are speaking, eg is the speaker explaining, advising or warning?

How you say something is as important as what you say. Just think of the word *Hello*. If you're really excited about meeting someone, you will say *Hello* in a completely different way than if you see someone you really didn't want to meet.

When listening, you should try to work out if someone is saying something in an honest way or if they're being ironic or sarcastic, or if they're being humorous or if they're angry or upset.

You will hear the written instructions for each part on the CD and for Parts 2-4 you will have time to look over the questions before each part begins. Use this time to underline key words in the questions and answers. The more you can predict and anticipate what you're going to hear, the more you'll understand when you actually listen to the recording.

Remember you will hear each part twice, so don't panic if you're not sure of any answer after the first hearing.

In Part 1, you hear eight, unrelated 30-second monologues or recordings of people interacting. Each situation has a question which has three multiple-choice options. You decide on the correct one: A, B or C. Each correct answer gets one mark. You will have to read the multiple-choice options as you listen.

This part tests your understanding of gist, specific detail, how people feel, opinions, relationships between speakers, what people are trying to achieve, and other aspects of communication.

Make sure you understand the question. For example, here in question 1, the question is *What are they trying to do?*, not *What have they just done?* or *What are they going to do later on?*

As you listen, don't focus on any words or phrases in the recording that you don't understand. Just think about the bits you do understand!

If you hear a word or phrase that is in one of the answer options, this doesn't mean this option is the correct one. Listen for the whole meaning.

If you're really not sure of an answer, make a guess – don't leave any answers blank. Remember that you don't lose marks for incorrect answers.

Practise for this part by listening to short excerpts from radio programmes. Try to identify what the speaker or speakers are talking about and how they feel about it.

LISTENING PART 2

Questions 9 – 18

You will hear a young fashion model called Monica Mansfield talking about shopping. For questions **9 – 18**, complete the sentences with a word or short phrase.

SHOPPING WITH A FASHION MODEL

Monica plans to use the money she makes from modelling to go to | *university* | **9**

Monica didn't think her first shopping experience was very | *enjoyable* | **10**

Monica often buys the clothes of a couple of different | *designers* | **11**

Monica doesn't like to shop over the Internet because it's hard to | *exchange* | **12** things.

The most expensive dress Monica ever bought was dark green and reached the | *floor* | **13**

Monica most often buys T-shirts that have got | *writing* | **14** on the front.

Monica prefers to shop with other people, especially her | *best friend (Julia)* | **15**

The shop Monica likes best is a local | *second-hand/secondhand/second hand clothes* | **16** shop.

The one item of clothing Monica can't live without is her | *leather* | **17** jacket.

Monica needs to buy a | *pair of sunglasses* | **18** before her next trip.

GUIDANCE FOR CANDIDATES

In Part 2 you have to complete ten sentences with information you hear. Each correct answer gets one mark.

The questions always follow the order of the information in the recording, and the word(s) you have to fill the gaps with are always those you will hear in the recording. You don't have to change the words or rephrase them in a different way.

Although the instructions just say 'complete the sentences' and don't tell you how many words you can write, the answer is almost always between one and three words. If you've written more than three words, your answer is almost certainly wrong. Sometimes, there may be more than one possible way to fill a gap. However, you should only ever write one answer on your answer sheet.

In the time you have before you listen, read through the questions and think about what information is likely to be needed. Ask yourself what kind of word or phrase is probably required (a noun phrase? an adjective?) and try to think of possible words and phrases that might fit the gap logically. For example, in question 9 here, we probably need a place or an event. In question 10, the word *very* before the gap tells us that we probably need an adjective. Logically, the answer might be something like *successful* or *enjoyable*. The more you can predict what the answers might be before you actually listen, the more you're likely to understand when you do actually listen to the recording.

Don't get 'stuck' on a question. If you know you've just missed the answer to a question, don't spend time thinking about what it might have been. You need to keep listening to hear the answers to the remaining questions. You'll be able to listen out for the answer you missed the second time you hear the recording.

If you're really not sure of an answer, make a guess. You don't lose marks for incorrect answers.

LISTENING PART 3

Questions 19 – 23

You will hear five teenagers talking about summer camps. For questions **19 – 23**, choose from the list (**A – H**) what each speaker says about it. Use the letters only once. There are three extra letters which you do not need to use.

A We couldn't do an activity because of bad weather.

Speaker 1	B	**19**

B I was too old for some of the activities at the camp.

Speaker 2	G	**20**

C My family was worried about an activity I did at the camp.

Speaker 3	A	**21**

D I learnt a lot about technology at the camp.

Speaker 4	E	**22**

E I was taught how to react in difficult or dangerous situations.

Speaker 5	C	**23**

F My friends taught me how to do something interesting on the computer.

G The best thing about the camp was seeing a wild animal.

H One of the camp leaders got hurt at the camp.

GUIDANCE FOR CANDIDATES

In this part, there are five short monologues and eight options. You have to match each speaker to an option. Each correct answer gets one mark.

The different speakers will be talking about the same subject, eg travel, or doing the same thing, for example apologising.

It is particularly important here that you use the time before you listen to look through the statements so you know what you are listening for. For each statement, ask yourself before you listen what the speaker might actually say. For example, for option A here, perhaps the speaker says *It was pouring with rain so we weren't able to ... .* The more you can predict what you might hear, the more you'll understand when you actually listen to the recording.

Be very careful with 'word spotting' in this part. Speaker 1 here might mention bad weather, but that doesn't necessarily mean that option A is correct. They have to say that they couldn't do an activity because of bad weather for the answer to be correct. Perhaps they say that the weather was bad but that didn't stop them doing an activity.

Once you've chosen an option as the answer and are sure it's correct, put a line through the letter (A – H) so you don't use it again by mistake.

Once you've listened to the recording twice, if you're really not sure of an answer, make a guess using the remaining options. Remember that you don't lose marks for incorrect answers.

If you're in an English class or work at home with other students, one useful activity you can do to prepare for this part is to get one person to speak for 30 seconds or a minute on a subject of their choice. The other students listen to him/her and then write a short sentence summarising one aspect of what the student said – but they're not allowed to use any of the words they heard.

LISTENING PART 4

Questions 24 – 30

You will hear a radio interview with a man, Emmanuel Johnson, about how he began his career in the arts. For questions **24 – 30**, choose the best answer (**A**, **B** or **C**).

---

24   What job was Emmanuel originally supposed to do?
    A work as a businessman
    B work in the legal profession
    C work as a director

25   What was Emmanuel's first job in the arts?
    A He became his wife's assistant.
    B He worked behind the scenes.
    C He performed on stage.

26   What did Emmanuel discover when he was a child?
    A He had a talent for art.
    B He had a health problem.
    C He wasn't artistic at all.

27   Why did Emmanuel start work in the family law firm?
    A He was sure he would be good at the work.
    B He couldn't find any other work.
    C He didn't want to let his family down.

28   Where did Emmanuel and Lucasta first work professionally together?
    A London
    B abroad
    C in their office

29   Why did Lucasta stop working?
    A She grew too old.
    B She wanted to retire.
    C She got a better offer.

30   What does Emmanuel say about David Goldstein?
    A He is an old friend.
    B He only met him recently.
    C He doesn't trust him.

⌐GUIDANCE **FOR CANDIDATES**⌐

In this part, you hear a person or people discussing a subject for about three minutes. You have to answer seven multiple-choice questions, each with three options. Each correct answer gets one mark.

The seven questions rephrase, report or summarise the ideas expressed in the recording. The questions often start with *What, Who, When, How, Why* or *Where.*

Remember that the questions always follow the order of the information in the recording.

For an option to be right, it must fully answer the question. For example, in question 25 here, it's possible that all three options are correct as statements, but only one of them was his first job. Be very careful that the option you choose actually answers the question.

Always read through the questions and options before you listen. Underline key words or phrases in the questions. For example, in question 25, the key word is *first.*

Be very careful with 'word spotting' in this part. The speaker might mention *London* but that doesn't mean that option A in question 28 is definitely correct. You're listening for ideas, not specific words or phrases.

Don't get 'stuck' on a question. If you know you've just missed the answer to a question, don't spend time thinking about what it might have been. You need to keep listening to hear the answers to the remaining questions. You'll be able to listen out for the answer you missed the second time you hear the recording.

Once you've listened to the recording twice, if you're really not sure of an answer, make a guess. Remember that you don't lose marks for incorrect answers.

To practise this part, when you do a practice test, cover the options and only look at the questions. Listen and write your own answers and then see if your answers are similar to the correct options in the test.

SPEAKING PART 1

2 minutes (3 minutes for groups of three)

Good morning/afternoon/evening. My name is _____ and this is my colleague _____.

And your names are?

Can I have your mark sheets, please? Thank you.

First of all we'd like to know something about you.

- Where are you from, (Candidate A)?

- And you, (Candidate B)?

- What do you like about living (here/name of candidate's home town)?

- And what about you, (Candidate A/B)?

Select one or more questions from the following category, as appropriate.

Everyday life

- **What do you usually do in the evenings?**

- **Do you ever have extra activities after school? ...... (What kind?/How often?)**

- **Do you watch television in the evenings? ...... (What kind of television programmes do you watch?/Why?)**

- **Do you use a computer? ...... (What do you use it for?)**

- **What did you do last weekend?**

Students' own answers

GUIDANCE **FOR CANDIDATES**

For the Speaking paper, you'll be with another candidate and there will be two examiners, but only one of them will speak to you.

This is the time for you to show what you can do in English by speaking on your own and in conversation. There are four parts to the fourteen-minute test. Occasionally, there may be three candidates. If so, the test is the same but takes twenty minutes.

The examiner is there to ask you questions and help you to do the best you can. The examiner will not ask you tricky or silly questions. You need to know what you have to do in each part and speak as naturally as you can. You won't pass if you only answer with one word or are mostly silent. If you get stuck or can't remember a word, don't panic. Try and rephrase what you want to say. The important thing is to keep going and remember who you are speaking to and why. Don't worry about making mistakes; just think about getting your message across and responding to the examiner and your partner appropriately.

Arrive at the examination centre in plenty of time. When you go into the room, make sure there's no chewing gum in your mouth!

Remember: Don't give one word answers. Be polite. And at the end of the test, don't ask if you passed. The examiner won't tell you!

Part 1 is about your favourite subject – yourself! In the first part of the Speaking paper, you respond to a few questions from the examiner. You say your name, where you are from and what you like about living there.

A good answer to the question *Where are you from?* might be *I'm from a suburb of Athens called Peristeri.* That's all you need to say. You shouldn't say something you've learnt by heart which is not relevant to the question, such as *I'm from Greece, which is an ancient country and my family consists of four members, my parents, my sister and me.*

You will then be asked general questions about your daily life – school, free time and/or your future plans. You should feel confident in this part of the test because you don't need to think up answers. You know what the questions are going to be and you can practise interviews alone, with a friend or in class.

Practice Test 1

SPEAKING PART 2

4 minutes (6 minutes for groups of three)

1 Education
2 People and animals

Interlocutor	In this part of the test, I'm going to give each of you two photographs. I'd like you to talk about your photographs on your own for about a minute, and also to answer a short question about your partner's photographs.
See photos A and B on page 174.	*(Candidate A)*, it's your turn first. Here are your photographs. They show **students studying in different environments.**
	I'd like you to compare the photographs and say **what are the advantages and disadvantages of students studying in these ways.**
	All right?
Candidate A	*(Speak for approximately 1 minute.)*
Interlocutor	Thank you. *(Candidate B)*, **which way of studying is better?**
Candidate B	*(Reply for approximately 30 seconds.)*
Interlocutor	Thank you.
See photos C and D on page 175.	Now, *(Candidate B)*, here are your photographs. They show **people and animals together.**
	I'd like you to compare the photographs and **say how relationships with animals can help people.**
	All right?
Candidate B	*(Reply for approximately 1 minute.)*
Interlocutor	Thank you. *(Candidate A)*, **which of these animals would you prefer to have as a pet?**
Candidate A	*(Reply for approximately 30 seconds.)*
Interlocutor	Thank you.

Students' own answers

GUIDANCE FOR CANDIDATES

In Part 2, you are given two photographs to compare. The examiner will tell you what to do and you should remember that in the one minute you have to speak you shouldn't just describe what you see. Talk about the similarities and differences in the photographs but remember to also answer the question above the photographs. Remember that you're talking about the main ideas in the photos: who the people are, where they are, what they're doing, etc. You don't need to describe all the tiny details.

Remember also that it's fine to tell the examiner that you don't know or can't tell something about the pictures. Here, you should speculate: *I'm not sure but it might be ..., Perhaps they're ..., It's difficult to tell, but maybe he's ...,* etc.

Talking on your own for one minute may seem like a long time, but there's always something more you can say about the photographs and what you think about them. Don't worry if the examiner stops you by saying *Thank you* before you've said all you want to say. It's because you're not allowed to speak for more than a minute but you won't lose marks for this.

When you have finished speaking, the examiner will ask your partner a question, eg if the photographs show different places to shop, the question might be *Where do you like to go shopping?*

You can practise for this part of the test by playing the game *Just a minute*. You have to talk on a subject for a minute without repeating the same ideas, words or phrases.

Bring to class your own photographs or use photos cut out from magazines to practise comparing and giving your reactions to them. Practise useful phrases such as *One similarity is that ..., In this photo there's ... whereas in the other one ...* . Practise comparatives and linking phrases.

SPEAKING PARTS 3 AND 4

8 minutes (11 minutes for groups of three)

Festivals

PART 3

Interlocutor	Now, I'd like you to talk about something together for about two minutes. *(3 minutes for groups of three)*

See written prompts on page 176.

I'd like you to imagine that a school is going to have a festival to raise some money. Here are some ideas for the festival and a question for you to discuss. First you have some time to look at the task.

Now, talk to each other about **which kind of festival would be the most popular.**

Candidates	*(Reply for approximately 2 minutes – 3 minutes for groups of three.)*
Interlocutor	Thank you. Now you have about a minute to decide **which two would be the easiest to organise.**
Candidates	*(Reply for approximately 1 minute – for pairs and groups of three.)*
Interlocutor	Thank you.

PART 4

Interlocutor

Select any of the following questions, as appropriate:

- **Have you ever been to a festival? ......** **(What kind of festival was it?)**

- **Do you think a festival should be for entertainment or for education?**

- **Are festivals a good way to meet new people? ...... (Why?/Why not?)**

- **Can you think of any problems that could occur at an outdoor festival? How could they be prevented?**

- **Do you think it's good for children to attend festivals? ...... (Why?/Why not?)**

- **Do festivals help promote tourism? ...... (How?)**

Select any of the following prompts, as appropriate:

- **What do you think?**
- **Do you agree?**
- **And you?**

Thank you. That is the end of the test.

Students' own answers

GUIDANCE FOR CANDIDATES

In Part 3 you're given spoken instructions with written prompts, which you have to talk about with your partner.

Remember that this is not a monologue; it's a conversation between you and your partner. You have to listen to what your partner says and respond.

One of you will have to start the conversation. If the other candidate doesn't immediately speak, look at the candidate, point to one of the prompts and say, *Right, shall we start with this one? What do you think about ...?*

Remember that you're not supposed to describe the prompts in detail; you're using them as ideas to discuss the issue and come to a conclusion.

Try to talk about all the ideas suggested by the prompts, and try to reach a decision, but if you don't have time to reach a decision, that doesn't matter – you won't lose marks.

You need to use language for agreeing and disagreeing and questioning in this part. It's absolutely fine to disagree with your partner, but be polite! Don't say *That's a ridiculous idea!* Say something like, *To be honest, I'm not sure I agree ...,* and then give a reason why.

Try to move the discussion forward. Do lots of practice in class where you have to come to an agreement using phrases such as *I see your point but ...,* *What do you think about ...?* and *Let's move on to the next one.*

GUIDANCE FOR CANDIDATES

The last part of the Speaking paper is always related to the topic of Part 3.

This part gives you the chance to really show how well you can respond to questions. Try to respond fully to any question you are asked – don't just give one-word or short-phrase answers.

Look at the questions about festivals in Part 4 here. When you give an answer, think about *who, what, where, when, how* and *why.* If you answer some of these questions in your response, it will be much fuller than if you only answer with a short sentence such as *Yes, I have been to a festival.*

Always listen to the other candidate's answers because you may want or need to agree or disagree with them.

Remember that most answers aren't black and white. For example in Part 4 here, there's a question *Do you think it's good for children to attend festivals?* The most sensible answer probably starts *Well, it depends on what kind of festival it is.* You would then go on to explain that some festivals are appropriate for children, but others might not be. Give examples where you can, and always try to give reasons for your opinions. You'll never lose marks for having strange or odd opinions, so don't worry about trying to say something you think the examiner agrees with. It's more important that your ideas are logical and are supported with sensible reasons.

If you attend an English class, you can practise for this part by having class discussions in pairs and groups on different subjects.

Practice Test 2

READING AND USE OF ENGLISH `PART 1`

For questions **1 – 8**, read the text below and decide which answer (**A**, **B**, **C** or **D**) best fits each gap. There is an example at the beginning (**0**).

Example:

0 A get   **B** become   **C** turn   **D** have

0	A	B	C	D
	☐	■	☐	☐

Do too many cooks spoil the broth? Maybe not ...

What does it take to **(0)** _____ the world's top chef? What do you have to cook to make your customers wait months and even years for a reservation? Well, renowned gastronomical genius Ferran Adriá knows the answer. About two million people every year would try to **(1)** _____ a table at his restaurant _elBulli_. But only 8,000 **(2)** _____ in getting one. For Ferran Adriá the key was **(3)** _____ with a highly-trained team of chefs – and a big one at that!

ElBulli, located on the north coast of Spain, only used to open for six months a year, and there were just fifty-two seats available. Adriá and his team of forty cooks created many groundbreaking dishes. Each meal **(4)** _____ about fifty dishes and cost about 300 euros per person! _ElBulli_ closed in 2011, but there are plans to reopen as a non-profit creativity centre.

Most of the staff that worked at _elBulli_ were trainee chefs who worked fourteen hours a day for no **(5)** _____. Even so, thousands of young cooks **(6)** _____ each year and the thirty-two lucky ones to be selected flew to Spain from all over the world. They had to be physically **(7)** _____ to work the long hours, but also mentally strong to remember what they had to do. Some of the young chefs weren't able to finish their apprenticeship, but those who did must feel proud about having worked at possibly the best restaurant of all **(8)** _____.

1	**A** order	**B** book	**C** purchase	**D** keep
2	**A** managed	**B** achieved	**C** won	**D** succeeded
3	**A** working	**B** leading	**C** employing	**D** getting
4	**A** added	**B** held	**C** counted	**D** included
5	**A** pay	**B** profit	**C** donation	**D** proceeds
6	**A** asked for	**B** demanded	**C** applied	**D** submitted
7	**A** unhealthy	**B** athletic	**C** fit	**D** trained
8	**A** occasion	**B** era	**C** period	**D** time

TIPS

Read through the whole text before you look at the multiple-choice options. As you do so, you will be thinking of a word or phrase that can complete the gap and getting a sense of the overall meaning. You might want to lightly pencil in any word or phrase that you think fits.

On your second reading, when you are deciding on the correct option, make sure you read the whole sentence with the gap in it and consider all four options.

Question 2: Which of these verbs is always followed by *in + -ing*?

Question 3: Here, you have to think about grammar as well as meaning. The first question to ask is *Which of these verbs can be followed by 'with'*? When you've chosen them, ask yourself which of them make sense here in terms of meaning.

Question 8: This is a phrase. If you're not sure of the answer, say all four options to yourself with the words *of all* before them. Which one sounds best to you?

41

Practice Test 2

READING AND USE OF ENGLISH `PART 2`

For questions **9 – 16**, read the text below and think of the word which best fits each gap. Use only **one** word in each gap. There is an example at the beginning (0).

Write your answers **IN CAPITAL LETTERS**.

Example: | 0 | W | E | R | E |

No longer extinct

Sometimes animals that **(0)** _WERE_ once thought to be extinct are 'rediscovered'. Such is the case with the Miller's grizzled langur, a type of monkey **(9)** _WHICH_ lives in the jungles of Indonesia. Scientists travel to these jungles every year **(10)** _TO_ study and photograph animals, and this year, a photograph containing a Miller's grizzled langur caught them **(11)** _BY_ surprise.

The scientists had planned **(12)** _ON_ capturing photographs of other animals, such as leopards. The monkey, believed extinct, was an animal the scientists hadn't seen before, so they didn't know what they were looking at. Images of the langur appeared several times in the scientist's photos, but it was difficult to determine what kind of monkey was in the photo because no photographs of the monkey existed. Eventually, scientists had to rely **(13)** _ON_ museum sketches.

Until that moment, scientists thought the monkey **(14)** _HAD_ become extinct years before. A land survey in 2005 found no evidence **(15)** _OF_ the monkey's existence. Scientists will now attempt to find **(16)** _OUT_ exactly how many monkeys there are.

A common grey langur

READING AND USE OF ENGLISH PART 3

For questions **17 – 24**, read the text below. Use the word given in capitals at the end of some of the lines to form a word that fits the gap **in the same line**. There is an example at the beginning (**0**).

Write your answers **IN CAPITAL LETTERS**.

Example: | **0** | C | O | N | C | E | R | N | E | D | | | | | | | | |

Help in old age

Would people be **(0)** _CONCERNED_ if you said you wanted to spend time in a developing country, working as a volunteer? If so, you could point out that you were not alone. Many teenagers today feel the need to do **(17)** _VOLUNTARY_ work to help the people around them.   **CONCERN**

VOLUNTEER

If you're **(18)** _INTERESTED_ in volunteering in your town, then why not contact one of the local charities for older people, such as our charity *Help in Old Age*?   **INTEREST**

The **(19)** _ELDERLY_ don't always have relatives to take care of them and our charity can put you in touch with someone in your **(20)** _NEIGHBOURHOOD_ who needs some support to live the life they want and stay active.   **OLD**

NEIGHBOUR

Thousands of people throughout the country already volunteer, and without them, charities such as ours **(21)** _SIMPLY_ wouldn't exist.   **SIMPLE**

If you are as **(22)** _PASSIONATE_ about caring for the people in your community as we are, then contact *Help in Old Age,* and we'll send you **(23)** _DETAILED_ information about opportunities in your area.   **PASSION**

DETAIL

Let's make a **(24)** _DIFFERENCE_ together; there are people who need us!   **DIFFER**

TIPS

For Part 3, the word at the end of the line must always be changed in some way. Read the surrounding sentence to decide what changes you need to make to the stem word. Should you make the word an adjective, a noun, a plural, negative, etc? In this task, all of them need a change of ending. Only one question requires you to also change the first letter of the stem word. Which question is it?

READING AND USE OF ENGLISH PART 4

For questions **25 – 30**, complete the second sentence so that it has a similar meaning to the first sentence, using the word given. **Do not change the word given.** You must use between **two** and **five** words, including the word given. Here is an example (0).

Example:

0   There's no need for you to bring any DVDs as I have plenty.

HAVE

You _____*DON'T HAVE TO*_____ bring any DVDs as I have plenty.

The gap can be filled by the words 'don't have to', so you write:

Example: | 0 | | *DON'T HAVE TO* |

Write **only** the missing words **IN CAPITAL LETTERS**.

25   Learning a musical instrument isn't as useful as learning a foreign language.
MORE
Learning a foreign language _*IS MORE USEFUL THAN*_ learning a musical instrument.

26   'Why didn't I take more photos while I was travelling around India?' said Tom.
HAD
Tom wishes _____*HE HAD TAKEN*_____ more photos while he was travelling around India.

27   Jenny said that it didn't matter to her where we ate.
MIND
Jenny said that _*SHE DIDN'T/DID NOT MIND*_ where we ate.

28   'Did you understand the end of the film?' Rosie asked Mark.
IF
Rosie asked Mark _*IF HE HAD UNDERSTOOD*_ the end of the film.

29   Marilyn prefers going camping to staying in hotels.
RATHER
Marilyn _____*WOULD RATHER GO*_____ camping than stay in a hotel.

30   Although I started work at this company ten years ago, I still enjoy it.
BEEN
I _____*HAVE BEEN WORKING*_____ at this company for ten years, but I still enjoy it.

Remember that for this part you must write between two and five words including the key word, which mustn't be changed in any way. If you write more than five words as your answer, you lose marks.

The second sentence must always convey a similar meaning to the first. You might have to change direct into reported speech as in questions 26 and 28, or find an alternative phrase for a particular function as in question 27 (saying something is not important) and question 29 (expressing preference).

Question 25: Is the answer going to be in a negative or positive form? What word follows *more*?

Question 27: Don't use exactly the same wording as the lead-in sentence (*it didn't matter*), just replacing one word with the key word. The correct answer here is NOT *it didn't mind*.

Question 30: This looks so easy, but students often get questions like this wrong because of carelessness. You know that only three words can go before *been – have, has* and *had* and that *was been* is ungrammatical. The subject of the sentence is *I* and the speaker is still working at the company, so what's the answer?

READING AND USE OF ENGLISH PART 5

Questions 31 – 36

You are going to read an article about hidden camera shows on television. For questions 31 – 36, choose the answer (**A, B, C** or **D**) which you think fits best according to the text.

Hidden camera shows

Ashley Tisdale

Ashley Tisdale, the *High School Musical* actress and singer, is invited to a children's ward in a hospital to visit the patients. She suspects nothing. Why should she? It's the kind of thing celebrities are asked to do all the time.

In one of the beds is Jonathan, a youngster in a coma following a skateboarding accident. Jonathan's mum explains to Ashley that Jonathan is a huge fan of hers and asks her to sing something for her poor son. She then slips out of the room. Ashley starts singing and – who would have believed it? – Jonathan begins to respond, smiling at Ashley and whispering 'Hi!'. No one witnesses this apart from the astonished star. Ashley rushes to find the mother and the doctor, who are equally speechless when they hear what's happened. But once they get back to the bed, Jonathan is still very much in a coma.

Ashley and Jonathan are then left alone one more time. Again he 'wakes up'. He confesses to her that he's only pretending to be in a coma because he doesn't want to go to school, and begs her not to tell anyone.

When Jonathan's mum and the doctor came back with some nurses, they ask Ashley to sing once more. Maybe she can wake him again. Ashley, now feeling extremely uncomfortable, agrees. Eventually, Jonathan starts to stir, lifts his head, looks at Ashley and says the now infamous words: 'You got Punk'd!' Ashley is, of course, one of the many victims of the MTV show *Punk'd*, which ran from 2003 to 2007. And *Punk'd* is just one of the many hidden camera shows that have entertained us since the dawn of television.

Humans have always enjoyed playing tricks on other people – and watching other people get tricked. It seems to be a fundamental part of human nature. From magicians and illusionists to April Fools' Day and playground pranks, the 'trick', in whichever form it takes, appeals to our sense of humour. And television was the perfect medium to take it to a whole new level.

The first hidden camera show was the hugely successful *Candid Camera*, which was first aired in the US in 1948. British, Australian and Canadian versions followed, and the show continued in various forms well into the early 2000s. Other similar shows have included *Scare Tactics, Just for Laughs, Gags* and *Beadle's About*. Whether the aim of the trick is to shock, scare, surprise or embarrass the victim, and whether the victim is a celebrity or an ordinary member of the public, the basic premise is always the same: the victim is put in a situation which they believe is real, but which in fact has been created by the producers of the show and won't go the way the victim supposes it will – ideally with hilarious results for the viewer.

Sometimes, of course, things go wrong. In one episode of *Punk'd*, wrestler Bill Goldberg was supposed to see a truck run over his motorbike (the producers had made an exact replica). However, the truck driver missed the bike. When the bike blew up for no apparent reason, Goldberg realised he was being tricked. And all victims – whether celebrities or not – have to give permission after the stunt for the footage to be shown. Sometimes they refuse, which can be costly in terms of time and money for the producers. Most, thankfully, do see the funny side and are happy for us to laugh at their misfortune. *line 35*

31 In the first paragraph, the question 'Why should she?' is used to show that the writer
    A isn't sure if Ashley is suspicious or not.
    B thinks it makes sense that Ashley isn't suspicious.
    C believes that Ashley should be suspicious.
    D wants to know what Ashley should be suspicious of.

32 Jonathan tells Ashley a secret
    A the first time he wakes up in front of her.
    B after he opens his eyes for the second time.
    C while she is singing one of her songs to him.
    D just after some nurses have been in the room.

33 What does the writer say in the fifth paragraph?
    A Humour has changed a lot over the years.
    B More tricks are played today than in the past.
    C It's quite normal to want to play tricks on people.
    D Television has totally changed the idea of the 'trick'.

34 According to the writer, what do different hidden camera shows have in common?
    A Viewers always find their tricks extremely funny.
    B The victims always react in the same way.
    C The victims are always the same kind of people.
    D The tricks are all based on the same general concept.

35 What does 'Most' refer to in line 35?
    A victims
    B celebrities
    C producers
    D viewers

36 Which statement sums up the writer's general attitude towards hidden camera shows?
    A Although they're popular, they sometimes do damage.
    B They create victims, which is not acceptable.
    C They are all the same, which is a bad thing.
    D They're popular and they're good fun.

TIPS

Question 34: Be careful of words such as *always* in the options. This word occurs in the text, but ask yourself if the text supports the use of the word *always* in options A, B and C.

Question 36: The final question often asks you to interpret an aspect of the text as a whole. Be careful with two-part options – ones that include two statements. One part may be true, but the other false.

READING AND USE OF ENGLISH PART 6

Questions 37 – 42

You are going to read an article about a modern type of performance art. Six sentences have been removed from the article. Choose from the sentences **A – G** the one which fits each gap (**37 – 42**). There is one extra sentence which you do not need to use.

Flash mobs!

Outside, it's a cold winter's day. Inside a large, urban shopping centre, teenagers are hanging around, mothers are pushing prams, and pensioners are window shopping. In short, it's a typical British scene on a typical British day.

But then, without warning, a pop song starts to play loudly over the tannoy. One of the teenage boys walks lazily to the centre of the concourse, and springs into action – dancing crazily to the music. **37** G Within the space of a few seconds, more than sixty people are dancing to the music – all in time and all in step. Onlookers are initially baffled, then start smiling and clapping. Many of them film the event with their mobile phones or video recorders. They now know what they're witnessing: a flash mob.

According to the online encylopaedia Wikipedia, both the concept and the term 'flash mob' were created by Bill Wasik, an editor at Harper's Magazine, in 2003. **38** E Since then, hundreds – possibly thousands – of flash mobs have been carried out around the world, in almost every kind of public space imaginable: on high streets and beaches, in shopping centres, shops, train stations, airports, university campuses, school assembly halls, lecture theatres – even prisons!

Each flash mob has its own unique style and properties, but most flash mobs follow a similar formula. Often, the organisers appeal for willing participants using social media such as Facebook or Twitter. Initial instructions and dance routines are given via email or video download. There are usually several rehearsals before the big day. **39** A

While it's happening, a few lucky passers-by witness it live. The vast majority of people who watch it, however, will see it later online. Some of the most popular flash mobs on YouTube have been watched more than 10 million times (just put 'flash mob' into the search bar on YouTube to find some examples). Some interesting variants on the traditional formula have been tried over the years. **40** F Organised by the group *Improv Everywhere*, this event differed from standard flash mobs in that much of it was completely silent – and there were no rehearsals.

Participants were divided into two groups based on their birthdays. Each group downloaded instructions on what to wear (white shorts for one group, black shirts for the other group), what to bring (an MP3 player or smartphone with headphones, a camera with a flash, a glow stick, etc) a starting location and an MP3 file. **41** D The result was a spectacular show. Type 'The MP3 Experiment Eight' into the search bar on YouTube to see it for yourself.

Several companies, such as T-Mobile, recognising the popularity and appeal of flash mobs, have jumped on the bandwagon and produced advertisements based on the flash mob concept. **42** B You can judge for yourself how successful you think they've been by putting 'The T-Mobile Dance' or 'The T-Mobile Welcome Back' into YouTube.

One thing's for sure: flash mobs provide the participants, onlookers and online viewers with a huge amount of enjoyment and pleasure. For this reason alone, they're a modern, popular art form that should be celebrated.

A   These aren't in the final location, of course, and then the event takes place.

B   Although some people have criticised them for using what is essentially a non-profit art form for commercial purposes, the adverts have generally been well received, managing to retain the spirit, warmth and innocence of the original concept.

C   Some of them had rehearsed for hours, others for only a few minutes.

D   At a specified time, they all pressed play and followed the instructions through their headphones.

E   Within a year, the phrase had entered the Concise Oxford English Dictionary.

F   A famous example is MP3 Experiment Eight, a flash mob that took place in New York City in July 2011 with over 3,500 participants.

G   He's joined by two of his friends, then some of the mothers pushing prams, then some of the pensioners.

READING AND USE OF ENGLISH `PART 7`

Questions 43 – 52

You are going to read a newspaper article about teenagers and politics. For questions **43 – 52**, choose from the people (**A – D**). The people may be chosen more than once.

Which person

was originally interested in politics because of something they read?	**43**	D
has been very successful in politics outside of school?	**44**	C
looked up to a famous political figure?	**45**	B
was inspired to get involved in politics by a teacher?	**46**	C
prefers not to have to make important decisions about their school?	**47**	D
likes having responsibilities at school?	**48**	A
was discouraged from becoming politically active?	**49**	A
didn't expect to enjoy studying certain subjects?	**50**	B
won't have as much time for politics in the future?	**51**	D
doesn't mind not doing as much sport as they used to?	**52**	B

> **TIPS**
>
> A good way to approach this task is to read the questions first and underline the key words. The correct matching answer from the text(s) will express the whole idea of the question, not just part of it. Try to keep the questions in mind as you read through the text(s). Remember that you are trying to locate very specific information, opinions or attitudes and you should know what you are looking for before you read.
>
> Question 43: Although several texts mention things you can read, only one mentions reading a book that caused the writer to become interested in politics.
>
> Question 45: To get the right answer here, you need to find not just a famous political figure, but one that the writer admired. Be careful not to read things into the text(s) that are not actually stated. Elena from Greece (A) has a grandfather who was a mayor. You may suppose that Elena admired her grandfather, but the text doesn't say that. As a mayor, he was a political figure, but the text doesn't say that he was famous. Other texts mention political figures, but only one text says (using other words) that the person was admired by the writer. Which is it?

Power to the (young) people!

There are many young people out there who feel it's their responsibility to participate in politics. They choose to have a say in how things work at school and in their community. Budding politicians from different countries and backgrounds have told us their stories. Here's what four of them said.

Elena, Greece

I've always been interested in politics, because it runs in my family. My grandfather worked in the town hall for years and he was even elected mayor once. I remember the stories he used to tell me about famous politicians he had met. But when I told him last year that I was running for school president, he advised me not to. He was worried that I'd be too busy to focus on schoolwork, and in a way he was right. I've already had to retake some exams this term because I've been attending so many meetings. But it's worth it. I really enjoy making important decisions such as what books we should use, what school rules need changing and what school trips to take. My teachers and the other students say I'm doing a really good job. So, who knows? I might become the mayor of our town one day!

Arjit, India

My parents were surprised when I told them that I wanted to register for a course on politics. I remember watching documentaries about the amazing political leader, Mahatma Gandhi, and wanting to be like him. This is my first year at the Netagiri (leadership) school. We only have lessons on Saturdays, and I have to cycle for two hours to get there, but I don't mind. Most of my friends think I'm crazy. My brother can't see why I pay to spend my free time in a classroom. I tell them that the fee is only 50 rupees and that studying politics is as important as studying maths. It's true that some of the lessons are not that interesting, but Mr Ranjan, our teacher, has just started teaching us about social psychology and economics. I didn't know that they'd be so fascinating! I miss playing football on Saturday mornings now, but there's no other place I'd rather be than in class.

Dave, UK

When I was younger, I hadn't even heard of important political figures like Winston Churchill and Margaret Thatcher. I was only interested in playing rugby at the weekends and going out on my bike after school during the week. It all started when Mr Lloyd, our new history teacher, came to our school. I was an ignorant fourteen-year-old then and, thanks to Mr Lloyd's classes, I learnt a lot about the Second World War and the political scene in Europe and the US at the time. I'm now eighteen and I've just been elected a member of our local council! I'm quite well-known now because I'm one of the youngest politicians in the country. My parents are really proud, and my sister has a collection of newspaper articles about me. It's hard work studying at university, as well as doing council work, but I'm determined not to let my family and my voters down.

Jessica, USA

No one in my family expected me to be so interested in politics. My father liked watching chat shows on television about politics and famous politicians, but that was about it. My teachers at school were not very inspiring either, so it was reading Nelson Mandela's autobiography that got me started. My friends insist that I should get involved with the school council, but I don't want that responsibility. I'm happy just having my blog. I can upload my thoughts on local and national issues whenever I have time. I normally write one post every Saturday and I usually get about twenty comments in the first week. The topics can be anything from sports competitions at school, problems in our town, new laws or international issues. I probably won't have as much time for my blog when I start uni, but I'll try to write for it at least once a month.

Practice Test 2

WRITING PART 1

You **must** answer this question. Write your answer in **140 – 190** words in an appropriate style.

1 In your English class you have been talking about the environment. Now your English teacher has asked you to write an essay for homework.

Write your essay using **all** the notes and giving reasons for your point of view.

'Most teenagers don't do enough to help the environment.'

Do you agree?

Notes

Write about:

1 volunteering

2 recycling

3 .... (your own idea)

Students' own answers

WRITING PART 2

Write an answer to **one** of the questions **2 – 5** in this part. Write your answer in **140 – 190** words in an appropriate style.

2 You have seen this announcement in a new English-language magazine for teenagers.

Stories wanted	Your story must include:
We are looking for stories for our new English-language magazine for teenagers. Your story must **begin** with this sentence:	• a detective • a crime
Maria unlocked her front door and was shocked to see that somebody had been in her house.	

Write your **story**.

3 You have received the following letter from your English-speaking friend.

> *Our teacher has asked us to write about how people spend special or traditional days in different countries. What preparations do you have to do on the days running up to the special day? Could you describe a typical special or traditional day in your country?*
>
> *Thanks very much!*
>
> *Love, Carl*

Write your **letter**.

4 You see this announcement in an international English-language magazine for young people.

We're looking for articles about unusual collections. Have you, or any of your friends, ever collected anything unusual? Tell us about it – describe the collection and explain why it's so unusual. The best articles will be published in next month's issue.

Write your **article**.

5 Question 5 always consists of a question on the set text. Only answer question 5 if you have studied the set text. Here is an example of the kind of question you might be asked:

Your English class has had a discussion about different scenes in the book. Now your English teacher has asked you to write an essay about the scene that surprised you most. You should describe the scene and explain why it was surprising.

Write your **essay**.

Students' own answers

TIPS

Question 2: Your story will probably have four paragraphs. In the first paragraph, after the sentence which you must use, provide details about the main character, her situation and her feelings. In the main body paragraphs, describe what Maria does about her situation and what happens as a result. In the last paragraph, describe how the story ends and how your main character feels.

Question 3: Note that you're writing a letter to your friend, so this is an informal letter. Use paragraphs and remember to answer both your friend's questions.

Question 4: This article will be written for an English-language magazine aimed at young people, so you can assume that the reader will have similar interests to you, the writer. The main purpose of an article is to interest and engage your reader, so you should give your opinion and comment on the unusual collection that you are required to write about.

Question 5: Don't attempt this question if you haven't read (or seen a film version of) the set text and discussed the plot, characters, relationships and key scenes and events.

LISTENING PART 1

Questions 1 – 8

You will hear people talking in eight different situations. For questions **1 – 8**, choose the best answer (**A**, **B** or **C**).

1   You hear a football coach talking to his players before the start of the new season.
    Why is he talking to them?
    A to explain what went wrong the previous season
    B to express his gratitude that he is part of the team
    C to give them instructions for their next match

2   You overhear a conversation about a young woman called Beth.
    Where did she recently go on holiday?
    A Cuba
    B Spain
    C Paris

3   You overhear a conversation at a hairdresser's.
    How much is the woman going to spend?
    A twenty pounds
    B thirty-five pounds
    C fifty-five pounds

4   You hear an announcement at a supermarket.
    What is it about?
    A a new chocolate product
    B a three-for-one offer that has just started
    C three new yoghurt flavours

5   You hear part of an interview with an actor who won an Oscar.
    Why does he feel lucky?
    A because he has won a very important award
    B because he has worked with people he respects
    C because he is famous after only two films

6   You overhear a conversation between two sisters about a pair of trousers.
    Where is the pair of trousers?
    A under Lizzie's coat
    B in Maggie's cupboard
    C in the washing machine

7   You hear a presenter opening a music show.
    What new information does he give?
    A that the rock concert will start in ten minutes
    B that the pop singer will perform his new songs
    C that the artists' albums will be on sale

8   You hear part of an interview with a young motorcyclist.
    When will he be able to race again?
    A in two months
    B in three months
    C in five months

TIPS

As you will hear each part of the Listening paper twice, don't worry if you don't get the answer on the first listening. For Part 1, which has eight different situations, write an answer immediately after each second listening. Don't leave any question unanswered. Don't think about any previous answer – focus your attention on the next situation you will listen to.

For each of the eight situations you will both hear and read the context sentence. However, you will not hear the question and three options. Each question begins with a *Wh-* question word, so read the questions carefully to make sure you know what you are listening for.

Questions 1 and 5: The answer to a question may not be directly stated. You may hear information about all three options, but only one of them says <u>why</u> the person is speaking or feeling the way he/she does.

Question 2: All three places are mentioned, but you can get the correct answer by listening for what actually happened, not what was planned, supposed or thought.

LISTENING PART 2

Questions 9 – 18

You will hear a young inventor called Sophie Williams talking about a competition. For questions **9 – 18**, complete the sentences with a word or short phrase.

SOPHIE WILLIAMS: INVENTOR

The competition that Sophie won is held every | *two/2 years* | **9**

The mouse that Sophie invented produces a little | *heat* | **10** | when it's used.

The | *temperature* | **11** | of the mouse isn't unusual when it's set on the 'off' mode.

Sophie had some | *trouble* | **12** | during the initial design stages.

The mouse sometimes didn't work when she connected it to her | *laptop* | **13**

Sophie's | *IT teacher* | **14** | suggested the solution to the problem.

During the award ceremony, Sophie felt very | *nervous* | **15**

Journalists and important | *scientists* | **16** | attended the ceremony.

When Sophie heard she was the winner, she was taken | *by surprise* | **17**

Her next invention will be used on a(n) | *Christmas tree* | **18**

TIPS

Before you hear Part 2, you'll have 45 seconds to look through the ten questions. Use this time to think about the likely answer – is it a period of time, a person, a place, a feeling, etc? Remember you mustn't write more than three words. The information you have to fill in is in the order that you hear it and you write exactly what you hear – you don't need to change any words or paraphrase anything.

Question 15: You know the answer is going to be an adjective such as *happy* or *scared*. Maybe more than one adjective is mentioned, so don't just write down the first one you hear – listen for the one that completes the sentence.

LISTENING PART 3

Questions 19 – 23

You will hear five people talking about natural disasters. For questions **19 – 23**, choose from the list (**A – H**) which statement goes with each speaker's story. Use the letters only once. There are three extra letters which you do not need to use.

A   They didn't need transport to escape the danger.

Speaker 1   *E*   **19**

B   A boat came to rescue them.

Speaker 2   *C*   **20**

C   They usually escape by car.

Speaker 3   *A*   **21**

D   They left their home when they shouldn't have.

Speaker 4   *H*   **22**

E   Luckily their home was not damaged.

Speaker 5   *B*   **23**

F   They are more frightened of natural disasters than ever.

G   A family member rescued them.

H   They were advised to leave but didn't.

TIPS

For Part 3, use the 30 seconds you have before you hear the first speaker to read through the questions so you know what you're listening for. As you listen to each speaker, try and decide which of the eight statements is a paraphrase of something you hear that speaker say. Don't make a final decision until you've heard a speaker twice. Remember that no statement is true for more than one speaker.

Option B: Boats are mentioned by two of the speakers in this Part 3 task, but do these speakers actually say that a boat came to rescue <u>them</u> or was the boat for others? Perhaps the correct speaker for option B doesn't say the word *boat* at all!

LISTENING PART 4

Questions 24 – 30

You will hear a radio interview with Dave Oliver, who is the organiser of *Medieval Norwich*, a festival held every year in Norwich. For questions **24 – 30**, choose the best answer (**A, B or C**).

---

24 What does Dave think has had the biggest impact on the increase in popularity of the festival in Norwich?
   A other festivals in the area
   B social networking sites
   C the festival's website

25 When did Dave first get the idea to start a medieval festival?
   A when he was a student at school
   B when he was studying at university
   C when he was working in a library

26 Why was it difficult to organise the festival in the beginning?
   A because it was difficult to find the right location
   B because it wasn't easy to get funding
   C because it was hard to find performers

27 According to Dave, what's the most popular part of the festival?
   A the food market and the stalls with crafts
   B the fancy dress competition
   C the ancient fight

28 Which of Dave's responsibilities is the most difficult?
   A helping find children
   B giving directions
   C telling people where to camp

29 What activity in *Medieval Norwich* does Dave personally enjoy?
   A making his own wooden sword
   B dancing in the medieval dance workshop
   C taking part in the medieval theatre performance

30 What advice does Dave give to people who might go to *Medieval Norwich* next year?
   A Bring a blanket if you're planning to camp there.
   B Bring equipment to eat with.
   C Bring warm clothes in case of bad weather.

TIPS

Before you hear the speakers in Part 4, you'll have one minute to look through the questions. You can use this time to underline the key words in the questions and options. This will help you focus as you listen. For example, for question 25 you are listening not for when Dave first went to or became interested in medieval festivals, but for when he first got the idea to start one.

Remember that the questions follow the order of the information you hear in the recording.

When you listen the first time, you can lightly underline the answer you think is correct and cross out any option you're fairly sure is not the right answer. If you can rule out one of the options, you can listen the second time to decide between the two remaining options or to confirm the option you underlined.

Always circle an answer for every question on the question paper, even if you're just guessing – it will help you avoid making mistakes when you are transferring your answers to the answer sheet at the end.

SPEAKING PART 1

2 minutes (3 minutes for groups of three)

This part is always the same. See page 34 of Test 1.

Select one or more questions from the following category, as appropriate.

Family and friends

- **How do you celebrate important days, like New Year's Eve or birthdays, with your family?**
- **Where does your family usually spend the summer holidays?**
- **What do you and your friends do at the weekend?**
- **Who do you admire most in your family? ...... (Why?)**
- **Which member of your family are you closest to? ...... (Why?)**
- **Do you and your friends have the same interests? ...... (What are they?)**

Students' own answers

TIPS

In Part 1, you and your partner respond to simple questions from the examiner. The first two questions are always the same and you just need to answer in a natural way without saying too much. The next questions are on a general theme – here it's *Family and friends* – and you have the chance to give more than very short answers; give some details and/or reasons during your answer; you don't need to wait for the examiner to ask you a follow-up question such as *Why?* or *Tell us about it.*

Practice Test 2

SPEAKING PART 2

4 minutes (6 minutes for groups of three)

1 Entertainment
2 The arts

Interlocutor	In this part of the test, I'm going to give each of you two photographs. I'd like you to talk about your photographs on your own for about a minute, and also to answer a short question about your partner's photographs.
See photos A and B on page 177.	*(Candidate A)*, it's your turn first. Here are your photographs. They show **people having fun in different ways**.
	I'd like you to compare the photographs and say **why people might choose these types of entertainment.**
	All right?
Candidate A	*(Speak for approximately 1 minute.)*
Interlocutor	Thank you. *(Candidate B)*, **do you enjoy going to theme parks?**
Candidate B	*(Reply for approximately 30 seconds.)*
Interlocutor	Thank you.
See photos C and D on page 178.	Now, *(Candidate B)*, here are your photographs. They show **people taking part in different creative activities.**
	I'd like you to compare the photographs and say **what the advantages and disadvantages of each creative activity are for the people taking part in them.**
	All right?
Candidate B	*(Speak for approximately 1 minute.)*
Interlocutor	Thank you. *(Candidate A)*, **which of these creative activities would you like to be good at?**
Candidate A	*(Reply for approximately 30 seconds.)*
Interlocutor	Thank you.

Students' own answers

TIPS

In Part 2 you speak on your own for a minute about two related photos. The examiner gives you the photos, tells you what they show, asks you to compare them and gives you a question to answer. The question is also written above the photos. When the minute is up, the examiner will ask your partner a question related to your photos.

When you get your photos – which your partner can also see – talk about the similarities and differences between them first and then go on to answer the question. You shouldn't describe people and places in great detail. Keep speaking and try to introduce what you want to say with natural-sounding phrases such as *It looks like they're both ...*, *It seems to me that ...* and *I imagine that ....*

SPEAKING PARTS 3 AND 4

Travel and holidays

8 minutes (11 minutes for groups of three)

PART 3

Interlocutor

Now, I'd like you to talk about something together for about two minutes.
(3 minutes for groups of three)

See written prompts on page 179.

I'd like you to imagine that you and your friends are planning a holiday together. Here are some ideas for the holiday and a question for you to discuss. First you have some time to look at the task.

Now, talk to each other about **which type of holiday you would choose if you and your friends went on holiday together.**

Candidates

(Discuss for approximately 2 minutes – 3 minutes for groups of three.)

Interlocutor

Thank you. Now you have about a minute to decide **which two would be the least expensive.**

Candidates

(Reply for approximately 1 minute – for pairs and groups of three.)

Interlocutor

Thank you.

PART 4

Interlocutor

Select any of the following questions, as appropriate:

- **Did you go on holiday last summer?......
  (Where did you go?)**

- **Which is the safest/cheapest/most expensive way to travel in your country?**

- **Have you ever been on a camping holiday/ sightseeing holiday/cruise? Did you enjoy it? ...... (Why?/Why not?)**

- **Some people say that travelling abroad is the best way to learn a foreign language. Do you agree? ...... (Why?/Why not?)**

- **What are the most typical things that tourists do when they visit your country?**

Thank you. That is the end of the test.

Select any of the following prompts, as appropriate:

- **What do you think?**
- **Do you agree?**
- **And you?**

Students' own answers

TIPS

In Part 3, you and your partner speak to each other, so don't look at the examiner once you start your conversation. The examiner will give you some written prompts to look at, tell you the theme and give you two questions to answer.

When you're answering the first question, talk about all written prompts. Remember that this is a conversation, not two monologues, so as well as giving your views, ask for your partner's opinion and comment on what they say. Give yourselves time to try to agree on an answer to the second question, though if you don't agree, that's fine. What's important is that you have a discussion together. You're not talking about the written prompts; you're using it to explore the questions.

The questions you will be asked in Part 4 lead on from the theme in Part 3. You should try and give full answers and one way of doing this is to keep useful question words in your head, eg *Why, How, When, Where*. If you're answering the question *Did you go on holiday last summer?* you could say *Yes* and say **when** and **where** you went, **who** you went with and **what** you did. If you didn't go anywhere you could give reasons **why**.

If you look at the other questions in this practice test, you can see that thinking of the question *Why?* is useful to help you expand your answers for each one of them.

Remember – there's no 'right' answer or 'correct' opinion; you're only judged on how well you communicate in English, so show the examiners what you can do!

Practice Test 3

READING AND USE OF ENGLISH `PART 1`

For questions **1 – 8**, read the text below and decide which answer (**A**, **B**, **C** or **D**) best fits each gap. There is an example at the beginning (**0**).

Example:

0 A familiar   **B** successful   **C** accustomed   **D** suitable

0	A	B	C	D
	■			

The origin of tennis

Wimbledon and the US, French and Australian Open tennis tournaments are **(0)** _____ to millions of sports fans every where. But when and where did this popular sport begin?

(1) _____ to some history books, the modern form of tennis first started in 19th-century Britain, when a British army officer **(2)** _____ on the equipment and the rules for lawn tennis in 1874. Of course the game is much older than that, but historians disagree about its exact **(3)** _____.

Some say tennis was invented by the ancient Egyptians and there is some historical **(4)** _____ to suggest tennis was played in ancient times. Other historians think tennis first appeared in 11th-century France, where the game usually took **(5)** _____ outside and the hands were used to hit the ball.

As the game became better-known, it **(6)** _____ to other countries, and the hand was **(7)** _____ with the racquet. The English king, Henry VIII, played an indoor **(8)** _____ of the game in one of his palaces. From that time on, tennis has grown into the worldwide sport we know and love today.

1	**A** Writing	**B** Concerning	**C** Regarding	**D** According
2	**A** decided	**B** put	**C** made	**D** took
3	**A** opening	**B** origins	**C** background	**D** beginning
4	**A** evidence	**B** proof	**C** information	**D** truth
5	**A** place	**B** part	**C** account	**D** hold
6	**A** grew	**B** widened	**C** travelled	**D** spread
7	**A** replaced	**B** switched	**C** introduced	**D** transformed
8	**A** edition	**B** version	**C** sort	**D** type

TIPS

Remember to read through the whole text before you look at the multiple-choice options. As you do so, you will be thinking of a word that can complete the gap and getting a sense of the overall meaning. You might want to lightly pencil in any word that you guess fits.

When you are deciding on the correct option, make sure you read the whole sentence with the gap in it and consider all four options.

Question 5: Sometimes you can discount an option because it doesn't fit grammatically, but on other occasions, all the options after a particular word – in this case the word *take* – are possible in English. However, only one fits with the meaning in the text. Remember that people *take part* and events *take place*.

READING AND USE OF ENGLISH `PART 2`

For questions **9 – 16**, read the text below and think of the word which best fits each gap. Use only **one** word in each gap. There is an example at the beginning (**0**).

Write your answers **IN CAPITAL LETTERS**.

Example: | **0** | *O F* |

Child stars

This week saw the modelling debut **(0)** _OF_ Cassie Andrews, daughter of the famous fashion model Dana. Cassie appeared at a fashion show in Paris and was an instant success with the press and public. But the **(9)** _MOST_ interesting part of the story is that Cassie is only ten years old. Is this a bit **(10)** _TOO_ young for a child to begin a career in modelling? Some people think **(11)** _SO_.

There are many sad stories about child stars **(12)** _WHO/THAT_ started acting or modelling at a very young age and experienced terrible problems **(13)** _AS_ a consequence. The teenage years are a difficult time for anyone, but if you **(14)** _ARE_ followed everywhere by journalists who photograph everything you do, the pressure can be too much.

But there are a **(15)** _FEW_ success stories. Shirley Conrad made several hit films before her twentieth birthday and then had a complete change of career. She moved into the world of politics and eventually became one of **(16)** _THE_ first women to be elected to parliament. She often said that her early experience with acting gave her the confidence to go into politics.

TIPS

As with Part 1, you should read the whole text through before you decide on the answers. Remember that all the missing words are simple ones that you know well. For each gap, look at the words that come before as well as after the gap and think about what type of word would fit – is it a preposition, relative pronoun, auxiliary verb, etc? Never fill a gap with more than one word.

Question 11: You know many words that often follow *think*: you can think *about* or *of* something/someone and think *that* something is true. But none of these fit the gap here because the gapped sentence is about something said earlier and the word you need ends the sentence.

Question 15: Be careful you don't rush to put in a word because the answer looks easy. If you don't read carefully, you might fill this gap with *some* or *many* because you didn't notice the little word *a* before the gap.

READING AND USE OF ENGLISH PART 3

For questions **17 – 24**, read the text below. Use the word given in capitals at the end of some of the lines to form a word that fits the gap **in the same line**. There is an example at the beginning **(0)**.

Write your answers **IN CAPITAL LETTERS**.

Example: | 0 | D | I | S | A | D | V | A | N | T | A | G | E | D | | | | | | |

Lighting the room with water bottles

In the Philippines, many **(0)** _DISADVANTAGED_ people cannot afford electricity.   **ADVANTAGE**
So something as simple as lighting your home is nearly **(17)** _IMPOSSIBLE_.   **POSSIBLE**

Now people are hoping to solve this problem with an amazing new
(18) _INVENTION_. It involves using an ordinary plastic water bottle filled   **INVENT**
with a(n) **(19)** _MIXTURE_ of filtered water and a small amount of   **MIX**
bleach.

Liter of Light, the **(20)** _ORGANISATION_ that promotes the method, hopes   **ORGANISE**
to provide lighting to one million homes in the Philippines. The 'lights'
are **(21)** _EASILY_ installed by cutting a hole in the roof the same   **EASY**
(22) _WIDTH_ as the bottle. The water-filled bottle is then inserted in   **WIDE**
the hole and sealed with glue. Although it only works during the day,
the water bottle provides light to homes that would otherwise be dark
inside.

People who were previously **(23)** _UNABLE_ to pay for indoor lighting   **ABLE**
will now be able to spend more time inside the home. It is relatively
(24) _INEXPENSIVE_ to install the water bottles, costing less than a pound,   **EXPENSE**
so everyone can afford it.

TIPS

For Part 3, the word at the end of the line must always be changed in some way. Read the surrounding sentence to decide what changes you need to make to the stem word. Should you make the word an adjective, a noun, a plural, a negative, etc?

For two of the answers here you need to keep the stem word as it is and just add a prefix. Which are they? One word needs a change which is not a prefix or suffix – which one? Think about how to add a suffix to a stem word ending in e or y, such as questions 20 and 21. Do you keep these letters, remove them or put another letter in their place?

READING AND USE OF ENGLISH PART 4

For questions **25 – 30**, complete the second sentence so that it has a similar meaning to the first sentence, using the word given. **Do not change the word given.** You must use between **two** and **five** words, including the word given. Here is an example (**0**).

Example:

0   A friendly taxi driver drove us into town.

DRIVEN

We _____*WERE*_____ *DRIVEN INTO TOWN BY* _____ a friendly taxi driver.

The gap can be filled by the words 'were driven into town by', so you write:

Example: | **0** | | *WERE DRIVEN INTO TOWN BY* |

Write **only** the missing words **IN CAPITAL LETTERS.**

---

25   Going camping appeals to Rudy.
KEEN
Rudy _____*IS KEEN ON*_____ going camping.

26   We had no difficulty in finding your house.
DIFFICULT *WAS NOT/*
It *WASN'T DIFFICULT TO FIND* your house.

27   Nobody but Henry gave her a birthday present.
ONLY
Henry was *THE ONLY ONE/PERSON TO* give her a birthday present.

28   It might rain, so don't forget your umbrella if you go out!
CASE *AN/YOUR*
If you go out, take *UMBRELLA IN CASE IT* rains!

29   Would you like to see a film tonight?
FEEL
How do you ____*FEEL ABOUT SEEING*____ a film tonight?

30   'You're too young to go to the theatre on your own,' said Frank's father.
OLD *HE WAS NOT/*
Frank's father told him *WASN'T OLD ENOUGH* to go to the theatre alone.

TIPS

Question 25: You've probably learnt a list of adjectives + prepositions + *ing*, eg, *interested in, scared of, enthusiastic about*. Which preposition comes after *keen*? And which verb usually goes before adjectives like *interested* and *keen*?

Question 27: Be careful when the verb changes tense in the second sentence. In the lead-in sentence, it's in the past – *gave*, but it's *give* in the second, so you can't put the word *who* before it. What can you put?

Question 30: Remember to put the verb in the correct tense for reported speech. When you use a negative, you can put it in a contracted form, eg *did not = didn't*, but remember all contractions except *cannot* count as two words.

READING AND USE OF ENGLISH `PART 5`

Questions 31 – 36

You are going to read an extract from a novel. For questions **31 – 36**, choose the answer (**A, B, C** or **D**) which you think fits best according to the text.

Leaving home

When I went to university at the age of eighteen, I think it was a relief to both of us. We had grown apart; she had grown old, and I had grown up. We were like strangers to each other, and it was clear we were not getting on as we once had, when there had been six of us in the house and, as the baby of the family, I had enjoyed everyone's attention. But then my four older brothers and sisters had spread their wings, only rarely returning to visit at Christmas and occasionally in summer. Having flown the coop, they brought back to their little brother stories of the outside world, amazing tales of the fabulous lives they led far away in the big city, so different from our little nest they had left so empty.

We lived in an old but grand house on the top of a small hill outside a village in the countryside. We were not rich and not poor. My father had left us some money in his will, and this was enough to keep us in some comfort, financially if not emotionally. I had been too young to even attend his funeral, and his absence caused me less emotional discomfort than it did for the rest of the family. But somehow I failed to appreciate my mother as much as I should have and certainly caused her more sadness than her other children. She spent the middle years of her life bringing us up alone; alone in every sense of the word, as there were no uncles, aunts or cousins nearby. She had to try very hard just to keep in touch with distant family members who had spread across the world over the years.

line 29   I thought at the time that my mother had exhausted herself with her efforts with my siblings and had very little left to give to me. She had produced four fine young adults who were well on the way to making successes of their lives, but at some point – and I set the date as the day Judith, my youngest sister, left – it seemed to me that she had stopped making that effort, and she had just stopped caring for me. Somehow, I thought, she perhaps felt she had done enough, that I would learn from example and didn't need any personal guidance. From that day it was just the two of us in the huge old house on the hill, I grew further and further away from her until I couldn't leave for university quickly enough.

So off I went, without a backwards look or a wave goodbye, with few regrets – on either side, as far as I was concerned.

I assumed my mother would appreciate the solitude she had never had, having married young. I now know she was heartbroken to be abandoned by her youngest child and I was never to be so deeply loved again. But I had grown tired of being the baby of the family and was only interested in my future as an adult and not my past as a child. In reality, I was neither. This ignorance about myself and other people was just one example of my general immaturity. I knew everything, or so I thought – the one sure sign that someone has a lot to learn and a lot of growing up to do. I don't know how anyone put up with me. Indeed, as an adult, I find it impossible to stand this sort of thing in others. Of course, my older and wiser brothers and sisters saw the situation much more clearly and were careful to protect my mother from the worst of my behaviour, which really amounted to not calling her, not attending family gatherings at Christmas and being generally distant. I spent my university years, and several years after, avoiding those closest to me, something which I bitterly regretted in later life.

TIPS

Question 31: You know you should read through the whole text quickly before you look at the questions, and doing this will help you with the first question here. The questions follow the order of the information in the text, so you can find the answer to question 31 in the first paragraph, but the information you need can also be found at the beginning of the third paragraph.

Question 36: Always read the stem question and the answer options carefully. The key word in this question is *now*. Option B mentions bad treatment, but was this from them to him? Don't choose an option if it is not supported by the text. We know the writer wasn't close to his relatives in the past, but is he still distant from them now? If the text doesn't give us the answer, we don't know.

31 How many people were left living at home when the author left?
   A five
   B one
   C two
   D six

32 In the first paragraph, what does the writer mean by 'flown the coop'?
   A left home
   B found jobs
   C got married
   D bought a house

33 What is the situation with the author's mother and father?
   A His father lives apart from the family.
   B They are divorced.
   C His mother is a widow.
   D His mother asked his father to leave.

34 What does the word 'siblings' mean in line 29?
   A children
   B family
   C parents
   D brothers and sisters

35 How did the author think his mother felt when he left home?
   A He thought she wouldn't enjoy being alone.
   B He knew it would break her heart.
   C He supposed she wouldn't mind him leaving.
   D He didn't care how she felt.

36 How does the author now feel about his family?
   A He wishes he had behaved better towards them.
   B He realises how badly they treated him.
   C He isn't close to them anymore.
   D He maintains a distance from them.

READING AND USE OF ENGLISH PART 6

Questions 37 – 42

You are going to read an article about a new way to teach poetry. Six sentences have been removed from the article. Choose from the sentences **A – G** the one which fits each gap (**37 – 42**). There is one extra sentence which you do not need to use.

Teaching poetry through hip-hop

Teachers by day, performance artists by night, these teachers have discovered an inspiring new way to teach an old subject.

Most of us would agree that the majority of school kids aren't too interested in poetry. It's a little bit boring, difficult to understand and even harder to write. However, we all know school kids are more enthusiastic about modern music. Two teachers at London's Kingsbury High have developed a way to use the poetic characteristics of modern music, in particular hip-hop lyrics, to engage students in learning poetry.

Sam Berkson and Chris Beschi are both teachers at Kingsbury High who also give poetry readings in the evenings at local entertainment venues. Together, the two teachers perform poetry in a hip-hop style for all of the students in Year 9, using poems from the school syllabus. **37** *E* From this reaction it is clear that the students are engaged by the teachers' technique.

The two teachers believe that kids view poetry as boring, hard to understand, and out of touch with their reality. Their technique involves creating a link between poetry and the kids' lives through things they're into, such as hip-hop. The teachers show them this connection. **38** *B* Before long, hopefully, students will want to go beyond an appreciation of it and want to create it as well.

Berkson and Beschi focus on poetry that has themes which relate to London's urban scene. Students at Kingsbury High come from diverse backgrounds and thus have a wide range of (possibly conflicting) interests. **39** *G* Through poetry that relates to their shared lives, students can learn to express their feelings about their surroundings.

Of course, there are many ways for young people to express themselves and their feelings creatively, such as through art or other forms of creative writing. These may even be preferred by some students. But it's good for students to be made aware of poetry, one of the oldest forms of self-expression, at the same time. Often, students are pressured to excel at other school subjects, such as maths and science. **40** *C* However, the skills acquired from learning poetry and performing it in front of the class are equally valuable. They allow students to communicate better and believe in themselves.

Berkson and Beschi admit that their teaching method doesn't work for everyone. This applies more to the teachers than to the students. Some teachers may have the ability to analyse and explain poetry to a class, but they will run into problems when they try to teach students how to write and perform it if they are not poets themselves. **41** *F*

Probably one of the most important things students can gain from this method is confidence. Many students at Kingsbury High lack a certain amount of inner strength. **42** *D* Through writing their own poetry and reading it aloud, students can learn how to command a crowd with the power of their voice and their ideas. And that's a lesson that extends well beyond the classroom.

A Because of that, they have many things in common which allow them to work well together.

B Once they see that, they are more likely to appreciate poetry.

C These are typically considered 'useful subjects'.

D They often lack the confidence to be leaders.

E The audience response is very loud when they have finished!

F For this reason, it needs a special kind of teacher, so the method does have limitations.

G However, they all share the experience of living and growing up in London.

TIPS

You should read the text first to get an overall idea of its meaning, ideas development and structure. When you're deciding which sentence fits a gap, make sure it fits with both what comes before it and what comes after it in the text.

When you're looking at the seven sentences **A – G**, pay special attention to the reference words such as *them, they, this, that* and *these*. Nearly all the sentences here contain one or more of these words. Work out what they refer to.

Question 37: You can try and guess what information/ideas will be included in the sentence which fills this gap. The sentence before the gap tells you that the teachers perform and the sentence after the gap tells you that the students are engaged because of *this reaction*. The sentence that fills the gap must be about the students' positive response.

Sentence C: You can work out that there must be at least two examples of *useful subjects* in the text immediately before Sentence C.

READING AND USE OF ENGLISH PART 7

Questions 43 – 52

You are going to read a newspaper article about different places where people have eaten. For questions **43 – 52**, choose from the people (**A – D**). The people may be chosen more than once.

Which person (or people)

didn't experience good food until they grew up?	**43**	D
liked the atmosphere?	**44**	C
liked the building?	**45**	A
didn't care that the food wasn't extraordinary?	**46**	C
probably ate the most expensive meal?	**47**	A
describes the wonderful flavour of the food?	**48**	D
had a social experience while eating?	**49**	C
felt guilty when they were eating?	**50**	A
ate a kind of food that is extremely popular nowadays	**51**	B
had a meal in a car?	**52**	B

My place for food

We asked four food writers about the most memorable place they have eaten in.

A Bruce

I once ate at an underwater restaurant in a luxury five-star hotel. It was in one big room, and you reached it by going down in a lift from the ground floor of the hotel. The walls, floor and ceiling were all made of glass, and behind the glass there was just the sea. You were entirely surrounded by water, and in the water there were thousands of brightly-coloured tropical fish swimming around. It was like being in the middle of a giant aquarium. It's an engineering miracle, really, and it must have cost a lot to build, which is why the prices were so high, I suppose. Of course, the menu included some fantastic seafood, but it felt a little strange sitting there eating your fish while his friends swam around you, watching you with their accusing eyes! I could imagine what they might say to each other about me as every mouthful went down. I ate very quickly and took the lift back upstairs!

B Melanie

One of the most memorable meals I've had was actually fast food. This was years ago, before all those American chains started to appear all over the UK, so it was quite new to me. I was driving across the United States for a summer break, all the way from one side of the country to the other. We were in Texas and went through a small town in the middle of the night, and the only place to eat that was open was a 24-hour drive-through restaurant. We'd never even heard of anything like that before. You stopped and gave your order into a microphone outside the restaurant. Then you drove round the corner of the building to collect your food at a little window. It was like an adventure. We told everyone all about it when we got home.

C Lena

I'm lucky because I lived in London a few years ago, where you can find any kind of food you want. There are thousands of restaurants with all sorts of cuisines from all over the world. But my favourite place to eat was actually a little café on the corner near my house. The food was nothing special, no different from anywhere else. The place was even a bit dirty and needed to be painted, especially the bathroom, but I knew everyone in there, so it was like a little community. You went in, saw a familiar face and had a chat while your food came. I generally popped in for breakfast – eggs, bacon, toast and a cup of tea. Not very healthy, I know, but it was the feeling of being with friends I liked the best.

D Dave

When I was growing up, my mother used to cook terrible meals, and we never went out to eat, so I never really enjoyed eating. In those days in my country, people weren't very adventurous with food, and in general I found it tasteless and uninteresting. That's why I prefer foreign cuisine now, particularly Italian. I loved it from the first time I tried it. I was on a trip to Italy, just sightseeing and relaxing before I started my first job after university, when I discovered Luigi's, a small traditional restaurant in the hills above Pescara. I couldn't believe how tasty everything was. The whole family was involved in the business, either cooking or serving, or just growing the vegetables and fruit in their fields. The meat came from the butcher in the same village. Every dish was freshly cooked and full of wonderful-tasting ingredients.

WRITING PART 1

You **must** answer this question. Write your answer in **140 – 190** words in an appropriate style.

1 In your English class you have been talking about young people working. Now your teacher has asked you to write an essay for homework.

Write your essay using **all** the notes and giving reasons for your point of view.

Some teenagers have part-time jobs while they are still in school.
Is this a good or a bad thing for the teenagers?

Notes

Write about:

1 earning pocket money

2 less time for studying

3 .... (your own idea)

Students' own answers

For Part 1, being able to support your opinion with reasons and examples is another skill you will need to write an effective essay. The two prompts you are given help to guide and develop the essay and always clearly relate to the question or statement you need to deal with. You also need to think of a third idea of your own which is distinct from the two prompts given. Try brainstorming ideas for different topics because it is very useful practice for this. Remember that if you miss out any of the three essay prompts, you will be penalised.

WRITING PART 2

Write an answer to **one** of the questions **2 – 5** in this part. Write your answer in **140 – 190** words in an appropriate style.

2   Your school is having a story-writing competition and you decide to enter. Your story must begin with this sentence:

When Mary woke up, she didn't expect her day to be so difficult.

Your story must include:

- an appointment
- an accident

Write your **story**.

3   Your teacher has asked you to write a review for the school magazine of a book you have read recently. Review the book, giving your opinion and saying whether or not you would recommend it.

Write your **review**.

4   You have seen this announcement in your local newspaper.

> How does technology like the Internet and mobile phones affect the way we live today? We are looking for articles about the effect of modern technology on our lives.

Write your **article**.

5   Question 5 always consists of a question on the set text. Only answer question 5 if you have studied the set text. Here is an example of the kind of question you might be asked:

Your English class has had a discussion about the book you have read and now your English teacher has asked you to write an article for the school magazine. Write about an important event in the book. How does the event affect the main character?

Write your **article**.

Students' own answers

TIPS

Question 2: Before you write your story, take a little time to think of answers to some question words: *Who is Mary? Where is she when she wakes up? What difficulties did she have to face during the day? How did she deal with them? What happens in the end?* You can make short notes so you remember what to include. Use your imagination – the story can be as strange and surprising as you like. Try and use interesting adjectives, adverbs and expressions and remember to use time expressions, past forms and to link your ideas together.

Question 3: Don't choose this question if you can't remember much about any particular book. If you do have a book in mind, you should do three things: briefly describe what it is about, say what you think of it and whether others should read it. You can write the title and author of the book as a heading. Of course, it doesn't have to be a book you read in English. If the book is a novel, don't just retell the story; you should give your personal response. If you hated the book, say so and say why!

Question 4: It's important to plan an article. Make a short list of ways modern technology affects our lives for good or bad. Apart from the Internet and mobile phones, you could talk about the impact of new medical, energy or transport technology if you know anything about such things. Join the points you make with words and phrases such as *The Internet not only ... but also ..., As well as ..., having a mobile means you can ...*

You should give your article a title and try and get the reader interested in what you have to say from the beginning. You can use questions and address the reader directly, eg, *Have you ever stopped to think about what the world was like when your grandparents were your age?* You might want to use examples and anecdotes to liven up your writing, eg, *Yesterday I used Skype to talk to and see my aunt in Australia and my sister in London at the same time – and it was free!*

Question 5: Follow the instructions carefully. You won't do well if you write about an important event in the book and don't mention how the event affects the main character. In this article, you must address both questions in order to have a successful article.

LISTENING PART 1

Questions 1 – 8

You will hear people talking in eight different situations. For questions **1 – 8**, choose the best answer (**A**, **B** or **C**).

1 You hear a man talking on the radio about the weather.
What does he say to people who might be travelling?
   A All roads are closed across the country.
   B People can travel if they really want to.
   C Driving might be difficult but not impossible.

2 You hear two people having a conversation while they are waiting for a bus.
What problem do they have?
   A They are not sure what the time is.
   B The bus is late.
   C The girl has lost her watch.

3 You hear a voicemail message which a woman leaves for one of her colleagues at work.
What does she tell her colleague?
   A The Belfast office will definitely send the information.
   B The work can be completed on time if she gets some help.
   C She can't possibly finish the work by the right date.

4 You hear two schoolchildren discussing one of their teachers.
What do they say about her?
   A She has started to be nice to her students.
   B She is very strict with everyone.
   C She is fair to all their classmates.

5 You hear two people talking about their friend.
What happened to him?
   A He was seriously injured in a fall.
   B He escaped unhurt from a dangerous situation.
   C He has recovered after an accident.

6 You hear a travel agent talking about holidays.
What does the person say about choosing a holiday?
   A They can give you good advice.
   B It's difficult to choose a luxury holiday.
   C They have the best selection of modern holidays.

7 You hear two teenagers talking.
What does the girl say about school?
   A She is too tired to do her exams.
   B She will have a rest in the summer holidays.
   C She has too much work to do.

8 You hear a couple talking about a film they have just seen together.
What do they say?
   A They both think the film was too long.
   B The woman doesn't like films about boats.
   C The man prefers films about people and animals.

TIPS

Question 1: Read the options carefully.

A: You will hear some information about roads and closures, but is it the <u>roads</u> that are closed?

B: To be the correct answer, the wording in the option must reflect what you actually hear. Does the speaker say people are only allowed to travel if they really <u>want</u> to?

C: Can people still drive despite bad conditions?

Question 3: Sometimes there will be more than one phrase or sentence that points you in the direction of the correct answer. Is the speaker 100% sure that Belfast will send the information or that she won't finish the work on time? If there is any doubt about either of these things, then the correct answer has to be something else.

LISTENING PART 2

Questions 9 – 18

You will hear a radio programme about the problems facing young people today. For questions **9 – 18**, complete the sentences with a word or short phrase.

Young people and the world today

The lack of | *money* | **9** | in the economy can cause young people problems.

According to the speaker, being a teenager is never | *easy* | **10**

The speaker says that going to university is now | *more expensive* | **11** | than it used to be.

The alternative to going to university is getting a(n) | *job* | **12**

The speaker advises young people to discuss their | *intentions* | **13** | with their parents.

In most countries, more people are | *unemployed* | **14** | than ever before.

In spite of the bad economic situation, the | *majority* | **15** | of young people are feeling confident about the years ahead.

Africa has always had problems with | *poverty* | **16**

In some countries in Africa, young people are sometimes forced into | *the army* | **17** | by the government.

In some places in the world, the law cannot | *protect* | **18** | child workers.

TIPS

Although you should read through the questions and guess what word or type of word(s) might complete the sentences, don't write anything in the gaps until you listen. Remember that you only write words that you hear in the text; don't try to paraphrase using your own words to fill the gaps.

The word(s) you fill the gap with have to fit so the sentence makes grammatical sense, so for question 11 you're listening for a comparative word or phrase and for question 15 the answer can't be a number or a percentage.

LISTENING PART 3

Questions 19 – 23

You will hear five people talking about their favourite place. For questions **19 – 23**, choose from the list (**A – H**) what each speaker says. Use the letters only once. There are three extra letters which you do not need to use.

A   I go to this place to listen to really loud music.

Speaker 1 | F | **19** |

B   My favourite place is exciting but impersonal.

Speaker 2 | C | **20** |

C   I go to this place to be completely alone.

Speaker 3 | B | **21** |

D   I enjoy meeting strangers in my favourite place.

Speaker 4 | E | **22** |

E   Nobody else knows I go there.

F   The most important thing about the place I go to is the feeling of freedom.

Speaker 5 | G | **23** |

G   My favourite place is a meeting point for a group of friends.

H   My favourite place is special because I get lots of exercise there.

TIPS

For Part 3, use the 30 seconds you have before you hear the first speaker to read through the questions so you know what you are listening for. As you listen to each speaker, try and decide which of the eight statements is a paraphrase of something you hear that speaker say. Don't make a final decision until you've heard a speaker twice. Remember that no statement is true for more than one speaker.

Remember that *all* the information in each of the statements A – H must be true for a particular speaker, so if a speaker mentions escaping from their troubles, but *not* by being alone in a special personal space, then statement C isn't the right match. Perhaps no speaker actually says the word *problems*, but does give an example or two of specific problems they get away from by being completely by themselves. This may be the person you're looking for to match with C.

Speaker 4: You might think that this matches statement D because he is with strangers in his favourite place, but does he say he *enjoys* meeting them?

LISTENING PART 4

Questions 24 – 30

You will hear a radio interview with Neil Stanton, a fiction writer from Blackpool. For questions **24 – 30**, choose the best answer (**A**, **B** or **C**).

24 What reason does Neil give for why he's a fiction writer?
   A It's a glamorous way to make a living.
   B He had early success as a writer.
   C He enjoys the endless possibilities.

25 How does Neil say he gets his best ideas for stories?
   A by visiting faraway places
   B by spending time with other people
   C by spending time by himself

26 After deciding on an idea, how does Neil begin planning a story?
   A He starts with the ending in mind.
   B He writes about the people in the story.
   C He writes a description of the plot.

27 What aspect of writing gives Neil the most trouble?
   A His stories are often too long at first.
   B He finds it difficult to make all parts of a story interesting.
   C He has trouble thinking of a conclusion.

28 What kind of characters does Neil say are his favourite?
   A those who make a lot of noise
   B those who do the unexpected
   C those who are very productive

29 What books does Neil say he enjoys reading these days?
   A books about the subject he studied
   B books which are similar to his own stories
   C books about times gone by

30 What does Neil advise first-time writers to do?
   A Don't worry about the finer details at first.
   B Spend a lot of time on the details.
   C Go back and fix mistakes straight away.

TIPS

The correct option for each question will be a rephrasing, a report or a summary of what is said. To help you focus, use the minute you have to look at Part 4 to underline the key words in the stem questions and options. For question 24, you might underline the words *why*, *glamorous*, *early success* and *endless possibilities*.

Be careful of 'word spotting' – that is choosing an answer because you hear a word from an option in the text. You will hear Neil say *glamorous*, but listen for the context – perhaps Neil says that being a fiction writer just <u>seems</u> glamorous to others or that it is glamorous but that's not <u>his</u> reason for choosing it as a career. Remember that the correct option is usually a paraphrase of something in the text rather than a repetition.

Make sure you listen carefully to the whole of each section (Neil's responses to the questions) before you decide on your answer; in this Practice Test, the key information you need to get the right answer is often towards the end of the section.

SPEAKING PART 1

2 minutes (3 minutes for groups of three)

This part is always the same. See page 34 of Test 1.

Select one or more questions from the following category, as appropriate.

Future plans

- **What will you do when you leave school? ...... (Tell us about your plans.)**
- **Do you want to go to university or get a job?**
- **Do you want to do something else before going to university/getting a job? ...... (What?)**
- **What would you like to study at university? ...... (Why?)**
- **What job do you think you will do? ...... (Why?)**
- **Do you want to work/study in your country or another country? ...... (Where? Why?)**

Students' own answers

TIPS

TIPS

After you've given your name, said where you're from and what you like about living there, for Practice Test 3 you'll be asked one or two questions about your study and work plans. It's up to you to give more than a short, simple answer. Give reasons for your answers or if you're undecided, say why and give some possibilities of what you might do. If you only say one or two words, the examiner can't give you a good mark.

Practice Test 3

SPEAKING PART 2

4 minutes (6 minutes for groups of three)

1 Education
2 The environment

Interlocutor	In this part of the test, I'm going to give each of you two photographs. I'd like you to talk about your photographs on your own for about a minute, and also to answer a short question about your partner's photographs.
See photos A and B on page 180.	*(Candidate A)*, it's your turn first. Here are your photographs. They show **students at school and university.** I'd like you to compare the photographs and say **what the differences are between studying at school and studying at university.** All right?
Candidate A	*(Speak for approximately 1 minute.)*
Interlocutor	Thank you. *(Candidate B)*, **do you think it's a good idea to go to university after school?**
Candidate B	*(Reply for approximately 30 seconds.)*
Interlocutor	Thank you.
See photos C and D on page 181.	Now, *(Candidate B)*, here are your photographs. They show **some environmental problems.** I'd like you to compare the photographs and say **what environmental problems modern technology can cause.** All right?
Candidate B	*(Speak for approximately 1 minute.)*
Interlocutor	Thank you. *(Candidate A)*, **why do you think there are so many environmental problems today?**
Candidate A	*(Reply for approximately 30 seconds.)*
Interlocutor	Thank you.

Students' own answers

TIPS

When you're comparing your two photos, don't worry if you don't know or can't remember a particular word you want to say. Maybe you start a sentence like this, *Well, here we can see a factory with lots of smoke coming from a …* and you can't remember the word *chimney*. It's fine if you say, *Oh, I've forgotten the word for that thing sticking up in the sky, but anyway there's a lot of pollution*. The important thing is to keep going.

After you've compared the photos, remember to give your answer to the question written above the photographs. The question is connected with the photos, so even though you have no experience of studying at university, for example, you can still say something using what you see in the photo, eg, *I imagine you'd have more opportunities to discuss things with your teacher in small groups at university.*

SPEAKING PARTS 3 AND 4

8 minutes (11 minutes for groups of three)

Museums and art galleries

PART 3

Interlocutor	Now, I'd like you to talk about something together for about two minutes. *(3 minutes for groups of three)*

See written prompts on page 182.

Here are some reasons why many teachers take their students to museums and art galleries on school outings and a question for you to discuss. First you have some time to look at the task.

Now, talk to each other about **whether it's a good idea for students to go to museums and art galleries on school outings.**

Candidates	*(Discuss for approximately 2 minutes – 3 minutes for groups of three.)*
Interlocutor	Thank you. Now you have about a minute to decide **which two things are the most important for teachers to think about when they choose a museum or art gallery for a school outing.**
Candidates	*(Reply for approximately 1 minute – for pairs and groups of three.)*
Interlocutor	**Thank you.**

PART 4

Interlocutor

Select any of the following questions, as appropriate:

- **Why do people visit museums and galleries?**
- **Do you think museums and galleries are just for tourists, or do they have another purpose?**
- **What kind of galleries and museums are most important? ...... (Why?)**
- **Do you think a country should spend a lot of money on museums and galleries? ...... (Why?/Why not?)**
- **Do you think the things in museums and galleries should be sold if the country needs money?**
- **Are galleries and museums just for art, or should there be other things in them, too? ...... (What things?)**
- **Do you think visitors to galleries and museums should have to pay to get in? ...... (Why?/Why not?)**

Select any of the following prompts, as appropriate:

- **What do you think?**
- **Do you agree?**
- **And you?**

Thank you. That is the end of the test.

Students' own answers

TIPS

Part 3 is a discussion between you and your partner, so you don't just take turns to talk about the written prompts – you share your thoughts and opinions about the written prompts related to the question. You're having a conversation about why teachers take their students on school outings to museums and galleries. You are free to say what you like on the subject, but try to justify your views on the different ideas about museums and art galleries outlined in the written prompts. Remember to leave time to answer the second question and give reasons for your choice.

The questions in Part 4 ask you to give your opinions and support them with reasons. Don't just answer in short sentences, eg, *People visit museums to learn about the past*. Introduce what you are going to say, eg, *I suppose there are different reasons – maybe it depends on your age – school kids might only go because they're forced to by their school for example ...*

Maybe you'll be asked a question that you've never thought about before. You'll always have something to say if you remember to talk about your own personal experience and what happens in your country before giving an opinion. You can also ask your partner what they think.

83

Practice Test 4

READING AND USE OF ENGLISH PART 1

For questions **1 – 8**, read the text below and decide which answer (**A**, **B**, **C** or **D**) best fits each gap. There is an example at the beginning (**0**).

Example:

0 **A** ended **B** gone **C** become **D** turned

0	A	B	C	D
	▭	▭	■	▭

TV cooking programmes for kids – *great entertainment or cheap exploitation?*

Reality TV shows have **(0)** ______ extremely popular in recent years. Initially **(1)** ______ just adults, they now frequently include children and teenagers as well. **(2)** ______ the most successful of these kinds of programmes are talent shows, and in **(3)** ______, cooking competitions.

A heated debate has arisen amongst commentators as to the **(4)** ____ and wrongs of allowing children to take part in these shows. Those in favour claim that the programmes teach viewers good eating **(5)** ____ and promote a healthy lifestyle. Supporters also believe the programmes demonstrate that hard work and dedication can lead to success, which serves as a great example to children watching the show.

(6) ______, some people are concerned about the effect of these shows on the participants because of the competitive element. The stress caused by the desire to win the show at all costs can lead to tears and even complete emotional **(7)** ______ in extreme cases. Far from developing confidence in the young competitors, the experience can lead some children to feel worthless and **(8)** ______. Should TV producers really be subjecting children to such a negative experience in the name of entertainment?

1	**A** featuring	**B** appearing	**C** holding	**D** consisting
2	**A** During	**B** Between	**C** Through	**D** Among
3	**A** special	**B** particular	**C** extreme	**D** individual
4	**A** rights	**B** advantages	**C** positives	**D** plusses
5	**A** traditions	**B** customs	**C** habits	**D** styles
6	**A** Besides	**B** Despite	**C** However	**D** Although
7	**A** touchdown	**B** breakdown	**C** countdown	**D** lowdown
8	**A** loose	**B** unsteady	**C** uneven	**D** insecure

READING AND USE OF ENGLISH PART 2

For **questions 9 – 16**, read the text below and think of the word which best fits each gap. Use only **one** word in each gap. There is an example at the beginning (0).

Write your answers **IN CAPITAL LETTERS**.

Example: | **0** | *A* | *T* | | | | | | | | | | | | | |

The Montessori experience

Are you happy (0) __AT__ school? Some students complain that much of (9) __WHAT__ they learn at school is not particularly useful, nor can it be put into practice in real life. It seems, however, that this is not a recent phenomenon. As early as the end of the eighteenth century, there were teachers who complained about the educational system because they found (10) __IT__ lacked both flexibility and practicality.

Maria Montessori, an educator from Italy, realised that the schooling system was not as effective as it could be because it did not take into account the physiological and psychological needs of children. She devised a new system (11) __WHERE__ children would feel safe and comfortable, learning from experience rather (12) __THAN__ being taught. At schools which follow the Montessori system, everything, even furniture, (13) __IS__ tailor-made to fit the needs of the students.

Many students find the business (14) __OF__ receiving their termly or yearly marks a nerve-wracking experience, but this is not an issue for children being educated at a Montessori school. The Montessori system does not believe (15) __IN__ traditional methods of testing. Teachers communicate with parents either through written reports describing the student's progress (16) __OR__ through meetings during the year.

READING AND USE OF ENGLISH `PART 3`

For questions **17 – 24**, read the text below. Use the word given in capitals at the end of some of the lines to form a word that fits in the gap **in the same line**. There is an example at the beginning **(0)**.

Write your answers **IN CAPITAL LETTERS**.

Example: | **0** | T | E | C | H | N | O | L | O | G | I | C | A | L | | | | | |

The windmills of hope

When most of us think about **(0)** *TECHNOLOGICAL* advances, our minds usually turn to space travel, microchips, nanotechnology and robots, but technology doesn't have to be **(17)** *EXTREMELY* advanced to make **(18)** *IMPROVEMENTS* in people's lives.

TECHNOLOGY

EXTREME

IMPROVE

William Kamkwamba left school at fourteen because his family's **(19)** *POVERTY* meant that he had to start work to support them. Once he'd begun working on the family farm, he realised that he needed to do something drastic to **(20)** *ENSURE* his family's survival. He started looking for junk and spare parts and, in his free time, built a turbine from what he had found. To everyone's surprise, the turbine worked. It not only produced electricity, but also pumped water for the family farm.

POOR

SURE

His **(21)** *SUCCESSFUL/ SUCCESS* story soon became well-known, and articles were written about him and his achievement. People from all over the world sent money to William, which he used to study farm technology.

SUCCEED

He used his new **(22)** *KNOWLEDGE* and the **(23)** *DONATIONS* he had been sent, to add water storage tanks. Now William's village has water on tap for the first time in its history. Stories like William Kamkwamba's should be a(n) **(24)** *INSPIRATION* to all of us.

KNOW, DONATE

INSPIRE

READING AND USE OF ENGLISH PART 4

For questions **25 – 30**, complete the second sentence so that it has a similar meaning to the first sentence, using the word given. **Do not change the word given.** You must use between **two** and **five** words, including the word given. Here is an example (0).

Example:

0   The cake was so big that it wouldn't fit on the table.

    SUCH

    It ___WAS SUCH A BIG CAKE___ that it wouldn't fit on the table.

The gap can be filled by the words 'was such a big cake', so you write:

Example: | 0 | *WAS SUCH A BIG CAKE*

Write **only** the missing words **IN CAPITAL LETTERS**.

---

25   I think this recipe needs more milk than we've got.
    ENOUGH
    I don't think we ___HAVE (GOT) ENOUGH MILK FOR___ this recipe.

26   This is the best computer game I've ever played.
    BETTER
    I've never ___PLAYED A BETTER COMPUTER GAME___ than this one.

27   Do you know how far away Hong Kong is?
    IDEA
    Do you ___HAVE ANY IDEA___ how far away Hong Kong is?

28   He started doing charity work when he was a student.
    INVOLVED
    He has ___BEEN INVOLVED IN/WITH___ doing charity work since he was a student.

29   Carl is the only person who would have used your MP3 player.
    MUST
    It ___MUST HAVE BEEN CARL___ who used your MP3 player.

30   I won't tolerate another argument between you!
    PUT
    I won't ___PUT UP WITH (ANY) MORE___ arguing between you!

READING AND USE OF ENGLISH `PART 5`

Questions 31 – 36

You are going to read a report on eco-tourism. For questions **31 – 36**, choose the answer (**A**, **B**, **C** or **D**) which you think fits best according to the text.

Eco-tourism:
Suitable for all

Background

In the last decade of the twentieth century and the first few years of the twenty-first century, eco-tourism was regarded as a luxury that few could afford. It meant luxurious hotels which used organic products, ranging from organically-grown cotton to toilet paper which had not been chemically bleached. It used expensive solar-powered systems and other modern technologies which conserved energy, whilst at the same time providing costly, quality services.

line 11 All that came to an end when eco-tourism was severely hit by the recent economic crisis. However, this section of the holiday industry is now showing signs of recovery. By changing its approach to include anything from conservation-based adventure programmes to high-end luxury hotels, eco-tourism is managing to increase the number of customers and therefore improve its chances of success in the tourism industry.

Current trends

According to Ron Erdmann, Director of Research at the Office of Travel and Tourism Industries, the number of people taking part in environmental or ecological travel started rising again after 2007. Eco-tourism has grown to mean much more than just luxury bungalows or tents in unspoilt areas and it now focuses on supporting local communities – a model of holiday that considers both travellers and local communities. One of the leaders in eco-tourism is the country of Costa Rica, where almost 49 per cent of the two million visitors in 2010 took part in eco-tourism activities during their stay, bringing an income of nearly a billion dollars to the country. The manager of *Lapa Rios*, one of the most successful green resorts in Costa Rica, explained that one of the main benefits of eco-tourism is that it protects areas from the sort of damage that ordinary (non-eco) tourists usually cause.

Eco-Tourism worldwide

Destinations like the Galapagos Islands, Ecuador, Nepal, Bhutan and Patagonia are also seeing an increase in the numbers of tourists that visit them hoping to have a holiday full of natural beauty. These areas are famous for their unspoilt surroundings and rare flowers and animals, and for the perfect landscapes and the

unique architecture which have remained unchanged for centuries. Trekking and backpacking are among the cheapest options in some of these locations, but there are other much more luxurious and costly choices as well. The director of the safari service *Roar Africa*, Deborah Calmeyer, says, 'Our clients often spend up to $30,000 per person for a personal African adventure that's environmentally-friendly.' Her company shares the aims of its partner organisation, *Singita*, a tourism operation whose purpose is to protect wildlife and its habitat as well as to prevent the illegal killing of animals.

The future

In the opinion of Steve Case, who is also working on a project in Costa Rica, the future of eco-tourism lies in the cooperation between the local people and the hoteliers. He also believes it is essential that the impact of waste on the resort is neutralised either by recycling it or by re-using it, so that the location can retain its beauty and character, and the tourism industry can continue. Bruce Poon Tip, director of *GAP Adventures*, agrees with him and adds that the goal is to help local people and that is the reason why his company uses small-scale accommodation, local means of transport and businesses owned by the locals in every area they visit.

Conclusion

It certainly seems as if eco-tourism is here to stay; more and more travellers are aware of the impact that travelling can have on the environment and are demanding that measures should be taken to reduce the damage or even reverse it.

31 What do we learn in the first paragraph about eco-tourism?
   A It was only for wealthy people.
   B Plenty of people could afford it.
   C It didn't use advanced technologies.
   D It didn't exist before the end of the twentieth century.

32 What does 'all that' refer to in line 11?
   A modern technologies
   B the economic crisis
   C organic products
   D expensive green holidays

33 What is one of the advantages of eco-tourism?
   A Many visitors take part in ecologically friendly activities.
   B Local communities are engaged in ecology.
   C Tourist activities cannot be done in some areas.
   D Some areas remain unspoilt.

34 What do travellers expect when they visit places like the Galapagos Islands or Nepal?
   A to find places undisturbed by modern civilisation
   B to spend some time in a costly hotel
   C to go on a safari
   D to have a cheap holiday

35 What should be done to ensure that eco-tourism has a future?
   A People should not dump their waste.
   B Local economies should be involved.
   C Waste should not be produced.
   D Travellers should not stay at hotels.

36 What is this report mainly seeking to inform readers about?
   A inexpensive tourist destinations
   B general trends in eco-tourism
   C the financial situation in eco-tourist areas
   D companies that offer eco-tourism services

READING AND USE OF ENGLISH PART 6

Questions 37 – 42

You are going to read a magazine article about choosing a career. Six sentences have been removed from the article. Choose from the sentences **A – G** the one which fits each gap (**37 – 42**). There is one extra sentence which you do not need to use.

The right job

There are more choices than ever, but what is the best job for you?

Many young people worry about their future and spend hour after hour considering what to do when they finish school. **37** *E* For the rest of us, it's a case of just waiting to see what comes along or even randomly selecting a job; after all, luck often plays an enormous part in the choices young adults make. Unfortunately, there is no straightforward advice that young people can follow, but there are a few things which can make choosing a suitable career a little easier.

The first thing you should do is focus on what your interests are. **38** *A* Planning out your future life is no easy feat, and this sort of self-awareness is vital. Knowing what your strengths and weaknesses are helps a lot, too. What are you good at? Do you find problem-solving easy? Are you comfortable working under pressure, or do you prefer a more relaxed pace? If you find it difficult to answer these questions yourself, take an aptitude test. This will help you identify what you excel at and areas in which you don't do so well. The results can then help you determine professions that are either suitable or totally inappropriate for you.

It is also important to know what your values and priorities in life are. What's more important to you? Is it wealth and fame or a comfortable family life? **39** *G*

A more practical activity that can be of benefit is taking a gap year between school and university and working as a volunteer. **40** *B* You'll also gain new skills and experience that will prove invaluable to you later in life and in your future career. After all, employers want to hire either experienced and skilled people, or those who can show initiative, a willingness to work and enthusiasm. **41** *D* It may well be this experience that sets you apart from the other applicants and gets you the job.

Another step that can be taken when contemplating a career is to ask people who are already working in that particular field about its positive and negative aspects. However, make sure you ask more than just one person, as different people have different perspectives.

Finally, you should never forget that whatever you choose, you don't necessarily have to do it forever. **42** *C* The important thing is to feel content with your life. As work plays such a major part in it, having a fulfilling career needs to be a priority.

A Ask yourself what kind of activities you enjoy doing most: are they physical or intellectual activities, indoor or outdoor, with other people or alone?

B This will give you more time to decide what you want to do, while at the same time providing you with the opportunity to help those in need.

C You could change your mind while still at university or you could even retrain when you're older and are already working.

D Having worked as a volunteer proves that you have all of these attributes and makes you a more attractive candidate.

E It is only a rare few who make up their minds early on regarding their choice of career and know what skills and qualifications will get them there.

F A rise in unemployment is making it increasingly difficult to find a good job.

G A steady, secure job with an average salary or a high-risk job with more potential for great wealth?

READING AND USE OF ENGLISH PART 7

Questions 43 – 52

You are going to read an article about different buildings that share a common characteristic. For questions **43 – 52**, choose from the buildings (**A – D**). The buildings may be chosen more than once.

Which building(s)

is the oldest structure?	**43**	B
has a very small, yet visible lean?	**44**	D
was built during times of war?	**45**	B
is located near the coast?	**46**	C
has been moved back into a former position?	**47**	B
has transport running under it?	**48**	D
has the biggest unplanned lean?	**49**	A
sits on top of the remains of trees?	**50**	A
was most recently completed?	**51**	C
was meant to lean?	**52**	C

THE LEANING TOWERS OF THE WORLD

Most buildings are built to stand up straight, but these look as if they might fall over!

A The medieval steeple of Suurhusen

Until recently, the medieval steeple in Suurhusen, Germany, could claim the title of tower that leaned the most – amongst towers which started to lean by accident. Built in 1450, the steeple, or church tower, sits on foundations that the connecting church once covered after part of the church was torn down to make room for it. The foundation at the time consisted of tree trunks preserved in water, making them stable for building purposes. However, the land was drained in the 1800s, and the wood began to rot, resulting in the tower becoming unstable. In 1975, officials declared the tower a safety hazard and people were not allowed to enter until the foundations were stabilised again; a process that took ten years to complete. The lean of the steeple is measured at an angle of about five degrees, a full degree more than the Leaning Tower of Pisa.

B The Leaning Tower of Pisa

The Leaning Tower of Pisa is the most well-known leaning tower in the world. Construction on the tower began in 1173, and over 177 years passed before it was considered complete. The tower began to tilt after just a couple of floors were built on its shallow foundation of only three metres. It was obvious from the start that the tower would lean, but construction stopped only because of ongoing conflicts between the Republic of Pisa and neighbouring areas. Fortunately, the time that passed between building stages allowed the foundation of the building to settle into the ground, becoming more solid. Nonetheless, its tilt gradually increased in the centuries after its completion, and it was eventually closed to the public in 1990 after attempts to stabilise it failed. It was reopened in 2001 after engineers removed soil from underneath its raised side, causing the tower to return to its 1838 position.

C Capital Gate of Abu Dhabi

The world's furthest leaning tower was completed in 2011. The Capital Gate tower in Abu Dhabi was designed to lean at an incredible eighteen degrees. The foundation of the building is thirty metres deep, allowing for greater stability in the thirty-five-storey tower. The building incorporates all the features of a twenty-first century skyscraper and was built to withstand the forces of nature, including high winds and earthquakes. The building stands next to the Abu Dhabi National Exhibition Centre and contains, among other things, a luxury hotel with wonderful views of the harbour. Also known as the leaning tower of Abu Dhabi, the tower is one of the tallest structures in the city.

D Big Ben of London

One of London's most famous buildings, the clock tower of the Palace of Westminster – often referred to as Big Ben, after the bell inside – is leaning. Engineers discovered the structure was leaning several years ago, although only very slightly. Now they say the tilt is accelerating, and it can be noticed by the average person on the street. The blame lies with the various engineering projects that have been carried out in the ground below it since the late 1800s. These projects, including a sewage system and an underground car park, have succeeded in weakening the structure's foundation. In 1990, after the Jubilee underground line was completed underneath it, engineers carried out work in an effort to strengthen the tower. The tower, which has been continuously open since it was completed in 1858, has nowhere near the tilt of the Tower of Pisa and is still completely safe to enter. In fact, it would take about 4,000 years for Big Ben to reach the same position as Italy's famous leaning tower.

WRITING `PART 1`

You **must** answer this question. Write your answer in **140 – 190** words in an appropriate style.

1   In your English class you have been talking about success in life. Now your teacher has asked you to write an essay for homework.

Write your essay using **all** the notes and giving reasons for your point of view.

'A person isn't really a success until they are wealthy.'

Do you agree?

Notes

Write about:

1   self-satisfaction

2   power

3   .... (your own idea)

Students' own answers

WRITING PART 2

Write an answer to **one** of the questions 2 – 5 in this part. Write your answer in **140 – 190** words in an appropriate style.

2   You see this announcement in an international English-language magazine for young people.

We're looking for articles about social networking sites and teens. Have you, or any of your friends, ever used a social networking site such as Facebook or Twitter? Tell us about the experience – describe it and comment on the effects that these sites have on young people's social lives.

The best articles will be published next month.

Write your article.

3   You have seen this announcement in a new English-language magazine for teens.

Stories wanted

We are looking for stories for our new English-language magazine for teens. Your story must **begin** with this sentence:

Kate read the text message and decided to go over to her best friend's house immediately.

Your story must include:

• a favour

• a party

Write your **story**.

4   You have received a letter from your friend, Sam, telling you that he is worried about his brother at school and asking you for advice. This is an extract from the letter:

... life at the moment isn't very pleasant. There's a girl at school who's bullying younger children, and my little brother, Ken, is really scared of her. He hasn't told me or our parents anything, but I can see that he doesn't want to go to school and he's sad and very worried all the time. He's even stopped playing his favourite computer games! I don't know what to do. Should I tell my parents about it?

I really want to help Ken, but I don't know how. What can I do to make him feel better?

Write your **letter**.

5   Question 5 always consists of a question on the set text. Only answer question 5 if you have studied the set text. Here is an example of the kind of question you might be asked:

In your English class you have been reading a book. Now your teacher has asked you to write a review for the school magazine. Your review should include what you enjoyed and didn't enjoy about the book, giving reasons. Would you recommend this book to other people your age?

Write your **review**.

Students' own answers

LISTENING PART 1

Questions 1 – 8

You will hear people talking in eight different situations. For questions **1 – 8**, choose the best answer (**A, B** or **C**).

1 You hear two teenagers talking about a misunderstanding.
How does the boy feel?
A worried
B angry
C foolish

2 You hear a mother and her son talking about a concert.
What seems to be the problem?
A Ryan wants to go to the concert alone.
B Ryan's mother doesn't want him to go to the concert.
C Ryan wants to take his phone to the concert.

3 You hear two people talking. What do they decide to do?
A go to a pizza restaurant
B see a film at the cinema
C get a DVD and watch it at home

4 You hear a man talking about his job to a class of students.
What does he do while he is talking?
A He explains to students what his job involves.
B He comments on the origins of his profession.
C He tells the students how he became an archaeologist.

5 You overhear a boy leaving a voicemail message.
What is it about?
A arranging who is going to call Samantha
B arranging who is going to do which part of the project
C arranging a meeting

6 You hear a sister and a brother arguing about household chores.
What does Andrew want Jill to do?
A He wants Jill to do the washing-up for a week.
B He wants Jill not to tell a secret to their mother.
C He wants Jill to do his share of the chores.

7 You overhear a boy talking on the phone.
What is he talking about?
A He owes his friend some money.
B He wants to borrow some money from his friend.
C He bought a new version of a computer game.

8 You hear a conversation between two friends in a shop.
What do they agree about?
A that teenagers like pale colours
B that Dave's room isn't very light
C that the colour green is more suitable for girls

LISTENING PART 2

Questions 9 – 18

You will hear a young sailor called Jasmine Schultz talking about sailing solo. For questions **9 – 18**, complete the sentences with a word or short phrase.

Jasmine Schultz: Sailing Solo

Jasmine says that originally her | *parents* | **9** | weren't keen on her plans.

She started organising the journey | *(about) a/one year* | **10** | before she left.

She had to learn how to do | *first aid/first-aid* | **11** | before she left.

If there was | *stormy weather* | **12** | , she had communication difficulties.

She found the experience of sailing very near | *dolphins and whales* | **13** | amazing.

Jasmine is going to miss the feeling of | *being alone* | **14** | at sea most of all.

On her journey, she covered a distance of | *27,000/ twenty-seven thousand* | **15** | nautical miles.

She believes that being | *determined* | **16** | leads to success.

Jasmine thinks that she is | *(much) more mature* | **17** | than before she went on her journey.

Jasmine hopes that her | *screenplay* | **18** | will end up being produced.

LISTENING PART 3

Questions 19 – 23

You will hear five people talking about memorable experiences they have had. For questions **19 – 23**, choose from the list (**A – H**) what each speaker considers was an important lesson that they learned. Use the letters only once. There are three extra letters which you do not need to use.

A   I could take care of myself.

Speaker 1 | D | **19** |

B   Actions have consequences.

Speaker 2 | A | **20** |

C   Money makes the world go round.

Speaker 3 | B | **21** |

D   Dreams can come true.

Speaker 4 | G | **22** |

E   Don't try to take on too much at once.

Speaker 5 | H | **23** |

F   Too much freedom can cause trouble.

G   Determination can pay off.

H   Don't be afraid of new circumstances.

LISTENING PART 4

Questions 24 – 30

You will hear a conversation between two people, Celia and Adam, who took part in an expedition to Mongolia, and a friend of theirs called Terry, who wants to know what it was like. For questions **24 – 30**, choose the best answer (**A**, **B** or **C**).

24   What did Adam and Celia enjoy while travelling on the train?
   A   the company of the people they met
   B   the views they saw from the window
   C   the luxury of travelling first class

25   Why is Genghis Khan thought of as an important person?
   A   He conquered many countries.
   B   He fought many wars against Europe.
   C   He created an enormous empire.

26   What does Adam say about Gandan Monastery?
   A   There is a very large statue there.
   B   It's the only Buddhist monastery in the country.
   C   It's very tall.

27   When is the best time to visit Mongolia, according to Celia?
   A   In the winter, although the conditions may be harsh.
   B   In the summer, although the weather may not be good.
   C   Any time except in the summer.

28   Why did Adam and Celia visit the singing dunes?
   A   to listen to the people who live there sing
   B   to hear funny stories about them
   C   to hear the strange sound they make

29   How is hunting in Mongolia different from other places in the world?
   A   Kazakhs use birds instead of dogs for hunting.
   B   Kazakhs only hunt birds.
   C   Kazakhs need to train their hunting animals.

30   Why is Karakorum important?
   A   There are many famous statues there.
   B   There are many ruins there.
   C   It was the place where Genghis Khan started from.

Practice Test 4

SPEAKING PART 1

2 minutes (3 minutes for groups of three)

This part is always the same. See page 34 of Test 1.

Select one or more questions from the following category, as appropriate.

Home town

- **Do you have friends who live in your area? What do you do together?**

- **Are there any parks in your town/city/village? How often do you visit them?**

- **Do you like spending time in your town/city/village at the weekend? What do you do?**

- **Is there anything you would like to change about your town/city/village? ...... (Why?)**

- **What's your favourite place to visit in your town/city/village? ...... (Why?)**

Students' own answers

SPEAKING PART 2

4 minutes (6 minutes for groups of three)

1 Children's activities
2 Free time

Interlocutor	In this part of the test, I'm going to give each of you two photographs. I'd like you to talk about your photographs on your own for about a minute, and also to answer a short question about your partner's photographs.
See photos A and B on page 183.	(*Candidate A*), it's your turn first. Here are your photographs. They show **children doing different activities**.
	I'd like you to compare the photographs, and say **how the children in the photographs might be feeling**.
	All right?
Candidate A	(*Speak for approximately 1 minute.*)
Interlocutor	Thank you. (*Candidate B*), **which activity would you most like to do?**
Candidate B	(*Reply for approximately 30 seconds.*)
Interlocutor	Thank you.
See photos C and D on page 184.	Now, (*Candidate B*), here are your photographs. They show **people doing different things in their free time**.
	I'd like you to compare the photographs, and say **what are the advantages and disadvantages of spending free time in these different ways**.
	All right?
Candidate B	(*Speak for approximately 1 minute.*)
Interlocutor	Thank you. (*Candidate A*), **do you like going shopping?**
Candidate A	(*Reply for approximately 30 seconds.*)
Interlocutor	Thank you.

Students' own answers

SPEAKING PARTS 3 AND 4

Health and fitness

8 minutes (11 minutes for groups of three)

PART 3

Interlocutor

See written prompts on page 185.

Now, I'd like you to talk about something together for about two minutes. *(3 minutes for groups of three)*

Here are some ways young people stay healthy and fit and a question for you to discuss. First you have some time to look at the task.

Now, talk to each other about **whether some ways of staying healthy and fit are better than others.**

Candidates

(Discuss for approximately 2 minutes – 3 minutes for groups of three.)

Interlocutor

Thank you. Now you have about a minute to decide **which two things are the most important for young people who want to stay healthy and fit.**

Candidates

(Reply for approximately 1 minute – for pairs and groups of three.)

Interlocutor

Thank you.

PART 4

Interlocutor

Select any of the following questions, as appropriate:

- **How important is to keep healthy? ......** **(Why?/Why not?)**

- **What do you do to keep fit?**

- **What do you think is the best way to encourage young people to eat healthy food?**

- **Did our grandparents have a healthier lifestyle than we do now? ......** **(Why?/Why not?)**

- **Should there be a school lesson about health and fitness?**

- **What advice would you give to someone who wants to be healthier?**

Select any of the following prompts, as appropriate:

- **What do you think?**
- **Do you agree?**
- **And you?**

Thank you. That is the end of the test.

Students' own answers

Practice Test 5

READING AND USE OF ENGLISH PART 1

For questions **1 – 8**, read the text below and decide which answer (**A, B, C** or **D**) best fits each gap. There is an example at the beginning (**0**).

Example:

0 A aimed   **B** drawn   **C** calculated   **D** considered

```
0 | A === | B ▢ | C ▢ | D ▢ |
```

Fitness farms

Fitness farms are health spas or centres that are **(0)** _____ at people who want to lose weight and get fit. Fitness farms combine healthy eating with rigorous exercise to help clients lose weight and **(1)** _____ up. People often go to fitness farms as a last **(2)** _____ after unsuccessfully trying diets or other weight-loss programmes.

(3) _____ some fitness farms are concerned with how much weight their clients lose, others are more **(4)** _____ on helping clients change their attitudes towards food and exercise. Because of this, some farms offer **(5)** _____ where they continue to offer support to clients after they have left the farm, ensuring that they don't revert to their old eating **(6)** _____ and unhealthy ways.

It's not just people's weight that changes at fitness farms; quite often clients feel more confident and have higher self-esteem after attending a course. So not **(7)** _____ does a stay at a fitness farm impact on the client's physical well-being, but ex-clients also **(8)** _____ that they are generally more enthusiastic about leading healthier and more active lifestyles.

1	**A** fit	**B** exercise	**C** tone	**D** sound
2	**A** decision	**B** place	**C** choice	**D** resort
3	**A** As	**B** While	**C** Despite	**D** However
4	**A** geared	**B** emphasised	**C** pointed	**D** focused
5	**A** packs	**B** packages	**C** packets	**D** parcels
6	**A** customs	**B** methods	**C** habits	**D** traditions
7	**A** hardly	**B** barely	**C** only	**D** simply
8	**A** find	**B** distinguish	**C** detect	**D** uncover

READING AND USE OF ENGLISH `PART 2`

For questions **9 – 16**, read the text below and think of the word which best fits each gap. Use only **one** word in each gap. There is an example at the beginning **(0)**.

Write your answers **IN CAPITAL LETTERS**.

Example: | **0** | *O* | *F* | | | | | | | | | | | |

Aye-aye

There are plenty **(0)** _*OF*_ weird and wonderful creatures on Planet Earth, but the aye-aye lemur from Madagascar **(9)** _*HAS*_ to be one of the most unusual animals around.

(10) _*WITH/ HAVING*_ big ears, sharp rat-like teeth and long bony fingers, the aye-aye is anything **(11)** _*BUT*_ cute. Measuring only about seventeen inches long, aye-ayes spend every night jumping from tree to tree and hunting for food. These lemurs use the rare technique of knocking on trees and listening for insects moving inside the wood. Their days are spent sleeping on piles of leaves that they build into nests in the trees. Aye-ayes normally live and hunt alone in the forests and leave a trail of scent behind **(12)** _*THEM*_ to let other aye-ayes know where they've been. When they do meet, however, they often fight aggressively with **(13)** _*EACH*_ other. Males can travel up to four kilometres a night in their search for food and normally roam over larger areas **(14)** _*THAN*_ the females. Females give birth about once every three years and feed their babies for a whole year before the young set off on their **(15)** _*OWN*_. Unfortunately, the species is now threatened by the destruction of its habitat and the superstitions of the Malagasy people. Sadly, many of the animals **(16)** _*ARE*_ killed as soon as they are spotted.

READING AND USE OF ENGLISH `PART 3`

For questions **17 – 24**, read the text below. Use the word given in capitals at the end of some of the lines to form a word that fits in the gap **in the same line**. There is an example at the beginning (0).

Write your answers **IN CAPITAL LETTERS**.

Example: | **0** | P | R | E | F | E | R | E | N | C | E | S | | | | | | |

Boys will be boys … and rock stars!

Most young people love music, and in recent years the music industry has begun to cater for teens of all musical **(0)** _PREFERENCES_ . | **PREFER**

But for a group of **(17)** _YOUNGSTERS_ from California, the love of | **YOUNG**
music goes beyond listening to the radio and downloading their favourite tracks. Twin brothers Nick and Chris, and their friends Geddy, Charley and Brandon, combined their **(18)** _EXTRAORDINARY_ | **ORDINARY**
skills to form *Haunted by Heroes*, a rock band inspired by **(19)** _INFLUENTIAL_ classic rock acts such as *AC/DC* and | **INFLUENCE**
Motorhead. The young rockers met at nursery school when they were all three and have been inseparable ever since. Now, their time is divided between band **(20)** _REHEARSAL(S)_ in | **REHEARSE**
their parents' garages and going to school. Well aware of the **(21)** _IMPORTANCE_ of education, band members claim they can't | **IMPORTANT**
make it as **(22)** _MUSICIANS_ if they don't get good marks at school. | **MUSIC**

When they are not playing at **(23)** _FAMOUS_ American rock | **FAME**
venues, the boys enjoy skateboarding, snowboarding and hanging out with friends. Being in a rock band, something that many young kids can only dream of, has become a **(24)** _REALITY_ for | **REAL**
California's youngest performers.

READING AND USE OF ENGLISH PART 4

For questions **25 – 30**, complete the second sentence so that it has a similar meaning to the first sentence, using the word given. **Do not change the word given.** You must use between **two** and **five** words, including the word given. Here is an example (0).

Example:

0   The opening of the museum will be held on Monday.

PLACE

The opening of the museum _____*WILL TAKE PLACE*_____ on Monday.

The gap can be filled by the words 'will take place', so you write:

Example: | **0** | | *WILL TAKE PLACE* |

Write **only** the missing words **IN CAPITAL LETTERS**.

---

25   Adam was happy to help Darren with his homework.
MIND
Adam _____*DIDN'T / DID NOT MIND HELPING*_____ Darren with his homework.

26   I was about to leave when you phoned me.
POINT
I was *ON THE POINT OF LEAVING* when you phoned me.

27   I haven't seen Natalie since the weekend.
LAST
I _____*LAST SAW NATALIE AT*_____ the weekend.

28   I'd rather play netball than basketball.
PLAYING
I prefer _____*NETBALL TO (PLAYING)*_____ basketball.

29   'Do the washing-up, Tim,' said his mum.
TOLD
Tim's mum _____*TOLD HIM TO DO*_____ the washing-up.

30   I'm disappointed you weren't at my Halloween party.
WISH
I _____*WISH YOU HAD BEEN*_____ at my Halloween party.

READING AND USE OF ENGLISH PART 5

Questions 31 – 36

You are going to read a magazine article about hormones. For questions **31 – 36**, choose the answer (**A, B, C** or **D**) which you think fits best according to the text.

Happy hormones

What makes us feel good? Why can we, one day, feel on top of the world and the next, feel like everything's just too much for us? The fact is that how we experience different emotions is actually all down to science.

Our moods and emotions are influenced by chemicals called hormones, which travel through our bloodstream and send messages to different parts of the body. Our bodies produce hormones, which affect us in different ways. Some hormones cause a physical response. For example, the hormone adrenalin is responsible for the 'fight or flight' reaction (hearts beat faster, breathing increases and our bodies are ready to either face a dangerous situation and 'fight' it or run away from it). Other hormones affect our feelings rather than our actions and produce a more emotional response.

Hormones such as serotonin and dopamine make us feel cheerful and are important in the treatment of those who suffer from depression, anxiety and other emotional problems. Medical professionals have found that prescribing medication which stimulates the production of serotonin in the body is an effective way to treat these kinds of conditions. It can help people to feel more relaxed, happier, and in some cases, more able to cope with day-to-day life.

What we do, eat and how we live helps release these hormones naturally, but how can we produce enough of them to get the 'feel good' effect? First, let's have a look at what these hormones are and how they help.

Serotonin, known as the 'happiness hormone', is one of the chemicals at work when we feel happy. It relieves depression and reduces anxiety as well as helping us stay emotionally balanced. So what exactly makes our serotonin levels go up? Have you ever noticed how people always seem more cheerful on a bright sunny day? Well, it's not just a coincidence. Exposure to sunlight can help release serotonin in the brain and make you feel better than you do on damp dreary days. Eating more carbohydrates can have a similar effect, but although complex carbohydrates like nuts and wheat increase serotonin, their influence may only be temporary. For a longer lasting feeling of happiness, combine carbohydrates with healthy fats and a range of protein-rich foods like fish, meat and eggs, which contain an acid that is converted into serotonin. Getting a serotonin boost is great for the feel-good factor, but a lack of this hormone can cause a condition called serotonin deficiency disease. Sufferers have a very low level of serotonin, and this not only affects mood, stress and anxiety levels, but also sleep patterns.

Endorphins are also important hormones. Known to reduce anxiety and how sensitive we are to pain, they are essential for a healthy mind. Exercise stimulates the production of endorphins, so that's why you normally feel happier when you've been playing sport, for example. In fact, doctors recommend physical activity for mild depression, and many people find that it is effective in improving their ~~line~~ mood.

If it is a lack of concentration and the inability to focus that is a problem, then you are probably low in dopamine.

Phenylethamine is another amazing hormone, which can make us feel a kind of happiness similar to being in love. Cocoa beans contain this hormone, and this may well explain why chocolate is so popular!

Of course, we all know that eating well and getting plenty of exercise is good for a healthy lifestyle, but now we can see how important it is for having a happier and more positive outlook on life.

31 The writer says that hormones
   A are similar to feelings.
   B are natural responses.
   C control how we feel.
   D depend on our mood.

32 The hormones discussed in the third paragraph
   A are effective in preventing stress.
   B can only be found in medication for depression.
   C can help people with psychological problems.
   D are absent from people suffering from depression.

33 What can permanently increase the level of serotonin in the body?
   A staying inside and away from bad weather
   B eating only carbohydrates
   C eating plenty of nuts and wheat
   D eating a balanced diet

34 What does 'it' refer to in line 31?
   A exercise
   B a healthy mind
   C depression
   D endorphin release

35 Dopamine is a hormone that
   A can help you focus better.
   B is found in most healthy food.
   C is released when you can't concentrate.
   D reduces your energy levels.

36 What is the main message of the article?
   A natural remedies are better than medicine
   B we should regulate our hormone levels
   C we can help ourselves to improve our mental health
   D healthy eating is the key to emotional stability

READING AND USE OF ENGLISH PART 6

Questions 37 – 42

You are going to read a magazine article about alternative energy. Six sentences have been removed from the article. Choose from the sentences **A – G** the one which fits each gap (**37 – 42**). There is one extra sentence which you do not need to use.

Green planet

How the world is thinking about more environmentally-friendly energy sources.

With more emphasis on being 'green' these days, it's not surprising that environmentalists are trying to tackle issues related to energy production. For centuries people have been using non-renewable fossil fuels like coal and oil to create energy. While they have undoubtedly proved effective in supplying energy to millions, fossil fuels are increasingly seen as the means by which we are destroying our atmosphere and, indeed, our environment.

First and foremost, the burning of fossil fuels like coal and oil releases carbon dioxide into the atmosphere and this is a main factor contributing to the problem of global warming. Secondly, these fuels are quite simply running out. Non-renewable fuels are limited, so the more we use now, the less we have for the future, and it is only a matter of time before none of these resources remain. **37** C

In simple terms, the answer to this question is that we need to stop using non-renewable fuels and focus on other forms of energy production instead. **38** G We are now well on the way to having viable and cost-effective ways of generating energy without depleting the planet's natural fuel sources.

Alternative energy is the term applied to energy sources that don't use fossil fuels. **39** D Instead, it harnesses renewable resources like the sun, wind and geothermal heat in order to produce electricity.

Solar power is gaining in popularity all over the world as a cost-effective way of producing energy, whether for heating water or for producing electricity. For countries with hot climates (especially those close to the equator), solar energy is probably the best alternative energy option, due to the large amount of sunlight they receive. **40** F Some governments are now offering low-interest loans to help deal with this issue.

Wind power has been a controversial topic in recent years due to the unsightly appearance of towering wind

turbines. **41** A This is particularly true for areas of natural beauty, such as mountains and coasts, as they are often better sites for the turbines. These locations are home to people who make their living through farming, fishing or tourism and they see the turbines as a high-tech threat to their livelihoods. After all, nobody wants their peace and quiet interrupted by the sound of the gigantic blades turning. However, some people argue that the appearance of – and noise from – the turbines is a price worth paying for clean energy.

Another alternative energy source which is being used increasingly is geothermal energy, which involves harnessing the energy produced deep inside the Earth. Red-hot magma at the Earth's core transfers huge amounts of heat to the surrounding rocks; this layer is drilled down to and the heat is used as a source of energy. **42** E Though relatively costly, this alternative form of energy would not only meet the demand for energy, but would also be a real alternative in countries with little solar or wind energy potential.

Energy production is changing, and alternative methods of generating power are becoming more popular throughout the world. With the use of solar panels, wind turbines and geothermal power stations replacing the burning of fossil fuels, one hopes the world is set to be a greener place.

A Some people feel that the placement of these unattractive pieces of equipment totally ruins the appearance of an area.

B While many people have heard of alternative energy, most don't understand how it can directly affect them.

C So where does that leave us?

D The main advantage, then, is the fact that this form of energy doesn't produce harmful gases or use up natural resources.

E Water pumped down to this depth comes back up as steam, which drives the turbines to produce electricity.

F However, the solar panels and cells required to convert this into energy are relatively expensive to buy and install, meaning many people are unable to afford the initial costs.

G Governments are pumping resources into the research and production of alternative energy technologies and have made significant progress in recent years.

Practice Test 5

READING AND USE OF ENGLISH PART 7

Questions 43 – 52

You are going to read an advice leaflet about managing money. For questions **43 – 52**, choose from the people (**A – D**). The people may be chosen more than once.

Which person says

a change in their circumstances helped them learn something?	**43** D
they decided to spend only a proportion of what they earned?	**44** A
they are aware of others' spending habits?	**45** E
keeping a record of the money they have is very important?	**46** C
they often forget how they spent their money?	**47** B
asking a question can help put spending into perspective?	**48** B
they didn't understand the importance of money?	**49** D
they decided to change their bad spending habits?	**50** A
spending money on necessities must be the priority?	**51** C
making just a small change can have a big effect?	**52** A

Money matters

We asked four teenagers for their advice on managing money.

A Megan

When I was younger, I spent all the money I got. As soon as I had earned it, it was gone again. After a couple of years, I began wondering why I didn't have any savings. Things had to change. It was then that I opened a bank account and made up my mind that I would save twenty per cent of my wages every time I got paid. It wasn't actually that much, but it soon began to build up. It's such a good feeling knowing that I have money in the bank, and I would never go back to my old ways now. Even saving just a tiny amount each month can make quite a difference, so my advice would be for everyone to open an account and start saving. I find that I don't actually miss the money I put in the bank, but it makes a big difference in the end.

C Jamie

My money motto is 'be strict and know what you're spending'. I keep a budget so that I know exactly how much money I can spend on clothes, how much on going out with my friends and how much I need to save. I can't stand not knowing where my money is going, especially since I work so hard for it. I mean, I only work at the weekends and I don't really make a lot of money, but I find it goes a lot further if I keep track of it. Budgeting is just the best way to manage your money and helps you see what you *need* to spend your money on first before deciding what you *want* to spend it on. For me, it means that I have money goals. If I tell myself I'll save five pounds every week, then I definitely will. It's as simple as that!

B Laura

My money goes on stupid things, like a coffee here or a sandwich there, and even though that only means two or three pounds a time, it soon mounts up. The thing is that you never really take much notice of the small change that you have. I find that if I have change in my purse, it's soon gone, and I can never remember where or what on! One day I made a list of all the things I'd bought that week – small things like magazines or snacks – and it really surprised me. I'd spent 30 pounds on, well, nothing really! If I could give anyone advice, I would tell them to always ask themselves, 'Do I really need this?' You'll be surprised at how many times the answer is 'No'! I could kick myself because I know I could have had a new mobile phone or new clothes for that money instead of just throwing it down the drain. What a waste!

D Olivia

I always got pocket money from my parents, which was great! It meant that when I wanted a new jacket or to go to the cinema I knew that I had enough to cover it. The problem is that I never really learnt the value of money. I mean, my parents gave me money, and I spent it. There was never any question of saving it or being careful, because I knew that I'd get more the following week. Well, that was a mistake. When my dad lost his job, my pocket money stopped. Of course, I was used to a lifestyle where I could have anything I wanted, within reason that is. Without my pocket money I began to see how much I'd taken money for granted, and worse still, how much I had actually spent over the years. I soon found a part-time job and started earning my own money. It wasn't a lot, but it was enough. Not only did I become more responsible about money and how I spent it, but I felt good that I was working for it and not just relying on my parents. My advice to anyone is not to expect money to always be there and make sure you save enough for a rainy day.

WRITING PART 1

You **must** answer this question. Write your answer in **140 – 190** words in an appropriate style.

1 In your English class you have been talking about culture. Now your teacher has asked you to write an essay for homework.

Write your essay using **all** the notes and giving reasons for your point of view.

Some countries spend huge amounts of money preserving their cultural heritage.

Is this a good or bad thing for the citizens of these countries?

Notes

Write about:

    1   taking pride in one's past

    2   spending money on more important things

    3   .... (your own idea)

Students' own answers

WRITING PART 2

Write an answer to **one** of the questions **2 – 5** in this part. Write your answer in **140 – 190** words in an appropriate style.

2 You have seen this announcement in a magazine for teenagers.

Competition:
Teenagers and Diet

Are teens eating too much junk food? Are they eating enough fruit and vegetables? What do you think?

Send your articles – the best article will be published in next month's magazine.

Write your **article**.

3 Your teacher has asked you to write a review of a concert you have recently been to. The best reviews will go in the school newspaper. Review the concert, giving your opinion and saying whether or not you would recommend it.

Write your **review**.

4 You have seen a story-writing competition in an English-language magazine and you decide to enter. Your story must begin with this sentence:

Sarah was happy to see her friend after such a long time, but would she ever forget what had happened so many years ago?

Your story must include:

• an argument
• a secret

Write your **story**.

5 Question 5 always consists of a question on the set text. Only answer question 5 if you have studied the set text. Here is an example of the kind of question you might be asked:

Your English class has had a discussion about a book you were assigned to read. Now your English teacher has asked you to write an essay on whether or not you think the book would make a good film.

Write your **essay**.

Students' own answers

LISTENING PART 1

Questions 1 – 8

You will hear people talking in eight different situations. For questions **1 – 8**, choose the best answer (**A, B** or **C**).

1   You hear part of an interview with a film director.
    What does he say about his last film?
    A It was the most fun to work on.
    B It was a great deal of work.
    C It was better than his first films.

2   You overhear a woman leaving a voicemail message.
    What does she ask her son to do?
    A to go to his grandparents' house at six
    B to pass on a message
    C to call his sister

3   You hear a brother and sister talking about a holiday.
    What do they agree about?
    A that being outdoors is boring
    B that they should do everything together
    C that they want to spend time away from the hotel

4   You overhear two friends talking about a surprise party.
    What did Rachel do?
    A She ruined Monica's lunch.
    B She gave away a secret.
    C She cancelled Monica's party.

5   You overhear two friends talking about shopping.
    How do they feel about a friend's recent purchase?
    A It's OK that she spent money on a brand name.
    B She should have bought three pairs of boots.
    C She could have spent her money better.

6   You overhear two friends in the street.
    Where are they going?
    A to the theatre
    B to the cinema
    C to work

7   You hear a teacher give an important announcement to her class.
    What is her announcement about?
    A practising what to do in an emergency
    B acting appropriately while at school
    C leaving the classroom due to a fire

8   You hear a weather forecast on a television programme.
    What is the forecast for tomorrow?
    A sunny spells in the early morning
    B improved afternoon temperatures
    C frosty weather except in lowland areas

LISTENING PART 2

Questions 9 – 18

You will hear a head teacher called June Parnell talking about schools and education. For questions 9 – 18, complete the sentences with a word or short phrase.

TODAY'S SCHOOLS

Mrs Parnell says that some lessons today are more | *creative* | **9**

According to Mrs Parnell, reading and | *spelling* | **10** are two useful life skills.

When it comes to homework, Mrs Parnell says that panicking makes it more difficult to | *concentrate* | **11**

Mrs Parnell says that | *(national) standards* | **12** ensure that exams stay at the same level of difficulty each year.

Harry is starting at a | *secondary school* | **13** later in the year.

Fortunately, poorer families don't have to worry about the | *expense* | **14** of buying IT equipment because schools provide it.

Mrs Parnell says that | *extra tuition* | **15** is provided in the lunch break at many schools.

Students benefit from being given some | *revision tips* | **16** for exams.

| *(school) trips* | **17** are an example of more practical learning.

Mrs Parnell thinks that | *technology* | **18** has already caused many changes in education.

LISTENING PART 3

Questions 19 – 23

You will hear five people talking about their friends. For questions **19 – 23**, choose from the list (**A – H**) how each speaker feels about friendship. Use the letters only once. There are three extra letters which you do not need to use.

A   Being best friends takes a lot of effort.

Speaker 1	D	**19**

B   Family members make the best friends.

Speaker 2	G	**20**

C   Some friendships don't last as people get older.

Speaker 3	A	**21**

D   It's best to have something in common with your friends.

Speaker 4	C	**22**

E   Friendship is time-consuming, but it's worth it.

Speaker 5	E	**23**

F   You can't keep friends unless you see them face to face.

G   Long distances aren't a problem when it comes to friends.

H   Technology often destroys friendships.

LISTENING PART 4

Questions 24 – 30

You will hear an interview with a teenager called Kelly Turner, who recently returned from a trip abroad. For questions **24 – 30**, choose the best answer (**A, B** or **C**).

24 Why did Kelly go to Paris?
    A It was an educational visit with her school.
    B Her teacher wanted her to go.
    C Her parents thought it would be beneficial.

25 What's the best way of getting to Paris, according to Kelly?
    A by plane
    B by train
    C by car

26 What will Kelly always remember?
    A going on an excursion along the river
    B an incident involving her father
    C visiting a famous landmark

27 How are the catacombs best described, according to Kelly?
    A as an experience not to be missed
    B as a modern-day problem
    C as too frightening to be enjoyable

28 Why was Kelly anxious about eating the local food?
    A She dislikes foods that she's not familiar with.
    B She doesn't normally try foreign food.
    C She'd heard rumours about the kind of food locals eat.

29 What does Kelly say about Paris and French culture?
    A The fashion industry attracts the most tourism.
    B Art isn't something that interests the French people.
    C Paris is a city full of culture.

30 How does Kelly feel about the French language?
    A It's good to have the opportunity to speak French.
    B It's impossible to learn French at school.
    C It's best to talk to native speakers of the language.

SPEAKING PART 1

2 minutes (3 minutes for groups of three)

This part is always the same. See page 34 of Test 1.

Select one or more questions from the following category, as appropriate.

Daily routine

* **What's your routine in the morning?**

* **How do you get to school?**

* **What do you normally do at school each day? ...... (What are your favourite classes?)**

* **Do you do any after-school sports or activities? ...... (What kind?)**

* **What do you usually do in the evenings?**

* **What do you usually do before you go to bed?**

Students' own answers

SPEAKING PART 2

4 minutes (6 minutes for groups of three)

1 Work
2 Housing

Interlocutor	In this part of the test, I'm going to give each of you two photographs. I'd like you to talk about your photographs on your own for about a minute, and also to answer a short question about your partner's photographs.
	(Candidate A), it's your turn first. Here are your photographs. They show **people working in different jobs**.
See photos A and B on page 186.	I'd like you to compare the photographs and say **what the main differences between these jobs are**.
	All right?
Candidate A	*(Speak for approximately 1 minute.)*
Interlocutor	Thank you. *(Candidate B)*, **which one of these jobs would you prefer to do?**
Candidate B	*(Reply for approximately 30 seconds.)*
Interlocutor	Thank you.
See photos C and D on page 187.	Now, *(Candidate B)*, here are your photographs. They show **different kinds of housing**.
	I'd like you to compare the photographs, and say **what the advantages and disadvantages of living in these kinds of houses are**.
	All right?
Candidate B	*(Speak for approximately 1 minute.)*
Interlocutor	Thank you. *(Candidate A)*, **which of these houses would you rather live in?**
Candidate A	*(Reply for approximately 30 seconds.)*
Interlocutor	Thank you.

Students' own answers

SPEAKING PARTS 3 AND 4

8 minutes (11 minutes for groups of three)

Exchange trips

PART 3

Interlocutor	Now, I'd like you to talk about something together for about two minutes. *(3 minutes for groups of three)*
See written prompts on page 188.	**I'd like you to imagine that your cousin, Niko, has asked you for some advice about improving his English. Here are some ideas that could help him improve his English** and a question for you to discuss. First you have some time to look at the task.
	Now, talk to each other about **which way of improving his English would be the most effective.**
Candidates	*(Discuss for approximately 2 minutes – 3 minutes for groups of three.)*
Interlocutor	Thank you. Now you have about a minute to decide **which two ways of improving his English would be the least expensive.**
Candidates	*(Reply for approximately 1 minute – for pairs and groups of three.)*
Interlocutor	Thank you.

PART 4

Interlocutor

Select any of the following questions, as appropriate:

Select any of the following prompts, as appropriate:

- **What do you think?**
- **Do you agree?**
- **And you?**

- **Do you think that going on an exchange trip is a good way to improve your English?** ...... **(Why?/Why not?)**

- **Some people think that foreign exchange trips give language learners a big advantage. Do you agree?** ...... **(Why?/Why not?)**

- **Are there any disadvantages to going on exchange trips?** ...... **(What are they?)**

- **Would you like to go on an exchange trip?** ...... **(Why?/Why not?)**

- **What is the difference between going on a foreign exchange trip and going on holiday?**

- **Do you think that school exchange trips should be compulsory for every student?** ...... **(Why?/Why not?)**

Thank you. That is the end of the test.

Students' own answers

Practice Test 6

READING AND USE OF ENGLISH PART 1

For questions **1 – 8**, read the text below and decide which answer (**A**, **B**, **C** or **D**) best fits each gap. There is an example at the beginning (**0**).

Example:

0 **A** led   **B** controlled   **C** reigned   **D** held

0	A	B	**C**	D

Queen Elizabeth II

Queen Elizabeth II is Queen of sixteen Commonwealth states, and has **(0)** _____ as Queen of the United Kingdom for over 60 years. In fact, she has spent the second longest amount of time on the **(1)** _____ of any ruler in UK history; only Queen Victoria ruled for longer.

The Queen was just 26 years old when she **(2)** _____ to power. Her father, King George VI, lost his **(3)** _____ with heart disease while the young Elizabeth was in Kenya. It was Elizabeth's husband, Prince Philip, who **(4)** _____ the news to her on 6th February 1952, the day she both lost her father and gained her current title of Queen. She flew back to the UK immediately.

Elizabeth was officially **(5)** _____ as Queen at her coronation ceremony on 2nd June 1953, more than one year after her father's death. Even **(6)** _____ it was just a one-day event, the **(7)** _____ took sixteen months to complete and cost millions of pounds. It was at this ceremony that Elizabeth made a promise to uphold the **(8)** _____ of her nation.

1	**A** seat	**B** throne	**C** chair	**D** bench
2	**A** came	**B** got	**C** took	**D** arrived
3	**A** conflict	**B** life	**C** war	**D** battle
4	**A** informed	**B** broke	**C** said	**D** opened
5	**A** crowned	**B** capped	**C** topped	**D** covered
6	**A** so	**B** as	**C** though	**D** and
7	**A** foundations	**B** organisations	**C** appointments	**D** preparations
8	**A** laws	**B** rules	**C** theories	**D** measures

READING AND USE OF ENGLISH PART 2

For questions **9 – 16**, read the text below and think of the word which best fits each gap. Use only **one** word in each gap. There is an example at the beginning **(0)**.

Write your answers **IN CAPITAL LETTERS**.

Example: | **0** | B | E | | | | | | | | | | | | |

Teens and cosmetic surgery

It may not **(0)** _BE_ surprising to hear that many teenagers are not happy when they see their reflection in the mirror. What might perhaps surprise people, though, is that many teenagers aged thirteen **(9)** _TO_ nineteen undergo cosmetic surgery every year. Believe it or **(10)** _NOT_, in 2009 over 219,000 cosmetic procedures were performed on teenagers in the US alone.

Why are so many teenagers unhappy **(11)** _WITH/ABOUT_ their appearance? Many adults have plastic surgery so that they can look younger. In the case **(12)** _OF_ teenagers, of course, the situation is quite different. They undergo these operations in **(13)** _ORDER_ to fit in with their peers. They believe there is something wrong with **(14)** _THEIR_ body and changing it will make them feel better about themselves.

The procedures are painful and sometimes dangerous, but many teens are willing to **(15)** _TAKE_ the risk. Sadly, many are still unhappy afterwards and find themselves having further surgery a **(16)** _FEW_ years down the road.

READING AND USE OF ENGLISH PART 3

For questions **17 – 24**, read the text below. Use the word given in capitals at the end of some of the lines to form a word that fits in the gap **in the same line**. There is an example at the beginning (0).

Write your answers **IN CAPITAL LETTERS**.

Example: | **0** | H | A | R | M | F | U | L | | | | | | | | | |

Are computer games safe?

Some people worry that computer games might be **(0)** ___HARMFUL___   **HARM**

to children. Many games today are full of **(17)** ___VIOLENCE___ , but there   **VIOLENT**

isn't much research on the subject, as the popularity of video games is

somewhat recent. While most children know the difference between

fantasy and **(18)** ___REALITY___ , more studies are being conducted   **REAL**

to see if these games contribute to a lack of sensitivity and a rise in

aggression in children who play these games.

The **(19)** ___LATEST___ findings seem to support the theory that   **LATE**

children who play video games **(20)** ___FREQUENTLY___ or for long periods   **FREQUENT**

of time experience adverse effects from the games. They become

addicted to playing and have less time to **(21)** ___SOCIALISE___ with   **SOCIAL**

other people. This causes them to feel a sense of **(22)** ___ISOLATION___   **ISOLATE**

in the world, and even to become fearful of it. An obvious

(23) ___SOLUTION___ to this problem would be to make sure children are   **SOLVE**

not playing video games **(24)** ___EXCESSIVELY___ , and to make sure they are   **EXCESS**

doing their homework and spending time with their friends.

READING AND USE OF ENGLISH PART 4

For questions **25 – 30**, complete the second sentence so that it has a similar meaning to the first sentence, using the word given. **Do not change the word given.** You must use between **two** and **five** words, including the word given. Here is an example (**0**).

Example:

0 The party didn't cost Mary a lot of money.

FORTUNE

Mary didn't ____*SPEND A FORTUNE*____ on the party.

The gap can be filled by the words 'spend a fortune', so you write:

Example: | **0** | *SPEND A FORTUNE*

Write **only** the missing words **IN CAPITAL LETTERS.**

---

25 You ought to do your homework before you watch TV.
HAD
You ____*HAD BETTER DO*____ your homework before you watch TV.

26 She had no idea he was a police officer.
KNOW
Little ____*DID SHE KNOW*____ that he was a police officer.

27 I lent her some money last month and she still hasn't paid me back.
FROM *BORROWED SOME*
She ____*MONEY FROM ME*____ last month and she still hasn't paid me back.

28 She hid in the kitchen because she didn't want to be seen.
AVOID
She hid in the kitchen *(IN ORDER) TO AVOID BEING* seen.

29 Monica will probably need help around the house.
LIKELY
Monica ____*IS LIKELY TO NEED*____ help around the house.

30 We really should call Aunty Gill in Australia.
HIGH
It's ____*HIGH TIME WE CALLED*____ Aunty Gill in Australia.

READING AND USE OF ENGLISH PART 5

Questions 31 – 36

You are going to read a magazine article about a medical advance. For questions **31 – 36**, choose the answer (**A, B, C** or **D**) which you think fits best according to the text.

The Medical Mirror

Imagine looking into the mirror and having it check a number of vital health signs all at once, giving you a record of the results, even forwarding the results to your doctor. PhD student Ming-Zher Poh has been working on making this a reality as part of his research into health sciences and development. He is seeking to create a way for people to check such information in the convenience of their own homes.

So far, the mirror Poh has developed can monitor a person's heart rate and breathing rate as they stand still and look straight into the mirror. It can also detect variations in heartbeats, known as heart-rate variability, which indicate how well the nervous system is functioning. Every heartbeat is different, says Poh, and monitoring changes in a person's heartbeats over time can identify the onset of larger problems before they become serious health issues.

So how does the mirror collect data? Poh explains that the mirror measures changes in the light around the blood vessels near the surface of our skin. The blood in our body absorbs light, and when our heart beats, the blood in our veins increases slightly. This increase in blood means more light is absorbed, so there is less light near the veins. This change may only occur for a fraction of a second, but the mirror can detect this difference and measure it. Using light measurements for measuring vital signs is not an entirely new concept. When doctors place clips on the fingers of patients in order to measure their heart rate, there is an infrared light that shines from the clip into the blood vessels. As the blood flows quickly through the area of skin that has infrared light passing through it, the gauge in the clip measures the patient's blood flow. The mirror uses a similar technology, except that it uses the light surrounding the skin, rather than passing light directly through it.

Besides being a convenient way of measuring vital signs, the mirror has a unique advantage over conventional methods as it has no contact with the patient and Poh is hoping this will make it popular for hospital use. Blood pressure devices have to be fitted around the arm, and the clip mentioned above around the finger. These devices are not suitable for certain patients, such as burn victims who can't have anything touching their skin, or for babies and small children who either cannot or do not like being fitted with a device. The mirror, however, is ideal.

Although the mirror looks like any other mirror, it is actually equipped with a very small computer positioned behind the glass. The computer has a webcam that can see through the glass in order to capture an image of the person standing in front of the mirror. The person can't see through the mirror; they simply see their reflection. The results of the data collection can, however, be viewed in a special area of the mirror. Poh is very keen to make this project a reality. At the moment it is only in the development stage, but he is planning to start a company to further develop the technology. He has managed to correct some of the earlier flaws of the device through his research. It was an enormous challenge to create a device that could take such tiny measurements, given the distance the data has to travel from person to mirror, but the project has come on in leaps and bounds since it began.

The mirror will also assist people in quantifying their own data, a growing trend in medicine as people are encouraged to take more responsibility for monitoring their own health. Quantifying data simply involves measuring a vital sign and giving the measurement a figure. With the ability to do this themselves, a person could take daily or weekly measurements and the information could then be sent to a doctor's office over the Internet.

31   In the first paragraph, what best describes what Ming-Zher Poh is doing?
     A finding a cure for diseases
     B building sophisticated mirrors
     C making health checks easier
     D improving hospital procedures

32   In the second paragraph, Poh talks about
     A why each heartbeat is different.
     B what heartbeats show about a person's health.
     C how heartbeats relate to breathing.
     D how heartbeats change with age.

33   What is the main difference between the mirror and the clip mentioned in the third paragraph?
     A They measure different things.
     B They measure in different ways.
     C They measure at different speeds.
     D They measure different people.

34   What does 'this' refer to in line 29?
     A the fact that the mirror doesn't touch the skin
     B the convenience of the mirror
     C the mirror itself
     D the use of the mirror in hospital

35   In the fifth paragraph, the expression 'leaps and bounds' relates to
     A measuring data.
     B starting a company.
     C gathering materials.
     D the project itself.

36   According to the last paragraph, what best describes quantifying data?
     A assigning numbers to data
     B making data calculations
     C reporting data to doctors
     D getting data on your own

READING AND USE OF ENGLISH PART 6

Questions 37 – 42

You are going to read an article about managing credit card debt. Six sentences have been removed from the article. Choose from the sentences **A – G** the one which fits each gap (**37 – 42**). There is one extra sentence which you do not need to use.

Getting rid of **credit card debt**

We know that credit cards are bad for us, but sometimes we find ourselves unable to resist the urge to use them. The best advice for managing credit card debt is not to have it in the first place. But what happens if, in spite of everything, you do end up with a mountain of credit card bills? They're hard to get rid of, but there is still hope.

Probably the most important step is to make your credit cards impossible to use any more. This means picking up a pair of scissors and cutting up each and every one of them. Of course you'll still have your outstanding balances, but it signifies an enormous change in the way you live. And one immediate benefit is that your credit card balances will stop increasing. The next step is to tackle your account balances. Most people who've got credit card debt have been using more than one credit card. **37** A In having many different accounts, you're receiving numerous bills in the post each month, which means many different payments. The best move here is to pay off the smallest balance first. You'll pay it off more quickly, and that will be one less bill to pay.

Another useful technique is using any extra money you've got at the end of the month to pay extra on your credit cards. Most people would probably put this surplus amount in the bank, then later spend it on something they don't need. **38** G And if you make enough of these small payments, they can add up.

What if you find that you haven't got any extra money at all? You may have to take another difficult yet necessary step, which is getting a second job. This could be something part-time, or perhaps something you can do from home. **39** E

If you are really in a serious mess with your credit card debts, there are other, more drastic options. One is speaking to your credit card companies about making lower payments. This is necessary if your minimum payments are too high. **40** F It will almost certainly be damaged. But there are worse things that can happen.

The worst scenario of all would be what's called bankruptcy This is where you go to court because of your debts and a judge decides that you don't have to pay your debts back at all. **41** B The consequences, however, are that you won't be able to get any credit, such as for car or home loans, for many years. It's not a decision to be taken lightly.

Whatever steps we take to deal with our credit card debt, we will probably have to ask ourselves some important questions, such as how we got into this mess. People often blame the banks or the economy, but rarely themselves. **42** D We must face the facts – we are responsible for managing our own finances, and it is in our power to do so.

A   Perhaps they've been using several!

B   Some may think it's a wonderful idea, since you won't have to pay any more money on your credit cards.

C   After he agrees to this, you can start paying off your balances one by one.

D   It is up to us to realise that we have a problem and we are the ones who have to take steps to fix it.

E   The added income from your extra wages can make a difference, and can be put solely towards paying off the cards.

F   The companies will probably work with you in lowering them, but it will be at a cost – your credit rating.

G   If you send it to one of your creditors, however, then it is actually being spent usefully.

READING AND USE OF ENGLISH PART 7

Questions 43 – 52

You are going to read some articles on various treatments for acne. For questions **43 – 52**, choose from the treatments (**A – D**). The treatments may be chosen more than once.

Which treatment(s)

is beyond the reach of those with low incomes?	**43**	D
is related to substances that can remove colour?	**44**	A
works from inside the body to kill germs?	**45**	B
is a form of a vitamin and is taken as a pill?	**46**	D
is cheap and available from a doctor only?	**47**	B
goes on the skin and contains a vitamin?	**48**	C
is most likely to cure acne?	**49**	D
can cause problems if used in stronger forms?	**50**	A
can cause a change in the thickness of the skin?	**51**	C
requires the user to start with small amounts before moving on to higher ones?	**52**	A

Treatments for acne

Billions of people worldwide suffer from this painful skin problem. What can be done to overcome it?

A Benzoyl peroxide

The most common method of treating acne is with benzoyl peroxide. Benzoyl peroxide is a chemical cleansing agent related to other peroxides that have whitening effects. Every chemist's shop carries some sort of cream that contains benzoyl peroxide. It can often be found in other shops as well; for example, in some supermarkets in the cosmetics section. Creams that contain benzoyl peroxide contain different amounts, from 2.5% up to 10%. A person with acne often begins with the lower percentage and moves up to a higher one after the skin starts to tolerate the medicine. In higher amounts, though, it can cause skin to become too irritated, and doctors do not believe it to be more effective at that dosage. For persons with mild acne, benzoyl peroxide is often effective enough to clear up some if not all acne spots, but for those people with persistent acne problems, it is not likely to work as a long-term solution. That said, benzoyl peroxide is very easy to obtain, as a prescription is not needed, and it is a relatively affordable product.

B Antibiotics

For people with more than mild cases of acne, a dermatologist will often prescribe an antibiotic. There are several types of antibiotics used for the treatment of acne, one of the most common being tetracycline. Tetracycline is taken in pill form and works by killing off the bacteria that cause acne to form. Some people respond well to this treatment; others, however, will still have persistent symptoms of acne, even if to a lesser degree. Tetracycline does have some side effects that should be considered; mainly that the user's skin becomes more sensitive. It has also been known to cause teeth to become yellow if taken by a child, but cases of this are extremely rare, as children do not have the need for it. Tetracycline is fairly inexpensive, so would not be beyond the means of most people, providing a doctor writes a prescription for it.

C Topical retinoids

A person who suffers from acne will usually try a topical retinoid after benzoyl peroxide creams and antibiotics fail to work. Topical retinoids, like Retin-A, are applied in the form of a cream. They have similar effects to benzoyl peroxide, such as drying of the skin, but they contain retinoids, which are completely different substances. Retinoids are derived from vitamin A, and like most other acne treatments, they make the skin sensitive. Retinoids go so far as to thin the surface of the skin, and caution must be taken when using this treatment. Users are not allowed to undergo any hair removal treatments that might tear the skin. Also, sun exposure is prohibited whilst using the cream. Creams with small amounts of retinoids can be bought over the counter these days, but those with larger amounts must be prescribed by a doctor. Topical retinoids have become more affordable over the years, as more and more people are using them.

D Oral retinoids

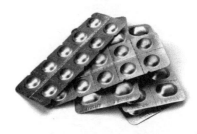

Perhaps one of the most effective acne treatments known today is the use of oral retinoids. Oral retinoids, like topical retinoids, are made from a form of vitamin A. A common oral retinoid is known by its brand name, Roaccutane. This treatment is used to treat the most serious cases of acne and is only available with a doctor's prescription. It is the most highly effective treatment on the market today, although it comes with the most serious side effects and is the least affordable treatment, with costs in the thousands of pounds, depending on the length of treatment. Roaccutane is taken in pill form, usually one a day, and the size of the pill depends on the weight of the individual. Its side effects include extreme drying of the skin and lips, and it can also cause an abrupt rise in blood sugar levels.

WRITING `PART 1`

You **must** answer this question. Write your answer in **140 – 190** words in an appropriate style.

1   In your English class you have been talking about sports. Now your teacher has asked you to write an essay for homework.

Write your essay using **all** the notes and giving reasons for your point of view.

'Professional athletes earn far too much money.'

Do you agree?

Notes

Write about:

  1   providing entertainment

  2   promoting sports

  3   .... (your own idea)

Students' own answers

WRITING PART 2

Write an answer to **one** of the questions **2 – 5** in this part. Write your answer in **140 – 190** words in an appropriate style.

2 You have seen a story writing competition in an English-language newspaper and you decide to enter.

Your story must begin with this sentence:

Jonathan felt nervous when the coach told him their star player was too ill to play.

Your story must include:

• a football match

• a goal

Write your **story**.

3 You have seen this notice in an English-language magazine for teenagers.

> **Articles wanted**
>
> We are looking for articles about special pets. Have you, or anybody that you know, ever had a special pet? Tell us about it – describe the pet and explain why it's so special.
>
> The best article will appear in our next issue.

Write your **article**.

4 You recently saw the following section of an article in the newspaper:

LUNCH MENU TO CHANGE

Schools in the Brighton area will stop offering fresh fruit and vegetables to students in order to cut costs.

Write a letter to the newspaper editor expressing your opinion about this decision. Write your **letter**.

5 Question 5 always consists of a question on the set text. Only answer question 5 if you have studied the set text. Here is an example of the kind of question you might be asked:

Your English class has had a discussion about a book you were assigned to read. Now your English teacher has asked you to write a letter to a friend telling them about an unusual event in a book you've read recently. You should write about the unusual event and say why it surprised you.

Write your **letter**.

Students' own answers

LISTENING PART 1

Questions 1 – 8

You will hear people talking in eight different situations. For questions **1 – 8**, choose the best answer (**A**, **B** or **C**).

1   You hear a reporter talking about travel.
    What will the reporter talk about first?
    A an empty village
    B an ancient site
    C a museum

2   You overhear two friends talking about books.
    What kind of book is Lindsay reading at the moment?
    A a crime novel
    B an autobiography
    C a love story

3   You hear part of an interview with a musician.
    What does she say about her professional training?
    A She had an easy time with it.
    B She found it challenging.
    C She was dissatisfied in the end.

4   You overhear two friends talking about shopping.
    What do they agree on?
    A the shop they want to go to
    B the quality of clothes in the shop
    C the cost of clothes in the shop

5   You hear two friends in a study hall.
    What are they going to do next?
    A continue studying
    B get something to eat
    C listen to music

6   You hear a girl leaving a voicemail message.
    What does she ask her mother to do?
    A pick her up from basketball practice
    B wait for her to have supper
    C record a sporting event on TV

7   You hear a girl talking about a play she has just seen.
    What did she think of it?
    A She hated everything about it.
    B She thought it got worse as it went on.
    C The way it looked was impressive.

8   You hear a woman talking to a class.
    What is her purpose in speaking to them?
    A to give thanks to everyone for joining the reading club
    B to postpone the reading club's first meeting
    C to inform students of the reading club's new location

LISTENING PART 2

Questions 9 – 18

You will hear a young musician named Eric Moseley talking about himself and his band. For questions **9 – 18**, complete the sentences with a word or short phrase.

PLAYING THE DRUMS WITH ERIC MOSELEY

The first instrument Eric played was | *(the) guitar* | **9**

Eric says you need a good | *sense of rhythm* | **10** | to play the drums.

In the summer, Eric intends to spend | *40/forty* | **11** | hours practising every week.

Eric finds | *classical* | **12** | music impressive when he hears drums in it.

Eric didn't know Frankie, the | *keyboard player* | **13** |, before they formed the band.

On the band's second tour, the fact that audiences were | *larger* | **14** | made him feel good.

At the first show, the audience consisted of about | *100/a hundred* | **15** | people.

At one of Eric's shows, someone threw a | *hamburger* | **16** | on stage.

The band will shortly spend some time in a | *(recording) studio* | **17**

The person Eric would most like to see at one of his concerts is his | *grandma* | **18**

LISTENING PART 3

Questions 19 – 23

You will hear five people talking about phobias. For questions **19 – 23**, choose from the list (**A – H**) what each speaker's phobia is. Use the letters only once. There are three extra letters which you do not need to use.

A   This person is very scared of large animals.

Speaker 1	*E* **19**

B   This person has got a fear of being in high places.

Speaker 2	*F* **20**

C   This person's fear is of a certain leisure activity.

Speaker 3	*G* **21**

D   This person is afraid of flying insects.

Speaker 4	*C* **22**

E   This person is afraid of a very small creature.

Speaker 5	*B* **23**

F   This person's fear has to do with darkness.

G   This person has got a fear of being on water.

H   This person has got a fear of zoos.

LISTENING PART 4

Questions 24 – 30

You will hear two teenagers talking about funny things that have happened to them, their friends and other people after accidentally falling asleep. For questions **24 – 30**, choose the best answer (**A**, **B** or **C**).

24 Why does Greg say he was tired in class?
   A His maths lesson was difficult.
   B His recent routine had exhausted him.
   C Someone played a joke on him.

25 When did Greg realise a joke was being played on him?
   A when the class bell rang
   B as soon as he woke up
   C when he saw people laughing

26 Who was sitting in front of Carla in the theatre?
   A a man on his own
   B about twenty-five people
   C a couple

27 How did Carla feel about the man's snoring?
   A She enjoyed it more than the movie.
   B It made her very upset.
   C It interfered with the film.

28 Where does Carla say her friend Rebecca has fallen asleep before?
   A on a piece of living room furniture
   B outside the house
   C under her brother's car

29 Why did Rebecca shout when she woke up?
   A She felt really embarrassed.
   B She was trying to get her brother's attention.
   C Her brother had closed the car door very loudly.

30 How does Rebecca feel about the incident now?
   A She's ready for it to happen again.
   B She feels it wasn't really so serious after all.
   C She can see the funny side of it.

SPEAKING PART 1

2 minutes (3 minutes for groups of three)

This part is always the same. See page 34 of Test 1.

Select one or more questions from the following category, as appropriate.

Holidays (past and future)

*   **What do you usually do during the school holidays? ...... (Who with?/Where?)**
*   **What are some things you have done on holidays in the past?**
*   **What is your favourite kind of holiday? ...... (Why?)**
*   **What kind of holiday would you hate to go on?**
*   **Is there any special place you would like to visit? ...... (Why?)**
*   **Who do you like to travel with? ...... (Why?)**

Students' own answers

SPEAKING PART 2

4 minutes (6 minutes for groups of three)

1 Clothing
2 Music

Interlocutor	In this part of the test, I'm going to give each of you two photographs. I'd like you to talk about your photographs on your own for about a minute, and also to answer a short question about your partner's photographs.
See photos A and B on page 189.	(*Candidate A*), it's your turn first. Here are your photographs. They show **people wearing different styles of clothing**.
	I'd like you to compare the photographs and say **why you think the people have chosen to wear those clothes**.
	All right?
Candidate A	(*Speak for approximately 1 minute.*)
Interlocutor	Thank you. (*Candidate B*), **which person's clothes do you prefer?**
Candidate B	(*Reply for approximately 30 seconds.*)
Interlocutor	Thank you.
See photos C and D on page 190.	Now, (*Candidate B*), here are your photographs. They show **people listening to music**.
	I'd like you to compare the photographs, and say **what the advantages and disadvantages are of listening to music in these different ways**.
	All right?
Candidate B	(*Speak for approximately 1 minute.*)
Interlocutor	Thank you. (*Candidate A*), **how important is listening to music to you?**
Candidate A	(*Reply for approximately 30 seconds.*)
Interlocutor	Thank you.

Students' own answers

SPEAKING PARTS 3 AND 4

8 minutes (11 minutes for groups of three)

Shopping and consumerism

PART 3

Interlocutor	Now, I'd like you to talk about something together for about two minutes. *(3 minutes for groups of three)*
See written prompts on page 191.	**Here are some reasons why many people shop online** and a question for you to discuss. First you have some time to look at the task.
	Now, talk to each other about **whether it's a good idea for people to shop online.**
Candidates	*(Discuss for approximately 2 minutes – 3 minutes for groups of three.)*
Interlocutor	Thank you. Now you have about a minute to decide **which two things are the most important for people who shop online.**
Candidates	*(Reply for approximately 1 minute – for pairs and groups of three.)*
Interlocutor	Thank you.

PART 4

Interlocutor

Select any of the following questions, as appropriate:

- **How important is it to shop for new things? ...... (Why?/Why not?)**

- **How often do you go shopping and what do you shop for? ...... (Who do you go with?)**

- **Does advertising affect what we buy? ...... (How?)**

- **What do you think is the best way to encourage young people to shop responsibly?**

- **Do you think shopping habits have changed since your grandparents' time? ...... (Why?/Why not?)**

- **Do our friends influence our shopping habits? Is this good or bad?**

Thank you. That is the end of the test.

Select any of the following prompts, as appropriate:

- **What do you think?**
- **Do you agree?**
- **And you?**

Students' own answers

Practice Test 7

READING AND USE OF ENGLISH PART 1

For questions **1 – 8**, read the text below and decide which answer (**A, B, C** or **D**) best fits each gap. There is an example at the beginning (**0**).

Example:

0 A taking   **B** having   **C** holding   **D** doing

0	A	B	C	D

Looking ahead

What will life be like in the future? Will we be **(0)** _____ pills instead of eating food and wearing silver space-suits? Will we be **(1)** _____ on the moon and going to school or work in flying cars? Perhaps not, but we can assume that we'll make great **(2)** _____ in technology which will change our lives in many ways.

In particular, there's no doubt that **(3)** _____ will be quicker and easier than it is now. High **(4)** _____ trains will take us from city to city in less time than ever. Planes will **(5)** _____ the journey from London to New York in an hour or two.

Our health is another area of our lives where we can expect great improvements. Doctors will work in better hospitals, which will be **(6)** _____ with machines to help people live longer, and with new medicines we might put a(n) **(7)** _____ to some of the diseases which are currently **(8)** _____ for so much ill health.

1	**A** staying	**B** living	**C** inhabiting	**D** visiting
2	**A** improvement	**B** development	**C** progress	**D** advance
3	**A** trip	**B** journey	**C** voyage	**D** travel
4	**A** time	**B** pace	**C** speed	**D** rate
5	**A** make	**B** do	**C** take	**D** go
6	**A** equipped	**B** given	**C** full	**D** used
7	**A** finish	**B** end	**C** stop	**D** finale
8	**A** cause	**B** blame	**C** responsible	**D** fault

READING AND USE OF ENGLISH PART 2

For questions **9 – 16**, read the text below and think of the word which best fits each gap. Use only **one** word in each gap. There is an example at the beginning (**0**).

Write your answers **IN CAPITAL LETTERS**.

Example: | **0** | *I* | *N* | | | | | | | | | | |

London

London is the capital of the UK and one of the largest cities **(0)** _IN_ Europe, with a population **(9)** _OF_ over seven million. It was founded **(10)** _BY_ the Romans in 43 AD, although there is evidence that people lived in the area long **(11)** _BEFORE_ that.

But it was not **(12)** _UNTIL_ the eleventh century that some of the key landmarks still standing today, such as the Tower of London and Westminster Abbey, were built. The Abbey was significant because it was **(13)** _WHERE_ the new king, William the Conqueror, was crowned on Christmas Day, 1066. Since then, most kings and queens of England have also **(14)** _BEEN_ crowned in the Abbey, and most of them were buried there, too, until the death of George II in 1760.

In the centuries following William's coronation, London grew as the power of England increased. The wealth of the world flowed **(15)** _INTO_ London, making it one of the richest cities in history. In the nineteenth century, the number of people living in London grew from one million to six million, and the population is **(16)** _STILL_ growing today.

READING AND USE OF ENGLISH PART 3

For questions **17 – 24**, read the text below. Use the word given in capitals at the end of some of the lines to form a word that fits in the gap **in the same line**. There is an example at the beginning **(0)**.

Write your answers **IN CAPITAL LETTERS**.

Example: | 0 | D | I | F | F | E | R | E | N | T | | | | | | | |

The developing world

Life in developed countries like Great Britain, Japan and the United States is very **(0)** ___DIFFERENT___ from life in the developing world. It is necessary to look at the conditions in a typical developing country in order to gain a(n) **(17)** _UNDERSTANDING_ of these differences.

DIFFER

UNDERSTAND

Developing countries are **(18)** ___CLEARLY___ at a disadvantage if they want to compete with their richer neighbours. But if a country is trying to improve living conditions for its citizens, some things are vital. The people of the country must be in **(19)** ___AGREEMENT___ with the government's plans, and the government in turn must be very progressive. In addition, the country needs **(20)** _IMAGINATIVE_ leaders.

CLEAR

AGREE

IMAGINE

Many rich countries have become **(21)** ___WEALTHY___ through their natural resources like coal or oil. However, drilling for oil or mining coal can be very expensive, and so poorer countries are often forced to seek **(22)** ___FINANCIAL___ help from international institutions, such as banks. These banks give developing countries **(23)** ___ASSISTANCE___ in the form of loans to help them start their projects.

WEALTH

FINANCE

ASSIST

This money can also be used to build transport and communication systems. These things are essential if a country wants to achieve long-term economic **(24)** ___GROWTH___.

GROW

READING AND USE OF ENGLISH PART 4

For questions **25 – 30**, complete the second sentence so that it has a similar meaning to the first sentence, using the word given. **Do not change the word given**. You must use between **two** and **five** words, including the word given. Here is an example (0).

Example:

0   They had never been there before.

FIRST

It was _THE FIRST TIME THEY HAD_ ever been there.

The gap can be filled by the words 'the first time they had', so you write:

Example: | **0** | *THE FIRST TIME THEY HAD*

Write **only** the missing words **IN CAPITAL LETTERS**.

---

25   Would you like to go and see a film tonight?
TO
How about _____ _GOING TO THE_ _____ cinema tonight?

26   Mandy was late for work because her alarm didn't go off.
GOT
If her alarm had gone off, Mandy _____ _WOULD HAVE GOT TO_ _____ work on time.

27   'It was James who broke the window!' said Peter.
ACCUSED   _ACCUSED_
Peter _____ _JAMES OF BREAKING_ _____ the window.

28   It wasn't difficult to find a seat on the bus.
DIFFICULTY   _HAD NO/_
We _LITTLE DIFFICULTY (IN) FINDING_ a seat on the bus.

29   I think she should have a holiday.
WERE
If _____ _I WERE HER_ _____ , I'd have a holiday.

30   Bad weather led to the match being cancelled.
RESULT
The match was cancelled _____ _AS A RESULT OF_ _____ bad weather.

READING AND USE OF ENGLISH PART 5

Questions 31 – 36

You are going to read an extract from a novel. For questions **31 – 36**, choose the answer (**A, B, C** or **D**) which you think fits best according to the text.

Louis couldn't remember a time when he hadn't been Daniel's friend, and he didn't want to. Daniel was his first friend and definitely his best friend. He couldn't imagine a time – no, *the* time, because he knew it was coming – when he wouldn't be Daniel's friend. They had met at school, on their first day. Louis had been holding on to his mother's hand and Daniel had been standing slightly apart from all the other nervous children and worried parents … alone but serene. When his mother had to talk to the teacher for a moment, Louis slipped his hand out of hers and went to stand next to Daniel. Although they didn't exchange a word, from that moment they were friends and spent almost all their free time with each other.

All those years, they remained friends and did everything together. They studied together, they played together, and they even fought together once, when they chased away a boy who had threatened Louis in the playground for some reason. But now Louis was facing an unimaginable future. Daniel's father had been promoted and the family was relocating. When Daniel told him, Louis just looked at him. 'What?' asked Louis, shocked and upset.

'Well, …'

'What does that mean?'

'I don't know, do I?'

And that was that. They didn't talk about it again, they just went on doing things together as usual, as if nothing was going to happen. But it was always there, like a heavy, dark cloud above them. Louis felt helpless, and Daniel couldn't – or didn't – try to make things easier.

One afternoon, Louis walked over to Daniel's house. As he reached the house, he saw the family car in the road, full of luggage, and realised with a shock that the day had arrived. A big van was parked beside the car, with men carrying things out of the house and putting them in the van. Daniel's mother was tying something to the roof of the car. She saw Louis and greeted him in her usual loud and cheerful manner. She said something about the weather and travelling, and smiled. Louis couldn't believe her lack of understanding, her ignorance, and walked past her to the front door.

Inside the house, people were carrying things and shouting questions to each other and walking from room to room with things in boxes, putting stuff down and picking it up again and putting it somewhere else. He didn't recognise some of the people, and couldn't see Daniel anywhere. A removal man pushed past him without saying sorry. Louis didn't feel like helping and sat on a box in the kitchen until Daniel's father politely asked him to move. He went into the front garden and, with a sense of loss and uselessness, one hand in his pocket, stood looking at the house, without a word to say. It emptied itself of possessions as he watched. Afterwards, he walked home from Daniel's empty house without a clear thought in his head. He didn't feel anything. He walked as if he were in a daze. Familiar things looked neutral, without value. The tree on the corner, the garden gate, they had lost their meaning. Without his best friend, things had no significance any more. They looked like he felt – blank.

He sat in his bedroom and looked out of the window, and gradually his memory guided him back over the years of their friendship. He began to understand that he was feeling so bad only because he had felt so good before. He realised slowly that although unhappiness is the opposite of happiness, you can only really feel one if you have felt the other too. He took some small comfort from this even though he felt lonely and through his pain he could see, just perhaps, that he was lucky to have had such a great friend.

31 What does Louis realise in the first paragraph?
   A He can't remember his friend.
   B He hasn't got any other friends.
   C He has no imagination.
   D He will lose his friend soon.

32 What was the result of the boys' chat about the move?
   A They felt worse than before.
   B They realised they could not remain friends.
   C They ignored the situation and carried on as normal.
   D They continued to discuss it normally.

33 How did Louis interpret Daniel's mother's reaction when she saw Louis?
   A He thought she wasn't taking the situation seriously enough.
   B He assumed she was pleased that Louis had come to help.
   C He understood she was happy that they were finally moving.
   D He thought she wasn't being honest.

34 How did the removal man and Daniel's father treat Louis?
   A They both treated him like a stranger.
   B They were both rude to him.
   C They both felt he was in the way.
   D They both completely ignored his presence.

35 What do we learn about Louis after Daniel left?
   A He got lost on the way home.
   B He was numb because of his experiences.
   C He found his family inconsiderate.
   D He didn't recognise things he knew very well.

36 In the last paragraph, Louis
   A begins to be happy again because he is alone.
   B starts to accept the situation.
   C realises he must learn to forget.
   D becomes comfortable in his own room.

READING AND USE OF ENGLISH PART 6

Questions 37 – 42

You are going to read a magazine article about zoos. Six sentences have been removed from the article. Choose from the sentences **A – G** the one which fits each gap (**37 – 42**). There is one extra sentence which you do not need to use.

Zoos
old and new

Many people love visiting the zoo for a day out. But have you ever wondered if zoos have always been the same? Are zoos just for curious people who want to look at strange animals from other countries?

Although opinions differ, some archaeologists think that the very first zoo was in Hierakonpolis in Ancient Egypt. Remains of a large collection of animals from about 4,500 years ago have been found there, and experts think that the animals were kept in a special place by the city's rulers, like a zoo today. **37** D On the other side of the world, records show that a kind of zoo that was called a 'Garden of Intelligence' was established in China in about 1100 BC.

The Romans brought animals back to Rome from foreign countries, and some were kept in private collections. Others were less fortunate. **38** B This type of public 'entertainment', where animals and men would die for the amusement of the crowd, is very different from entertainment today where people generally do not consider it entertaining to watch animals suffer. It is generally agreed that the first modern zoo opened in London in 1828 and called itself a 'zoological garden'. The word 'zoo' didn't actually appear until some twenty years later, when a newspaper used it to describe Clifton Zoo in Bristol, England. Both of these places housed collections of animals not found in Britain.

The original purpose of European zoos was to allow scientists to do research on the animals, but zoos were soon opened to the public and became popular. This was because the nineteenth century was a time of discovery and learning for all, and zoos played their part in this. Curious members of the public could satisfy their thirst for knowledge by simply visiting the local zoo. **39** E

Like Europe, the United States saw the zoo gain in popularity in the nineteenth century. **40** A People began to question if it was right to take animals away from their natural habitat and put them in cages. This attitude contributed to the drop in visitor numbers to zoos, and London Zoo itself was threatened with closure by the 1980s.

Zoos were forced to change, just as public opinion had changed. Increasing environmental awareness and concern over the future of endangered habitats and species have shaped the development of the modern zoo. **41** G The areas where animals were kept have been re-designed to resemble their natural surroundings.

Today, zoos have become protectors rather than exhibitors. Animals faced with extinction have been given a better chance of surviving in a zoo and, in some cases, successful breeding programmes have actually increased the population. **42** C In short, zoos are thriving and are now seen as a place of education and conservation as well as entertainment, thus fulfilling all of their historical roles at once.

A However, this popularity eventually started to decline as there was a change in the public attitude towards keeping animals in captivity.

B Some of the more dangerous animals were kept not in private zoos, but were used to fight to the death in public shows at places like the Colosseum.

C Animals have even been released back into the wild as a result of such successes.

D Later in the same country, Queen Hatshepsut built a zoo in 1500 BC, and filled it with animals from all over Africa.

E There, on display for their education and interest, were examples of animals from all over the world.

F Visitors were not encouraged to feed the animals or get too close to the cages.

G Following the trend set by the growing ecological movement, zoos have taken a long look at their relationship with the natural world.

READING AND USE OF ENGLISH PART 7

Questions 43 – 52

You are going to read a magazine article about modern museums. For questions **43 – 52**, choose from the museums (**A – E**). The museums may be chosen more than once.

Which museum(s)

is located in the same place as an educational establishment?	**43**	B
is pleased to be the only one of its kind in the country?	**44**	A
changed its name?	**45**	C
has links to the people in its area through its activities?	**46**	A
has exhibits which were given to it as gifts?	**47**	D
is visited by over 1,000,000 people every year?	**48**	E
has a huge number of exhibits in quite a small space?	**49**	B
claims that it can keep visitors occupied for a very long time?	**50**	D
would not interest young children so much?	**51**	B
allows visitors to go inside a unique pair of exhibits?	**52**	E

State of the Art

We look at five of the most up-to-date museum experiences in the world today and find out what they can offer visitors.

A London Film Museum

The London Film Museum is proud to be unique in Great Britain. It is self-supporting even though the entry price is very low. The museum also supports the film industry in Great Britain, as well as the local community, through educational programmes and special events. The museum covers 27,000 square feet of space and features many familiar objects from some famous films. Some past exhibits include the *Star Wars* 30th Anniversary Exhibition which was voted Britain's number one attraction by a national newspaper, and an exhibition about the famous comic artist Charlie Chaplin called *The Great Londoner*, once again highlighting the museum's commitment to the surrounding area.

B MIT Museum

The Massachusetts Institute of Technology Museum introduces the curious visitor to inventions, ideas and innovations by using interactive exhibitions, experimental projects and its famous collections. The museum's various exhibits illustrate the world of technology, and the place is an inspiration for all ages to explore science and technology, although the museum is most suitable for visitors of twelve and above. The museum is situated in the grounds of the university, an impressive location, and is the only museum on the site. There are two floors of exhibits and although space is limited, the museum houses over one million items of historical interest including rare books, technical documents and photographs. There are also hundreds of machines and devices to see, such as early or important examples of telephones, thermometers and computers. In addition, there are temporary exhibitions dealing with different subjects; the current ones feature robots, holographs, the development of ship design and the relationship between computer graphics and the brain.

C The Museum of Science

The Museum of Science in Boston believes its role is to help change the way people think about science and inspire them to explore and develop their relationship with both the technological world and the natural world. In fact, when the museum opened in 1830, its original name was The New England Museum of Natural History, and it was largely concerned with animals. Over the years, however, the focus moved to science rather than nature. By 1951, it was the only museum dedicated solely to science in the United States. Today the museum still houses over 100 live animals, but the most popular attractions are the Planetarium, where visitors can view all the planets in the solar system, and the IMAX theatre, a kind of hi-tech cinema where special 3-D films are shown. The connection to cinema doesn't end there, as in 2004 the museum hosted *The Lord of the Rings* exhibition featuring many items from the movie. And in 2009, *Harry Potter: The Exhibition* featured at the museum.

D Rock and Roll Hall of Fame

Visit the Rock and Roll Hall of Fame in Cleveland and your admission will help fund their efforts to educate the world about the importance of rock and roll music in society. The museum embodies the music it celebrates; it is full of passion, energy and the spirit of the music concerned. A visit to the world of rock and roll can take you five hours or two days, according to their website! In its vast 150,000 square-foot space, there are seven floors; the ideal place for the special events and temporary exhibitions which change on a regular basis. The featured collections include items donated by the stars and the fans such as instruments, photos and private documents. In the museum shop, you can buy T-shirts, hats, and mugs with images of your favourite band on, as well as posters and CDs of all the artists in the museum.

E Auto and Technik Museum Sinsheim

The Auto and Technik Museum (or Car and Technology Museum as it's sometimes known in English), which is in Sinsheim in Germany, is the largest privately-owned museum of technology in the whole of Europe. It boasts more than 3000 exhibits in over 30,000m² of exhibition space. More than a million people visit the museum each year, to see up close the amazing collection of aeroplanes, sports cars, vintage cars, motorbikes, early agricultural machinery, and much much more. With both an Air France Concorde and a Tupolev TU-144 on display, this is the only museum in the world where you can see the two supersonic passenger planes which have flown commercially. Visitors don't just get to see them from the outside though, as the planes have been designed to be 'walk-through'. This is undoubtedly the highlight of any trip to the museum.

WRITING PART 1

You **must** answer this question. Write your answer in **140 – 190** words in an appropriate style.

1 In your English class you have been talking about space exploration. Now your teacher has asked you to write an essay for homework.

   Write your essay using **all** the notes and giving reasons for your point of view.

   In some countries the government spends huge amounts of money on space exploration.

   Is this a good or bad way for governments to spend money?

   Notes

   Write about:

   1   increasing knowledge

   2   ignoring citizens' needs

   3   .... (your own idea)

   Students' own answers

WRITING PART 2

Write an answer to **one** of the questions **2 – 5** in this part. Write your answer in **140 – 190** words in an appropriate style.

2   You have seen this announcement in an English-language magazine for teenagers.

Articles wanted:
Studying at home or abroad?

What are the advantages and disadvantages of studying abroad compared to studying in your own country?

Send us your article and win a free trip to the country of your choice!

Write your **article**.

3   You have been watching a popular TV series, and your teacher has asked you to write a review for the school magazine. You should describe the series and say whether you recommend it or not.

Write your **review**.

4   Your English-speaking pen-friend is thinking of going on holiday to a place in your country where you have been many times. Write a letter to your pen-friend describing the place and giving him/her some recommendations about what he/she can do there.

Write your **letter**.

5   Question 5 always consists of a question on the set text. Only answer question 5 if you have studied the set text. Here is an example of the kind of question you might be asked:

Your English class has had a discussion about the book you have read and now your English teacher has asked you to write an essay for homework.

Describe two characters from the book, and the relationship between them. How are the characters similar or different? What effect on each others' lives do they have?

Write your **essay**.

Students' own answers

LISTENING PART 1

Questions 1 – 8

You will hear people talking in eight different situations. For questions **1 – 8**, choose the best answer (**A**, **B** or **C**).

1   You hear an announcement on the radio.
    Which programme will be broadcast now?
    A a news report on a political story
    B an interview with a famous reporter
    C a drama series about a journalist

2   You hear a woman complaining on the telephone.
    Who is she talking to?
    A her doctor
    B a travel agent
    C a hotel receptionist

3   You hear a teacher talking to a student's mother.
    What is the problem with the student?
    A His performance in school is poor despite previous warnings.
    B He doesn't work hard enough in class.
    C He often arrives at school after the lessons have begun.

4   You hear someone talking on the radio about his job.
    Why does he do this particular job?
    A He felt that he had no choice.
    B It was easy to find a job in this area.
    C His family has always worked at sea.

5   You hear part of an interview with a young writer.
    What does she say about her new book?
    A It costs about the same as her first book.
    B It is sold in a different way to her first book.
    C It has sold more copies than her first book.

6   You hear an athlete talking about his training methods.
    What is the most important aspect of his training?
    A He must exercise very carefully to avoid injury.
    B He must not change the amount of training he does.
    C He must be in perfect condition before competing.

7   You hear two children talking about their recent holidays.
    What problem do they both complain about?
    A the lack of activities
    B the food
    C the weather

8   You hear a man talking about travelling.
    What advice does he give?
    A Take as much as possible with you when you travel.
    B Learn as much as you can about where you're going.
    C Taking unnecessary luggage is sadly unavoidable.

LISTENING PART 2

Questions 9 – 18

You will hear a famous person called Gilbert Horne talking about his career in the world of sport.
For questions **9 – 18**, complete the sentences with a word or short phrase.

A LIFE IN SPORT

According to Gilbert, the best place to learn how to compete in sport is at | *school* | **9**

His | *height* | **10** was the main reason he stopped playing basketball.

Gilbert's first major achievement in sport was becoming a tennis | *champion* | **11**

Gilbert says that dedication is necessary in order to succeed as a | *professional* | **12**

The most important thing about football for Gilbert is | *team spirit* | **13**

Gilbert found success after he was | *transferred* | **14** to the Melchester team.

Gilbert soon | *adapted* | **15** to his second club because he already knew their style of football.

Gilbert's first job after he stopped playing football was | *assistant manager* | **16**

Gilbert describes Dave Grobbs as a(n) | *master* | **17** of the game.

Gilbert says he is | *proud* | **18** of his association with every aspect of the football club.

LISTENING PART 3

Questions 19 – 23

You will hear five people talking about different types of transport. For questions **19 – 23**, choose from the list (**A – H**) what each speaker talks about. Use the letters only once. There are three extra letters which you do not need to use.

A   This person finds travelling the best part of their holiday.

Speaker 1	D	**19**

B   This person prefers to travel in comfort and style.

Speaker 2	E	**20**

C   This person often suffers from motion sickness.

Speaker 3	H	**21**

D   This person enjoys the freedom they get using this form of transport.

Speaker 4	A	**22**

E   This person finds their journey convenient but sometimes uncomfortable.

Speaker 5	G	**23**

F   This person finds a certain form of transport too unreliable.

G   This person feels safe and confident when they travel.

H   This person would prefer to use another means of transport.

LISTENING PART 4

Questions 24 – 30

You will hear a radio interview with an animal expert called Daisy Neame. For questions **24 – 30**, choose the best answer (**A**, **B** or **C**).

24 What does Daisy regret about her childhood?
   A Her father used to laugh at her animals.
   B Her parents didn't let her have a pet.
   C Her pets didn't survive in her house.

25 How did Daisy develop her relationship with animals?
   A She found employment with her neighbours.
   B She spent her free time collecting animals.
   C She worked with animals at the weekend.

26 How did Daisy learn about the animal world as a child?
   A She found material outside school to educate herself.
   B She was allowed to study zoology at school.
   C She attended courses on her favourite subjects.

27 What does Daisy say about going to university?
   A It was clear from the beginning what she was going to study.
   B Her parents helped her consider her options.
   C There was only a narrow choice of courses she could take.

28 What memory influenced Daisy in her choice of university course?
   A the way the local vet helped pets
   B how badly the shop owner treated his animals
   C how sick animals were treated where she worked

29 What did Daisy realise in her first job?
   A She needed more qualifications to become a good vet.
   B Her previous experiences were very valuable in her new job.
   C She had not learnt everything she needed to know at university.

30 What has Daisy been doing for the last six months?
   A She has been working with someone she used to know.
   B She has been preparing to open a business.
   C She has become a zoology teacher.

SPEAKING PART 1

2 minutes (3 minutes for groups of three)

This part is always the same. See page 34 of Test 1.

Select one or more questions from the following category, as appropriate.

Music

- **Is music very important to you?**
- **What kind of music do you like listening to?**
- **How do you listen to music – on the Internet, on an iPod or in some other way?**
- **Is there any music you really don't like?**
- **Would you like to play a musical instrument? ...... (Which one?)**
- **How do you find out about new music?**
- **Do you go to concerts to see your favourite musicians or bands?**
- **Do you like the same sort of music as your friends?**

Students' own answers

SPEAKING PART 2

4 minutes (6 minutes for groups of three)

1 Hobbies and activities
2 Children and places

Interlocutor	In this part of the test, I'm going to give each of you two photographs. I'd like you to talk about your photographs on your own for about a minute, and also to answer a short question about your partner's photographs.
See photos A and B on page 192.	*(Candidate A)*, it's your turn first. Here are your photographs. They show **people doing different hobbies and activities**.
	I'd like you to compare the photographs and **talk about how the people in the photographs might be feeling.**
	All right?
Candidate A	*(Speak for approximately 1 minute.)*
Interlocutor	Thank you. *(Candidate B)*, **which activity would you most like to do?**
Candidate B	*(Reply for approximately 30 seconds.)*
Interlocutor	Thank you.
See photos C and D on page 193.	Now, *(Candidate B)*, here are your photographs. They show **children's playgrounds in different neighbourhoods**.
	I'd like you to compare the photographs, and **talk about what it might be like to be a child living in these places.**
	All right?
Candidate B	*(Speak for approximately 1 minute.)*
Interlocutor	Thank you. *(Candidate A)*, **how is the place where you live different from the places in these photos?**
Candidate A	*(Reply for approximately 30 seconds.)*
Interlocutor	Thank you.

Students' own answers

SPEAKING PARTS 3 AND 4

8 minutes (11 minutes for groups of three)

PART 3

Interlocutor	Now I'd like you to talk about something together for about two minutes. *(3 minutes for groups of three)*

See written prompts on page 194.

Here are some reasons why people choose the job that they do and a question for you to discuss. First you have some time to look at the task.

Now, talk to each other about **whether people choose the job that they do for the right reason.**

Candidates	*(Discuss for approximately 2 minutes – 3 minutes for groups of three.)*
Interlocutor	Thank you. Now you have about a minute to decide **which two things are the most important to think about when you choose a job.**
Candidates	*(Reply for approximately 1 minute – for pairs and groups of three.)*
Interlocutor	Thank you.

PART 4

Interlocutor	*Select any of the following questions, as appropriate:*

> *Select any of the following prompts, as appropriate:*
> * **What do you think?**
> * **Do you agree?**
> * **And you?**

* **Do you think there are some jobs which are unsuitable for men or women? ......
(Why?/Why not?)**

* **Do you think men and women can work together in different jobs? ......
(Why?/Why not)?**

* **Do you think that men and women should be paid the same for doing the same job? ...... (Why?/Why not?)**

* **Would it be difficult for an older person to work for a young person?**

* **Do you think that everyone should have the same job opportunities – men, women, old, or young?**

* **What do you think is most important when trying to choose the right person for a job?**

Thank you. That is the end of the test.

Students' own answers

Practice Test 8

READING AND USE OF ENGLISH `PART 1`

For questions **1 – 8**, read the text below and decide which answer (**A, B, C** or **D**) best fits each gap. There is an example at the beginning (**0**).

Example:

0 A baggy   **B** loose   **C** slack   **D** free

0	A	B	C	D
	☐	■	☐	☐

Working with the Elderly

Have you been at a **(0)** _____ end since school broke up for the summer? Why not take part in a volunteer programme working with the elderly? The programmes available across the UK are as varied as the **(1)** _____ that volunteers may be asked to undertake.

(2) _____ on in years can create certain difficulties, and the elderly often have specific age-related problems. **(3)** _____ some elderly people may require assistance with **(4)** _____ tasks like dressing, washing and feeding themselves, others will have less **(5)** _____ needs. On many occasions, as a volunteer, the only thing you'll need to do is be a companion – a person for them to talk to.

Of course, elderly people enjoy doing things **(6)** _____ than talking. As many elderly people suffer from **(7)** _____ eyesight, they often appreciate being read to. Or they might enjoy being taken for a stroll in the local park.

Whichever programme you **(8)** _____ for, you'll see that being a volunteer is a highly rewarding way for you to spend your summer months.

1	**A** parts	**B** duties	**C** posts	**D** places
2	**A** Going	**B** Being	**C** Getting	**D** Putting
3	**A** However	**B** Despite	**C** As	**D** While
4	**A** main	**B** central	**C** basic	**D** chief
5	**A** demanding	**B** tough	**C** heavy	**D** hard
6	**A** besides	**B** other	**C** more	**D** addition
7	**A** poor	**B** worst	**C** loss	**D** lack
8	**A** opt	**B** choose	**C** select	**D** pick

READING AND USE OF ENGLISH PART 2

For questions **9 – 16**, read the text below and think of the word which best fits each gap. Use only **one** word in each gap. There is an example at the beginning (0).

Write your answers **IN CAPITAL LETTERS**.

Example: | **0** | O | N | | | | | | | | | | | |

Box-office gold

Hold **(0)** _ON_ to your popcorn! Matt Damon, star of box-office hits **(9)** _SUCH_ as *Ocean's Eleven* and *The Bourne Identity*, is back! Unlike these earlier films, **(10)** _HOWEVER/ THOUGH_ , *We Bought a Zoo* is not about spies, secrets and murder, but about a father and his two children suffering **(11)** _FROM/ AFTER_ the tragic loss of their wife and mother.

Damon stars **(12)** _AS_ Benjamin Mee, who moves his family out of the city and into the countryside after his son, Dylan (Colin Ford), gets **(13)** _IN(TO)_ trouble at school. Benjamin has decided to buy, renovate and re-open a struggling zoo. While his young daughter, Rosie (Maggie Elizabeth Jones), is delighted to **(14)** _BE_ living in a big house with a zoo full of animals as a back garden, young Dylan isn't quite **(15)** _SO/AS_ keen.

Although *We Bought a Zoo* might **(16)** _NOT_ be everyone's cup of tea – thriller fans take note – it's sure to delight both animal lovers and cinema-goers who enjoy a good comedy drama.

READING AND USE OF ENGLISH `PART 3`

For questions **17 – 24**, read the text below. Use the word given in capitals at the end of some of the lines to form a word that fits the gap **in the same line**. There is an example at the beginning (**0**).

Write your answers **IN CAPITAL LETTERS**.

Example: | **0** | S | E | C | O | N | D | A | R | Y | | | | | | | | | | |

Taking a gap year

A gap year is a year off between leaving (**0**) _SECONDARY_ school and going to university.

SECOND

Many young people see the gap year as (**17**) _BENEFICIAL_ because it allows them a short period of (**18**) _RELAXATION_ after so many years of study. Parents, on the other hand, do not always view the gap year quite so (**19**) _FAVOURABLY_. One of their main concerns is that their child might waste a year when they could be engaged in more useful (**20**) _EDUCATIONAL_ pursuits.

BENEFIT
RELAX

FAVOUR

EDUCATE

Some words of (**21**) _WISDOM_ for parents who are against their child's short 'time out': learning requires neither a teacher nor a classroom to be effective. Travelling the world, and encountering new cultures and customs, can prove (**22**) _(IN)VALUABLE_ to a young person in search of knowledge.

WISE

VALUE

A gap year is a time of great significance in the life of a young person. While it offers a brief escape from studying, it can also promote emotional and intellectual growth. A gap year can lead to the development of self-confidence, (**23**) _MATURITY_ and independence, which are all (**24**) _CHARACTERISTICS_ that cannot be 'taught' in any formal classroom setting.

MATURE
CHARACTER

READING AND USE OF ENGLISH `PART 4`

For questions **25 – 30**, complete the second sentence so that it has a similar meaning to the first sentence, using the word given. **Do not change the word given.** You must use between **two** and **five** words, including the word given. Here is an example (**0**).

Example:

0   We got here in half the time it took Sam.

TWICE

It took Sam ____*TWICE AS LONG AS US*____ to get here.

The gap can be filled by the words 'twice as long as us', so you write:

Example: | **0** | *TWICE AS LONG AS US*

Write **only** the missing words **IN CAPITAL LETTERS**.

---

25   My sister didn't get married until she was thirty.
WHEN
My sister ____*WAS THIRTY/30 WHEN SHE GOT*____ married.

26   You'll never find me even if you look everywhere.
NO
You will never find me ____*NO MATTER WHERE*____ you look.

27   I'm sure Tony didn't steal the money.
HAVE
It can't ____*HAVE BEEN TONY WHO/THAT*____ stole the money.

28   You need to study or you'll fail the test.
PROVIDED
You will ____*PASS THE TEST PROVIDED YOU*____ study.

29   Sally was the only one who didn't get into trouble.
APART
Everyone ____*GOT INTO TROUBLE APART FROM*____ Sally.

30   This is the fastest I can run.
ANY
I can't ____*RUN ANY FASTER THAN*____ this.

READING AND USE OF ENGLISH PART 5

Questions 31 – 36

You are going to read a leaflet about Fair Trade. For questions **31 – 36**, choose the answer (**A, B, C** or **D**) which you think fits best according to the text.

Fair Trade FOR A Fairer World

So what's so fair about fair trade?

Good question! First, for those of you who might not be in the know about fair trade, here's a brief explanation. In a nutshell, it's an initiative with the main aim of ensuring that the hard-working people all around the world who provide us with food to eat, things to use or clothes to wear are treated fairly. And part of that fair treatment is getting paid a fair amount of money for what they grow, produce or manufacture for us.

Why is fair trade necessary?

The answer to that question is: the world is not always a fair place. In the distant past, when people only consumed the food that they themselves were able to produce, things were probably a lot fairer. However, once countries started trading amongst themselves, two things happened. First, people could enjoy foods that they couldn't grow for themselves, and second, the producers of these foods, usually people from far-away countries, began to be exploited. This mistreatment took many forms, but the main one was that people were not paid what they should have been for what they were producing. And that is still happening today.

How does fair trade work?

That's an easy one! Let's take the banana, the world's best-loved naturally pre-packaged food, as an example. Now in the UK, the climate is such that it is unsuitable for growing many fruits, bananas being one of them. Therefore, if we are to have bananas to put on top of our breakfast cereal in the morning or add to our peanut butter sandwiches at lunchtime, then we must import them from countries like Ghana, Costa Rica and the Windward Islands in the Caribbean, where they grow successfully. The Fairtrade organisation asked major UK supermarkets to start selling only Fairtrade bananas, and after a lot of persuasion many of them agreed. What this meant was that,

while customers might unfortunately have to pay a bit more for their favourite fruit, the banana growers on their small farms were getting more of the profits from the sales of their tasty yellow crop. And when you consider that the average person in the UK consumes about 10kg of bananas annually, we're talking about a fair amount of profit!

How can I participate in fair trade?

That's the best question of all and it shows you've been paying attention! Each and every one of us can do our part to make sure that fair trade continues to grow, spread and become even more successful. One very good way is to get involved. A fun way to do that is to join the Take a Step campaign, which was launched by the Fairtrade Foundation. Each 'step' is like a promise you make to Fairtrade. These steps can include things like getting your canteen to use only fair trade ingredients in the preparation of school meals, or setting up a booth at your local supermarket to explain to customers all about fair trade and how it helps make the world a fairer place. And, of course, the biggest step of all is for you, your family and your friends to purchase foods and other goods that have been certified 'Fair Trade'; all you have to do is look for the label. Go on, take that first step!

31 In the first paragraph, the writer explains that fair trade
   A aims to help workers who produce things.
   B requires people to use their initiative.
   C encourages people to buy fewer things.
   D is popular all over the world.

32 In the second paragraph, what does the writer suggest about the world?
   A It was probably much fairer before countries began trading.
   B It may become a little less fair in the future.
   C It has never been a fair place.
   D It became fairer once food producers learned their trade.

33 In the third paragraph, the phrase 'naturally pre-packaged' is used because of the fact that
   A fruit never requires packaging.
   B all fruits are bought pre-packaged.
   C the banana's skin acts as packaging.
   D most foods need to be packaged.

34 What is the writer doing at the end of the third paragraph?
   A being ironic
   B being argumentative
   C emphasising a point
   D expressing disappointment

35 In the last paragraph, what does the writer say is the best way to participate in fair trade?
   A by starting the Take a Step campaign
   B by buying fair trade produce and products
   C by making a promise to the Fairtrade Foundation
   D by informing others about the importance of fair trade

36 What is the writer's main purpose in writing this text?
   A to persuade supermarkets to stock fair trade goods
   B to explain to people what fair trade does
   C to persuade people to take part in fair trade
   D to convince people fair trade goods are the best quality

READING AND USE OF ENGLISH `PART 6`

Questions 37 – 42

You are going to read a magazine article about people and their pets. Six sentences have been removed from the article. Choose from the sentences **A – G** the one which fits each gap (**37 – 42**). There is one extra sentence that you do not need to use.

Your pet: not just another furry face!

You've just had an argument with your best friend and you feel terrible. You walk into your house, slam the front door and, suddenly, a mass of fur comes hurtling towards you. Tongue lolling excitedly, tail wagging frenetically, you receive a sloppy doggy kiss. Admit it, you feel a bit better after such a welcoming greeting.

Pets, dogs and cats especially, can do that to you. They can lift your spirits and brighten your day with a single ecstatic bark or a steady contented purr. **37** B It could be that this unique relationship results from the fact that such a friendship is so satisfying and beneficial for both the two-legged and four-legged parties involved.

According to experts, man and wolves – the ancestors of every breed of dog on the planet – probably first teamed up during the most recent ice age. Wolves were allowed to join the human 'pack' as they had two very important characteristics: they were both ferocious and loyal. **38** G In return for their fierceness and devotion, wolves received a place beside the fire, food and affection.

Records indicate that our other four-legged friend, the cat, also has a long history with humans. While it is not known exactly when they were first domesticated, felines were considered sacred in ancient Egypt and their mummified bodies have been discovered in temples and among old ruins. In addition, ancient folklore provides another sort of record, as almost every culture makes some reference to felines as 'familiars' for those with supernatural powers. **39** A

In our modern world, dogs and cats are appreciated for many reasons. Medical professionals have long realised that canine and feline companions are ideal for people suffering from ailments such as deafness, blindness and epilepsy. **40** F It appears that our four-legged friends have a vital role to play as 'therapists' for those receiving mental health care.

There is also ample evidence that shows that the elderly live longer, healthier and happier lives when they have a furry friend to keep them company. Pets give the aged a sense of purpose. **41** C But in meeting their pets' needs, the aged feel more useful. Furthermore, taking a dog for a walk or changing a cat's litter box takes time and energy, so having a pet helps the elderly stay active. There is every indication that because of this, the general health of elderly pet-owners is better than their non-pet-owning counterparts. They tend to have lower blood pressure and are also less likely to develop heart problems.

Pet owners are well aware of the therapeutic benefits, both mental and physical, of having a cat or a dog. **42** D The happiness a pet feels upon seeing its owner is both obvious and infectious. Having a pet can only make a person feel better about things, regardless of what might be bothering them!

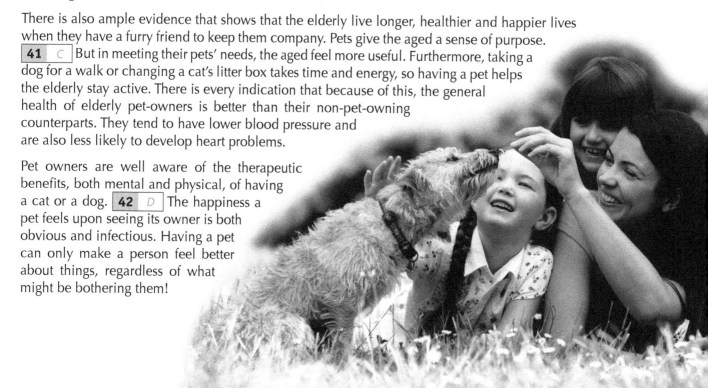

A Later, cats were encouraged into households because of their impressive skill in controlling vermin.

B This is one of the things that makes the relationship humans have with their pets so special.

C That's because pets have certain needs and can be very hard work at times.

D They have the gift of being able to make a person feel like somebody incredibly special, loved and needed.

E It's clear from all the available evidence that Egyptians were the first people to domesticate wolves.

F More recently, research has been done to study the possible positive effects of pet therapy on sufferers of dementia, depression, autism and even addiction.

G The former characteristic made them successful hunters, while the latter meant they were fantastic protectors.

READING AND USE OF ENGLISH PART 7

Questions 43 – 52

You are going to read an article about performers in a circus. For questions **43 – 52**, choose from the people (**A – E**). The people may be chosen more than once.

Which person says

they were recently injured in an accident?	**43**	E
the best part about circus work is pleasing the children?	**44**	D
they received a formal education for what they do?	**45**	A
they don't mind doing something dangerous?	**46**	D
the fact that they co-own something used to be a secret?	**47**	B
they regard the circus members as family?	**48**	C
they don't have brothers or sisters?	**49**	C
they went through a career change?	**50**	A
at the beginning of their career they were poorly paid?	**51**	B
their job isn't as risky as some people may think?	**52**	E

The circus is in town!
We asked five circus performers to tell us about their unusual lives.

A Clara the clown

I joined the circus relatively late in life; I wasn't born into it like some. Believe it or not, under all this paint – which takes forever to apply by the way – is a former banker! It's true! I was in banking for ten years. And I hated every minute of it! Then I saw an advert for Clown College. I applied, I got accepted, and eight weeks later I was a licensed clown. My whole family, except for Dad, was against the idea, but I've got no regrets. I love what I do and I really like the other clowns. We're a real team and we get along great. And the audience loves our show; we get an incredible number of laughs out of them!

B Sam the acrobat

There's no life like life under the big top! Stella, the circus's lion tamer, was working at this circus when I joined, before we were married. I fell in love the second I set eyes on her! Mr Bing Bailey was my first boss; a tough boss too. He worked us hard, and didn't pay us much. Then I inherited some money from my aunt, and Stella had some savings, so we pooled our money and we bought Old Bing out! It was a risk, but a good one. For years, people thought the circus still belonged to him. Stella thought it best to keep the buyout under our hats. She said it would make for better working relations. But I think everyone knows now and we all still get along fine!

C Crystal the fortune teller

I've been in this business for almost twenty years now. Sometimes I think it's time I packed up my crystal ball and retired, but I'll never do it. The circus gets into your blood; it becomes your life. And my fellow performers are everything to me; my parents passed away years ago and I was an only child, but now I feel as if I've got brothers and sisters again. I like my job and, OK, it's not all based on fact, but it is an art. To be a good fortune teller, you have to be incredibly observant. There are always signs; it just takes a special ability to read them.

D Angel the trapeze artist

Everyone dreams of being able to fly, and my job lets me do that! Admittedly, it's risky. There have been accidents, but that just makes it more exciting! As a trapeze artist, you have to have a lot of faith in your partner; you really need to trust them. I'm lucky; my partner is one of my cousins. We grew up together so he actually feels more like my brother. I love everything about my job: the fantastic costumes, the bright lights, the loud applause, everything! I think what truly makes it worthwhile is the look on the faces of the youngsters; they are totally in awe of what we do.

E Prometheus the fire eater

My family's been in the circus for generations. My great-grandparents had a travelling show in Poland, but they sold up before they emigrated to the UK in the 1920s and bought shares in another travelling show. But then they decided being owners wasn't exciting enough and that they preferred performing, so they decided to join a circus instead! And then there was my grandpa. He wasn't a fire eater like me; he was a human cannonball! Now that was dangerous! Not like fire eating; that's just an amazing magic trick. It's not really risky; if you're careful, you never get burnt … at least not on the job. Last week I was making chips and spilt oil on my hand – first degree burns! I'm fine now, though, and all set for tonight's performance!

WRITING PART 1

You **must** answer this question. Write your answer in **140 – 190** words in an appropriate style.

1 In your English class you have been talking about teens and physical fitness. Now your teacher has asked you to write an essay for homework.

Write your essay using **all** the notes and giving reasons for your point of view.

'All secondary school students should have to take part in physical education classes.'

Do you agree?

Notes

Write about:

    1   staying fit

    2   learning about team work

    3   .... (your own idea)

Students' own answers

WRITING PART 2

Write an answer to **one** of the questions **2 – 5** in this part. Write your answer in **140 – 190** words in an appropriate style.

2   You have seen this notice in an English-language magazine for young people.

> **Reviews wanted**
>
> We are looking for reviews of a summer camp for teenagers where you live. Your review should include information about what the camp is like, the kind of camp it is, the activities available there and the camp leaders. Would you recommend this camp to other teenagers?
>
> The best review will appear in our next issue.

Write your **review**.

3   You have seen this announcement on the notice board at your English language school.

> # Competition:
> ## The Perfect Teen Holiday
>
> What are the things that a holiday destination must have?
>
> Shopping facilities? Sports facilities? Music clubs and cafés? You decide!
>
> The best article will be published in next month's school paper.

Write your **article**.

4   A group of Japanese teenagers is coming to stay in your town and your teacher has asked you to write an email to their teacher about things the group could do during their stay. Mention some activities that young people in your town do for fun and where they usually do them. Then recommend the best places for the group to go to enjoy themselves, giving reasons for your recommendations.

Write your **email**.

5   Question 5 always consists of a question on the set text. Only answer question 5 if you have studied the set text. Here is an example of the kind of question you might be asked:

Your English class has had a discussion about the different scenes in the book you have read. Now your English teacher has asked you to write a letter to a friend about your favourite scene in the book. You should describe the scene and say how it made you feel, and also explain why this scene is your favourite.

Write your **letter**.

Students' own answers

LISTENING PART 1

Questions 1 – 8

You will hear people talking in eight different situations. For questions **1 – 8**, choose the best answer (**A**, **B** or **C**).

1   You hear two friends talking about a match they've just watched.
    What does the boy think of the final result?
    A It was unfair.
    B It was predictable.
    C It was surprising.

2   You hear an announcement on a local radio station.
    What will happen on Saturday morning?
    A There will be a chance to buy cheap clothes.
    B There will be some free refreshments.
    C There will be a performance by someone famous.

3   You hear a youth club leader talking to some teens about an excursion.
    Why is he talking to them?
    A to give them new information
    B to explain where they are going
    C to remind them about something

4   You hear a girl talking about a book she's just read.
    How does she feel about it?
    A She was dissatisfied with the ending.
    B She thought it was unnecessarily long.
    C She found it disappointing.

5   You overhear a girl talking on her mobile phone.
    What is she doing?
    A suggesting a solution to a problem
    B giving someone advice about something
    C apologising for something she has done

6   You hear two friends talking about a concert they have just been to.
    What do they agree about?
    A how crowded the venue was
    B how expensive the tickets were
    C how well the band performed

7   You hear a boy leaving a voicemail message.
    What is he doing?
    A asking someone for a favour
    B offering to do something for someone
    C turning down an invitation to a party

8   You hear part of an interview with a young actress.
    What does she say about her new film?
    A She disliked wearing so much make-up.
    B The film was shot entirely in one place.
    C Her character reminded her of her childhood.

LISTENING PART 2

Questions 9 – 18

You will hear a teenager named Jules talking about a charity called the Good Shepherd Centre. For questions **9 – 18**, complete the sentences with a word or short phrase.

Charity Work: Doing Your Part

Jules says the Good Shepherd Centre opened in | *1969* | **9**

People who stay temporarily in the homes of others are called | *sofa surfers* | **10**

Over | *80,000/eighty thousand* | **11** young people are affected by homelessness every year.

Jules says the homeless are put up in shelters, hostels and | *flats* | **12**

Being homeless can affect someone's | *mental and/& physical* | **13** health.

Jules says young people need skills to be competitive in the | *job market* | **14**

Jules says the garden produces | *vegetables* | **15** and herbs.

Night Out participants have only a(n) | *cardboard box* | **16** for warmth.

Individuals participating in *Night Out* must raise | *£350/350 pounds/three hundred and/& fifty pounds* | **17** or more.

You can't take part in *Night Out* until you | *complete the form* | **18** on the website.

LISTENING PART 3

Questions 19 – 23

You will hear five people talking about their eating habits. For questions **19 – 23**, choose from the list (**A – H**) what each speaker says about their eating habits. Use the letters only once. There are three extra letters which you do not need to use.

A   I have a bad habit of eating between meals.

Speaker 1	E	**19**

B   I eat the way I do because of my parents.

Speaker 2	D	**20**

C   I recently changed my eating habits for health reasons.

Speaker 3	C	**21**

D   I follow the advice in a saying when it comes to meals.

Speaker 4	F	**22**

E   I eat irregularly because of my lifestyle.

Speaker 5	A	**23**

F   I stopped eating something due to something I saw.

G   I have one very large meal every evening.

H   I once got food poisoning from something I ate.

LISTENING PART 4

Questions 24 – 30

You will hear a conversation between two friends about a project they are doing on advertising.
For questions **24 – 30**, choose the best answer (**A**, **B** or **C**).

24 Where has Tanya been doing her research?
   A at the library
   B in books
   C on the Internet

25 What will Tanya and Joe's project be about?
   A why people need to buy things
   B how companies have sold things
   C what adverts were like in the fifties

26 What does Tanya say about Vicary's test in New Jersey?
   A He asked people in a cinema for help.
   B He needed to use a special piece of equipment.
   C He showed cinema-goers a film.

27 What particularly impressed Tanya about the messages?
   A how greatly they seemed to increase sales
   B how quickly they were shown
   C how frequently they were flashed

28 What does Tanya say about Vicary's results?
   A They were quite persuasive.
   B They were made up.
   C They were repeated in later tests.

29 What surprises Tanya about the Vicary incident?
   A The truth never appeared in the news.
   B The newspapers covered it in such depth.
   C The American Congress banned stories about it.

30 What does Tanya think about subliminal advertising?
   A She thinks it sells products.
   B She thinks people are unaware of it.
   C She thinks it's ineffective.

Practice Test 8

SPEAKING PART 1

2 minutes (3 minutes for groups of three)

This part is always the same. See page 34 of Test 1.

Select one or more questions from the following category, as appropriate.

Likes and dislikes

- **Would you rather go to the cinema or the theatre? ...... (Why?)**

- **Where do you like going on holidays? ...... (Why?)**

- **What is your favourite subject at school? ...... (What do you like about *[subject mentioned]*?)**

- **Do you ever read books? ...... (Tell us about a good book you've read recently.)**

- **Do you have any hobbies? ...... (What do you like about *[hobby mentioned]*?)**

Students' own answers

SPEAKING PART 2

4 minutes (6 minutes for groups of three)

1 Food and eating out
2 Street performers

Interlocutor	In this part of the test, I'm going to give each of you two photographs. I'd like you to talk about your photographs on your own for about a minute, and also to answer a short question about your partner's photographs.
See photos A and B on page 195.	(*Candidate A*), it's your turn first. Here are your photographs. They show **people eating in different places**. I'd like you to compare the photographs, and say **what would be the advantages and disadvantages of eating at these different places**. All right?
Candidate A	(*Speak for approximately 1 minute.*)
Interlocutor	Thank you. (*Candidate B*), **do you enjoy eating out?**
Candidate B	(*Reply for approximately 30 seconds.*)
Interlocutor	Thank you.
See photos C and D on page 196.	Now (*Candidate B*), here are your photographs. They show **different kinds of street performers**. I'd like you to compare the photographs, and say **what people might find interesting about watching these different street performers**. All right?
Candidate B	(*Speak for approximately 1 minute.*)
Interlocutor	Thank you. (*Candidate A*), **which of these street performers would you like to watch?**
Candidate A	(*Reply for approximately 30 seconds.*)
Interlocutor	Thank you.

Students' own answers

SPEAKING PARTS 3 AND 4

8 minutes (11 minutes for groups of three)

PART 3

Interlocutor	Now, I'd like you to talk about something together for about two minutes. (*3 minutes for groups of three*)

See written prompts on page 197.

I'd like you to imagine that you are going to have an end-of-the-year party. Here are some ideas for the party and a question for you to discuss. First you have some time to look at the task.

Now, talk to each other about **why it might be important to have these things when you hold a party.**

Candidates	(*Discuss for approximately 2 minutes – 3 minutes for groups of three.*)
Interlocutor	Thank you. Now you have about a minute to decide **which two things are the least important when you hold a party.**
Candidates	(*Reply for approximately 1 minute – for pairs and groups of three.*)
Interlocutor	Thank you.

PART 4

Interlocutor

Select any of the following questions as appropriate:

- **How important is it for people to celebrate special occasions? ...... (Why?)**

- **Do people in your country tend to celebrate things like birthdays or name days?**

- **What sort of arrangements do people make for parties in your country?**

- **Do you think people spend too much money on celebration parties nowadays? ...... (Why?/Why not?)**

- **Would you ever consider having a theme party? ...... (Why?/Why not?)**

- **Some people say that celebrations should be small and for family members only. What do you think? ...... (Why?)**

Select any of the following prompts, as appropriate:

- **What do you think?**
- **Do you agree?**
- **And you?**

Thank you. That is the end of the test.

Students' own answers

SPEAKING PART 2 Photographs for Candidate A

What are the advantages and disadvantages of students studying in these ways?

SPEAKING PART 2 Photographs for Candidate B

How can relationships with animals help people?

SPEAKING PART 3 Written prompts

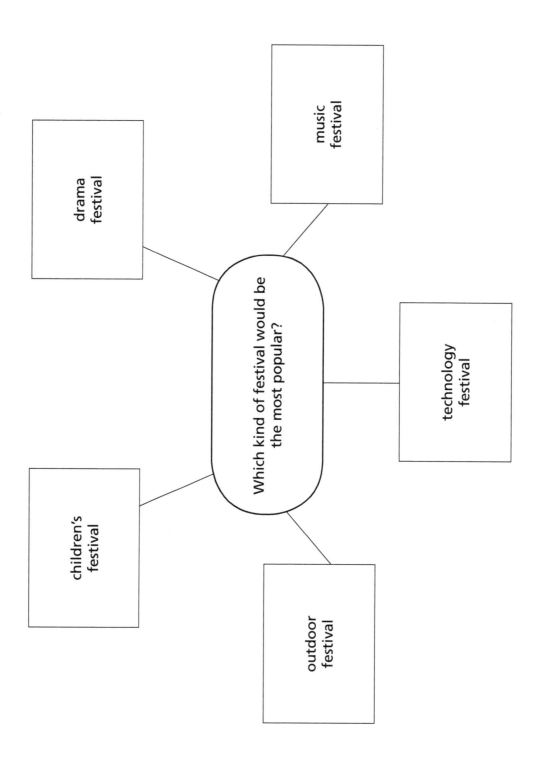

drama festival

music festival

technology festival

children's festival

Which kind of festival would be the most popular?

outdoor festival

SPEAKING PART 2 Photographs for Candidate A

| Why might people choose these types of entertainment? |

SPEAKING PART 2 Photographs for Candidate B

> What are the advantages and disadvantages of each creative activity for the people taking part in them?

SPEAKING PART 3 Written prompts

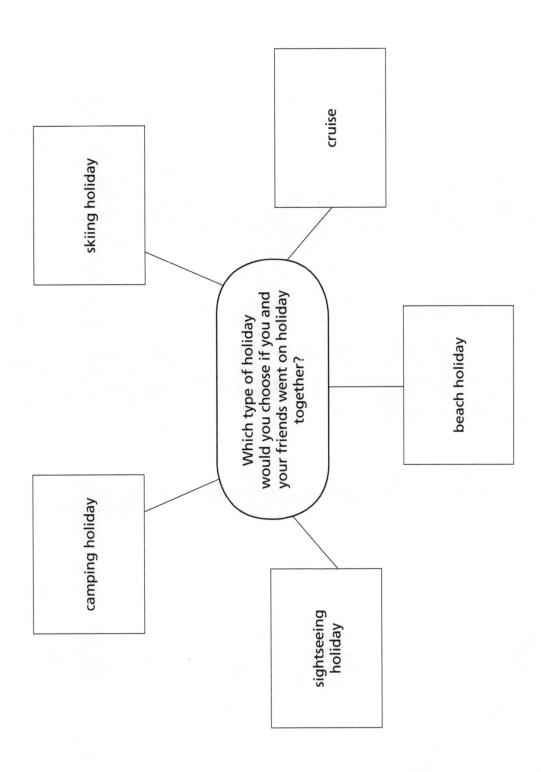

skiing holiday

cruise

Which type of holiday would you choose if you and your friends went on holiday together?

beach holiday

camping holiday

sightseeing holiday

SPEAKING PART 2 Photographs for Candidate A

What are the differences between studying at school and studying at university?

SPEAKING PART 2 Photographs for Candidate B

What environmental problems can modern technology cause?

SPEAKING PART 3 Written prompts

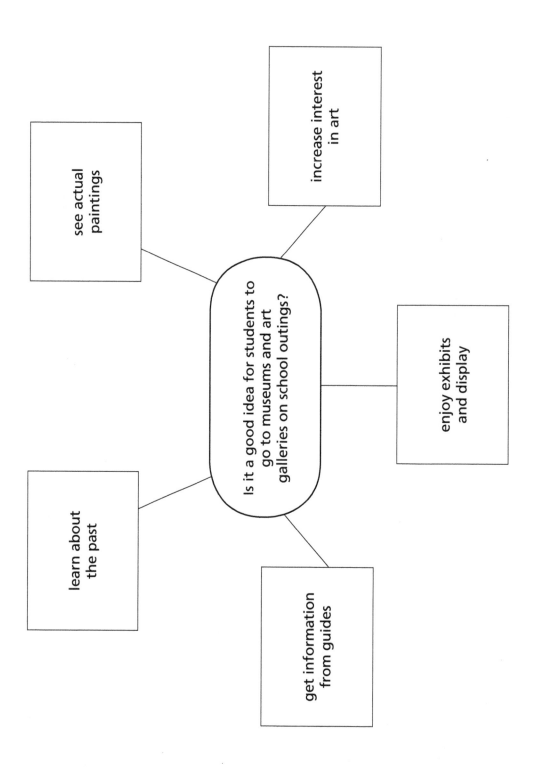

see actual paintings

increase interest in art

enjoy exhibits and display

Is it a good idea for students to go to museums and art galleries on school outings?

learn about the past

get information from guides

SPEAKING PART 2 Photographs for Candidate A

How might the children in the photographs be feeling?

SPEAKING PART 2 Photographs for Candidate B

What are the advantages and disadvantages of spending free time in these different ways?

SPEAKING PART 3 Written prompts

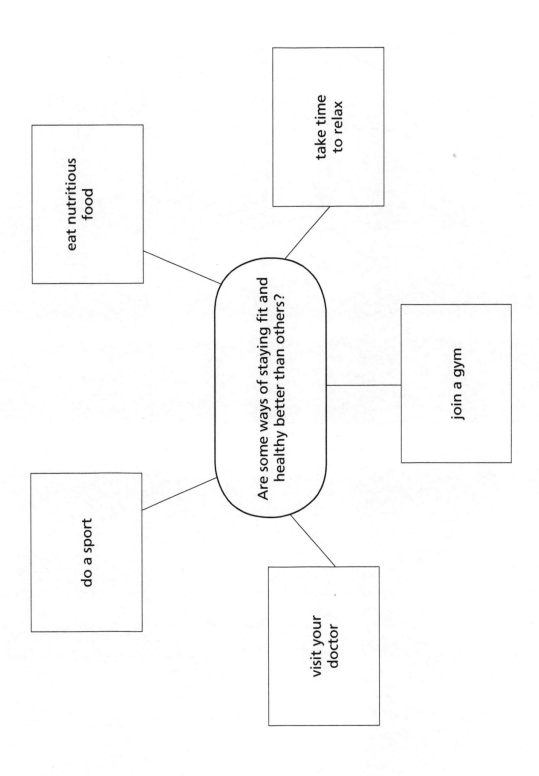

eat nutritious food

take time to relax

Are some ways of staying fit and healthy better than others?

join a gym

do a sport

visit your doctor

SPEAKING PART 2 Photographs for Candidate A

What are the main differences between these jobs?

SPEAKING PART 2 Photographs for Candidate B

What are the advantages and disadvantages of living in these kinds of houses?

SPEAKING PART 3 Written prompts

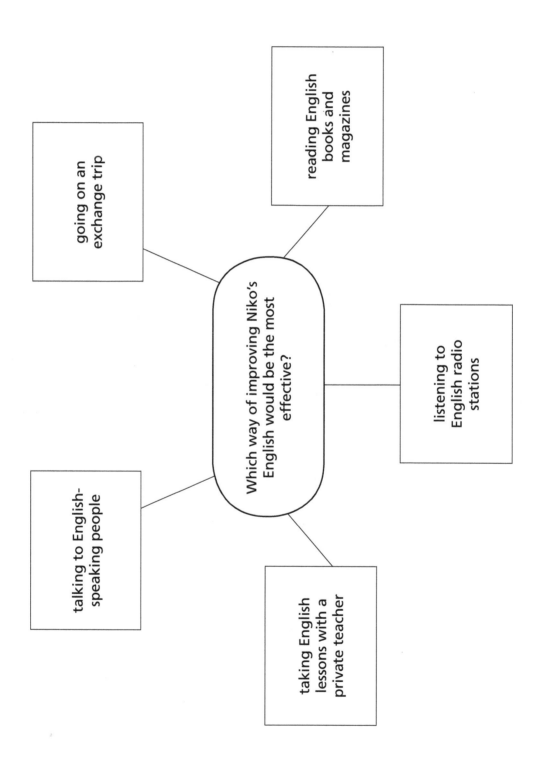

going on an exchange trip

reading English books and magazines

Which way of improving Niko's English would be the most effective?

listening to English radio stations

talking to English-speaking people

taking English lessons with a private teacher

SPEAKING PART 2 Photographs for Candidate A

Why do you think the people have chosen to wear these clothes?

SPEAKING PART 2 Photographs for Candidate B

What are the advantages and disadvantages of listening to music in these different ways?

SPEAKING PART 3 Written prompts

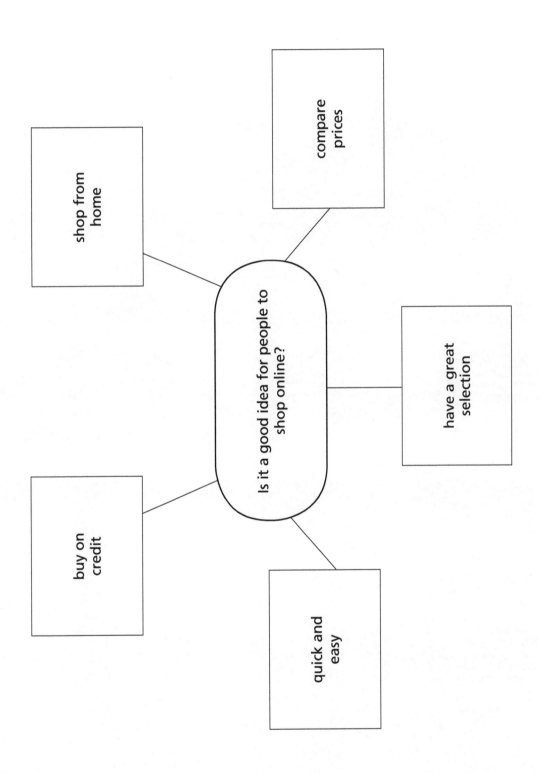

shop from home

compare prices

buy on credit

Is it a good idea for people to shop online?

have a great selection

quick and easy

SPEAKING PART 2 Photographs for Candidate A

How might the people in the photographs be feeling?

SPEAKING PART 2 Photographs for Candidate B

What might it be like to be a child living in these places?

SPEAKING PART 3 Written prompts

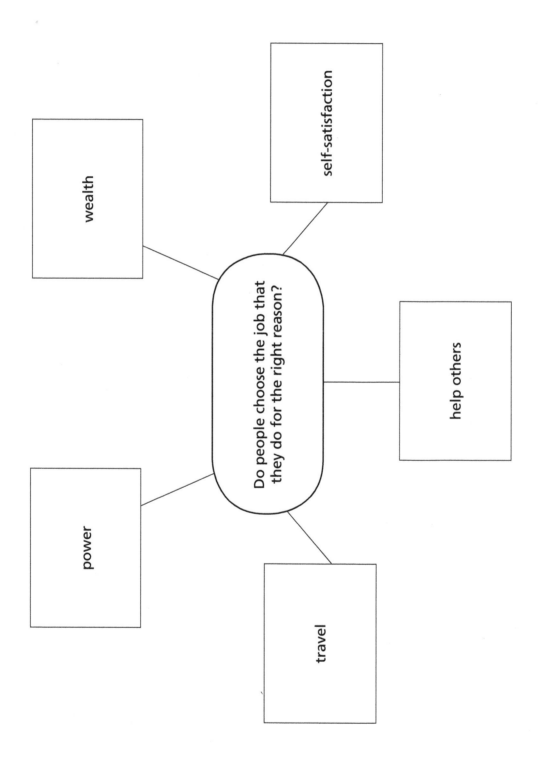

wealth

self-satisfaction

Do people choose the job that they do for the right reason?

help others

power

travel

SPEAKING PART 2 Photographs for Candidate A

What would be the advantages and disadvantages of eating at these different places?

A

B

SPEAKING PART 2 Photographs for Candidate B

What might people find interesting about watching these different
street performers?

SPEAKING PART 3 Written prompts

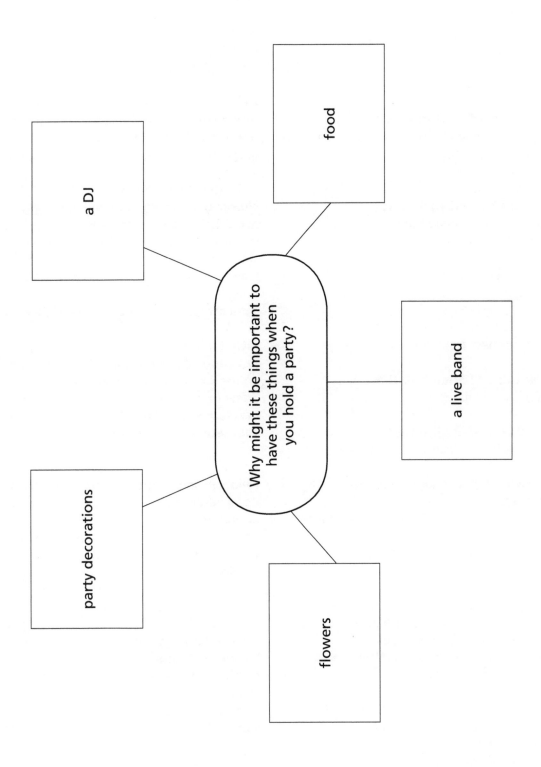

food

a DJ

a live band

Why might it be important to have these things when you hold a party?

party decorations

a live band

flowers

Glossary

Practice Test 1

Reading and Use of English Part 1
assignment (n) piece of homework
aspect (n) way of seeing
virtually (adv) almost
restrict (v) limit
inappropriate (adj) not suitable

Reading and Use of English Part 2
spice (n) spices are made from parts of plants and are usually used to flavour foods
scent (n) perfume
primarily (adv) mainly
ritual (n) set of fixed actions or words
tomb (n) building for a dead body
trace (n) small amount
aromatic (adj) nice-smelling
prosper (v) do well financially
odour (n) smell

Reading and Use of English Part 3
unplug (v) disconnect from the electricity source

Reading and Use of English Part 4
resemble (v) look similar to

Reading and Use of English Part 5
cashier (n) person customers pay at a supermarket check-out
in abundance (prep phr) in large amounts
impact (n) effect
start from scratch (phr) start from nothing, start again at the beginning
as it turns out (phr) what actually happens
eco-friendly (adj) not damaging to the environment
adorable (adj) lovable
renewable (adj) energy sources such as the sun, wind and waves that will not run out
degrade (v) change into simple chemical structures
fume (n) strong gas or smoke
consume (v) use up
fossil fuel (n) substance such as oil, gas or coal that comes from ancient plant materials and can be used to make heat or power
roughly (adv) approximately
discard (v) throw away, put aside
perceive (v) think of, regard as
tax (n) money paid to the government from income, goods or services
consumer (n) person who buys goods or services

charge (v) ask sb to pay sth
fall apart (phr v) break into pieces
along the lines of (phr) similar to
grab (v) quickly take hold of
issue (n) subject or problem
on-the-spot (adj) immediate
alternative (adj) different

Reading and Use of English Part 6
referee (n) person who judges in sports matches
undoubtedly (adv) definitely
wage (n) money paid to employees, usually every week
intimately (adv) very well
shocking (adj) surprising and upsetting
attitude (n) opinion or view
whistle (n) small thing a referee blows to start and stop play
trainee (n) person learning and practising new skills
send off (phr v) order a player to leave the game for breaking the rules
pitch (n) grass area where football is played
put yourself in someone's shoes (phr) think of yourself in another person's situation
angle (n) position
make up your mind (phr) decide
split second (n) very short period of time

Reading and Use of English Part 7
follow in someone's footsteps (phr) do what sb has done before you
alteration (n) change
draw inspiration from (phr) get creative ideas from
be into something (phr) have an interest in sth
fashion victim (n) person who buys new clothes just because they are in fashion
stand out (phr v) look different or special
scout (n) person employed to look for people with certain skills or talents
trendy (adj) fashionable
outfit (n) clothes you wear together
retailer (n) person or shop that sells to the public
firm (n) business, company
sample (n) small amount of sth that shows what the rest is like
stock (v) keep a supply of
take to (phr v) start to like
personalise (v) change sth to suit your character
market (n) people who might want to buy sth
apps (n) computer or mobile phone software designed to do specific things

sculpture (n) work of art, often made from metal, wood or stone

demand (n) amount of a product or service which people want to buy

cross my mind (phr) enter your thoughts

market (v) make available to the public

precious metal (n) metal such as gold which is valuable

wool (n) hair from a sheep

take off (phr v) become successful

Listening Part 1
confirm (v) make sure sth is accurate or true

resent (v) dislike being forced to do or accept sth

upcoming (adj) soon to happen

establishment (n) business or organisation

appreciate (v) value

décor (n) colour, style and arrangement of the things in a room

up-to-date (adj) modern

Listening Part 4
the legal profession (phr) all the people whose work is connected to the law

behind the scenes (phr) backstage at the theatre

let somebody down (phr v) disappoint sb by not doing what had been promised

Speaking
promote (v) encourage

Practice Test 2

Reading and Use of English Part 1
too many cooks spoil the broth (expr) if too many people are involved in sth, it can lead to problems

reservation (n) booking

renowned (adj) very well known, famous

gastronomical (adj) related to good food

key (n) the most important thing

groundbreaking (adj) completely new and different

apprenticeship (n) period of time spent working to learn a skill

Reading and Use of English Part 2
extinct (adj) no longer in existence

determine (v) decide, work out

sketch (n) drawing

survey (n) kind of research to discover information

Reading and Use of English Part 3
point out (phr v) bring to sb's attention, make clear

charity (n) organisation which gives money or help to people in need

Reading and Use of English Part 5
ward (n) room for people who are ill in hospital

patient (n) person receiving medical care

suspect (v) expect sth unusual might happen

celebrity (n) famous person, usually an entertainer

youngster (n) young person

slip out (phr v) leave without being noticed

witness (v) see

astonished (adj) very surprised

stir (v) move

infamous (adj) famous for bad reasons

victim (n) sb who has been hurt

the dawn of (phr) the start of

fundamental (adj) basic

illusionist (n) entertainer who does tricks in which amazing things seem to happen

prank (n) amusing practical joke

medium (n) way of expressing sth

take it to a whole new level (phr) develop, make more widespread

air (v) broadcast on TV or radio

embarrass (v) make sb feel uncomfortable

premise (n) idea or theory

hilarious (adj) very funny

wrestler (n) fighter who tries to throw his/her opponent to the ground

run over (phr v) hit or knock down with a vehicle

blow up (phr v) explode

apparent (adj) clear to see or understand

stunt (n) exciting action in a film or TV show

footage (n) what has been filmed

see the funny side (phr) view a serious event as being funny

misfortune (n) bad luck

suspicious (adj) suspecting sth strange or unusual will happen

Reading and Use of English Part 6
flash mob (n) group of people who meet for a specific purpose

urban (adj) related to a city

hang around (phr v) be in a place for no specific purpose

pram (n) wheeled vehicle for transporting a baby

pensioner (n) older person who has stopped working

window shopping (n) looking at shop window displays without buying

tannoy (n) public address system

concourse (n) large space in a public building

onlooker (n) viewer of a public event

baffled (adj) confused

concept (n) idea

term (n) specialised word to describe sth

carry out (phr v) do

Glossary

campus (n) buildings and land of a large school or university
assembly hall (n) place where all students/pupils can meet
property (n) characteristic
formula (n) plan
initial (adj) first
passer-by (n) member of the public who walks past
vast (adj) very big
variant (n) variation, difference
glow stick (n) a stick which can be held and is designed to light up
jump on the bandwagon (expr) join a popular trend
non-profit (adj) not intended to make money
commercial (adj) to do with business
well received (adj) generally thought of as positive
retain (v) keep
innocence (n) purity
specified (adj) exact, precise

Reading and Use of English Part 7
look up to (phr v) admire
figure (n) person
inspire (v) fill with confidence and ideas
it runs in the family (expr) a characteristic is shared by different generations of a family
mayor (n) elected leader of a town or city
run for (phr v) put yourself forward as a candidate for a job or position
register for (phr v) put your name down on an official list
fee (n) money paid for a service such as an educational course
fascinating (adj) very interesting
rugby (n) sport where two teams try to score points by carrying an oval ball across a line or kicking it between a set of posts
ignorant (adj) without knowledge
determined (adj) certain that you will do sth
voter (n) person who participates in an election by choosing a candidate
autobiography (n) story of someone's life, written by them
uni (n) university

Listening Part 1
previous (adj) earlier
gratitude (n) feeling of thankfulness
award (n) prize
album (n) CD with many songs on it

Listening Part 2
ceremony (n) formal event

Listening Part 4
medieval (adj) relating to the Middle Ages (1000 AD – 1500 AD)
funding (n) money to pay for sth
stall (n) large table from which things are sold in a public place
craft (n) hand-made product

Practice Test 3

Reading and Use of English Part 1
tournament (n) competition
lawn (n) stretch of usually well-kept grass
racquet (n) the piece of sports equipment used to hit the ball in games like tennis

Reading and Use of English Part 2
debut (n) first performance
instant (adj) immediate
the press (n) newspapers, TV and radio
consequence (n) result
hit (adj) successful
parliament (n) group of elected politicians who make the laws for a country

Reading and Use of English Part 3
bleach (n) chemical cleaner that removes stains and kills germs
install (v) put in a machine and connect it so it can be used
insert (v) put into sth else
seal (v) to close an opening so air or water cannot go in or out
relatively (adv) quite

Reading and Use of English Part 4
appeal to (phr v) if sth appeals to you, you like it

Reading and Use of English Part 5
relief (n) feeling of happiness that sth unpleasant has passed
grow apart (phr v) if two people grow apart, they become less close
spread your wings (expr) begin to be independent
fly the coop (expr) leave the family home
nest (n) literally, the place a bird lays its eggs in, metaphorically, any home
grand (adj) impressive, large
will (n) document which states to whom a person leaves their property when they die
funeral (n) ceremony for burying a dead body
discomfort (n) feeling of not being comfortable

sibling (n) brother or sister
well on the way to (phr) far along in the process of
without a backwards look (phr) without thinking about the past
assume (v) think that sth is true
solitude (n) state of being alone
abandon (v) leave
ignorance (n) not knowing much
immaturity (n) childishness
put up with (phr v) tolerate, be willing to accept
amount to (phr v) add up to, be the same as
gathering (n) when a small group of family or friends meet together
bitterly (adv) very strongly
widow (n) woman whose husband has died
maintain (v) keep

Reading and Use of English Part 6
lyrics (n pl) words of a song
engage in (phr v) be involved in, participate in
venue (n) place for performances
syllabus (n) plan of what will be studied on a course
out of touch (phr) not having any relevance to
link (n) connection
appreciation (n) understanding of the value of sth
diverse (adj) different
background (n) place and situation you come from
conflicting (adj) if two things are conflicting, they don't match or agree
excel (v) be extremely good at
run into (phr v) encounter, meet
gain (v) learn, find sth new
command (v) control
extend (v) go further than

Reading and Use of English Part 7
atmosphere (n) feeling of a place
miracle (n) amazing thing
chain (n) group of companies with the same name
pop in (phr v) go into a place for a short time
ingredient (n) one of the things needed to make a dish

Listening Part 1
fair (adj) reasonable, acceptable
recover (v) get better from an illness or accident

Listening Part 2
alternative (n) other option

Listening Part 3
impersonal (adj) without human warmth or interest

Listening Part 4
glamorous (adj) exciting and attractive
in mind (prep phr) in one's thoughts
plot (n) story of a film, book, etc

productive (adj) producing a lot
times gone by (phr) the past

Practice Test 4

Reading and Use of English Part 1
exploitation (n) a situation in which sb is treated unfairly
heated debate (n) discussion with strong opinions on both sides
arise (v) occur, begin to happen
commentator (n) person who talks on TV or radio about what's going on
demonstrate (v) show
dedication (n) commitment
serve as (phr v) help to be
at all costs (phr) whatever it takes
lead to (phr v) cause, create
subject somebody to (phr v) make sb experience sth (usually bad)

Reading and Use of English Part 2
phenomenon (n) thing or event
flexibility (n) ability to change easily
effective (adj) producing the result that was wanted
take into account (phr) consider, think about including
devise (v) make
tailor-made (adj) individually designed
nerve-wracking (adj) causing psychological stress

Reading and Use of English Part 3
advance (n) development
drastic (adj) extreme
junk (n) things people throw away
spare part (n) extra piece
turbine (n) machine that produces electricity
pump (v) make liquid or gas move from one place to another
storage tanks (n pl) places where things are kept
on tap (prep phr) ready to use

Reading and Use of English Part 5
decade (n) period of ten years
eco-tourism (n) tourism that aims to be friendly to the environment
regard (v) think about sth in a certain way
luxury (n) great comfort, sth which is pleasant to have but not necessary
organically-grown (adj) grown without chemicals
cotton (n) plant used to make cloth
bleach (v) make whiter
conserve (v) save
costly (adj) expensive
severely (adv) badly
high-end (adj) aiming at the rich

Glossary

trend (n) general way a situation is changing
bungalow (n) one-storey house
unspoilt (adj) natural, not damaged by human activities
income (n) money you earn
resort (n) holiday destination
benefit (n) advantage
unique (adj) if sth is unique, it is the only one of its kind
trekking (n) walking long distances in the countryside
backpacking (n) travelling with all your things in a backpack
purpose (n) aim
habitat (n) natural home of a plant or animal
hotelier (n) person who owns or runs a hotel
impact (n) the effect an event, situation, etc has on sth
neutralise (v) reduce the bad effect of
retain (v) keep
small-scale (adj) small in size
measure (n) official act which will deal with a problem
reduce (v) make less
reverse (v) change back to the way it was
undisturbed (adj) not touched or affected by
dump (v) throw away
seek (v) look for

Reading and Use of English Part 6
a case of (phr) a matter of, a question of
randomly (adv) by chance
straightforward (adj) easy and clear, not complicated
feat (n) sth difficult needing a lot of skill or strength to achieve
self-awareness (n) knowledge of yourself
vital (adj) essential
pace (n) speed
aptitude test (n) test to see if sb has the natural ability for a job
identify (v) name
determine (v) decide about
priority (n) thing you give most importance to
wealth (n) large amount of money or possessions
invaluable (n) very important
willingness (n) feeling of being ready to do sth
hire (v) employ
initiative (n) ability to make decisions without being told what to do
set someone apart from (phr v) show sb is different from
contemplate (v) think about
field (n) area of work
perspective (n) way of looking at things
content (adj) happy, satisfied
major (adj) important
fulfilling (adj) satisfying

intellectual (adj) related to the mind
attribute (n) quality
secure (n) safe
salary (n) monthly payment from your job
potential (n) possibility that sth will develop in a certain way

Reading and Use of English Part 7
structure (n) building
visible (adj) able to be seen
lean (n) position away from the vertical
former (adj) earlier
remains (n pl) what is left over
medieval (adj) of or from the Middle Ages (1000 AD – 1500 AD)
steeple (n) pointed tower which is often part of a church
claim (v) hold the record for
foundation (n) base of a building
tear down (phr v) knock down (a building)
make room for (phr) create space for
consist of (phr v) have or contain different parts
preserve (v) save sth from being harmed
stable (adj) steady
drain (v) remove the water
rot (v) decay
hazard (n) danger
degree (n) unit of measurement for angles
tilt (n) position away from the vertical
shallow (adj) not deep
ongoing (adj) continuing
conflict (n) disagreement
settle (v) become stable, stop moving
soil (n) earth, material on the surface of the ground in which plants grow
raised (adj) if sth is raised, it is higher than the things around it
incorporate (v) include in
skyscraper (n) very tall building
withstand (v) be strong enough not to be harmed (by cold, earthquakes, etc)
accelerate (v) go faster
sewage system (n) way that liquid waste is taken away

Writing
bully (v) threaten to hurt sb, or frighten them

Listening Part 1
misunderstanding (n) problem caused by a lack of communication
foolish (adj) silly
chore (n) household job

202

Listening Part 2
nautical mile (n) a measure of distance used at sea

Listening Part 4
conquer (v) take control of a foreign land
empire (n) group of countries ruled by one person or country
monastery (n) building in which monks (religious men) live
harsh (adj) hard
ruins (n pl) remains of old buildings

Practice Test 5

Reading and Use of English Part 1
rigorous (adj) careful and exact
client (n) customer
revert to (phr v) go back to an older way of doing things

Reading and Use of English Part 2
trail (n) path
aggressively (adv) with violence
roam (v) wander, travel over an area
superstition (n) belief which is not based on reason or knowledge, but on old unscientific ideas
spot (v) see, notice

Reading and Use of English Part 3
inseparable (adj) very close
claim (v) state that sth is true
make it (expr) succeed

Reading and Use of English Part 5
on top of the world (expr) very happy
down to (prep phr) due to, because of
bloodstream (n) the flow of blood around the body
cheerful (adj) happy
depression (n) a feeling of sadness that makes you think there is no hope for the future
prescribe (n) say what medical treatment sb should have
medication (n) medicine or drugs used to improve a condition or illness
treat (v) give medical care to
stimulate (v) cause or encourage to happen
cope with (phr v) manage
release (v) let a substance (eg a hormone) flow out
relieve (v) make better
coincidence (n) when two or more things happen at the same time in a way which is unlikely or surprising
exposure (n) amount of time a person leaves themselves open to sth
damp (adj) wet
dreary (adj) dull
wheat (n) plant used for making flour and then bread

temporary (adj) only for a short time
boost (n) increase
deficiency (n) lack of
outlook (n) way of seeing things
remedy (n) cure, solution to make sth better

Reading and Use of English Part 6
tackle (v) try to deal with
non-renewable (adj) not able to be used again
first and foremost (expr) as the main reason for sth
viable (adj) practically possible
cost-effective (adj) good value for money
deplete (v) make less, reduce
harness (v) capture and make use of
geothermal heat (n) heat inside the Earth
interest (n) money charged by banks to people who have borrowed from them
loan (n) sum of money which is borrowed and has to be paid back
controversial (adj) causing disagreement or discussion
unsightly (adj) ugly
towering (adj) very tall
livelihood (n) the way sb earns money
blade (n) the part of a wind turbine that catches the wind
core (n) centre
drill (v) use a machine to make holes
generate (v) create
solar panel (n) device to capture the sun's energy
ruin (v) destroy
steam (n) hot gas produced when water boils
initial (adj) first
pump (v) put in (money)

Reading and Use of English Part 7
circumstance (n) situation
proportion (n) part
put into perspective (phr) compare to other things so as to judge sth fairly
necessity (n) thing that is needed
savings (n pl) amount of money saved in the bank
build up (phr v) become larger
mount up (phr v) become larger
take notice of (phr v) pay attention to
small change (n) coins
purse (n) small bag used for carrying money
I could kick myself (expr) I realise I did sth wrong and wish I had avoided it
down the drain (expr) wasted, lost for no good reason
motto (n) short phrase expressing a rule
budget (n) financial plan
keep track of (phr) know where everything is
cover (v) afford to pay for
save for a rainy day (expr) save money for difficult times

Glossary

Listening Part 1
pass on (phr v) communicate to another person
give away (phr v) reveal
brand name (n) name by which an expensive product is sold
spell (n) short period of time
frosty (adj) icy
lowland (n) flat land that is near the level of the sea

Listening Part 3
time-consuming (adj) requiring a lot of time

Listening Part 4
beneficial (adj) helpful
incident (n) event, thing which happened
landmark (n) structure which is easy to recognise and identifies a place
catacomb (n) underground passage where bodies were buried
rumour (n) information passed from one person to another which may or may not be true
native speaker (n) person who speaks a language as their mother tongue

Practice Test 6

Reading and Use of English Part 1
Commonwealth (n) organisation of independent countries which in the past belonged to the British Empire
ruler (n) person who has power over a country
current (adj) of the present time
coronation (n) ceremony in which a person is made king or queen
uphold (v) defend or support a law or system

Reading and Use of English Part 2
fit in with (phr v) feel part of the same group as
peer (n) person of the same age group

Reading and Use of English Part 3
conduct (v) be responsible for doing or organising
sensitivity (n) ability to understand other people's feelings and problems
adverse (adj) negative
fearful (adj) frightened

Reading and Use of English Part 5
vital signs (n pl) basic physical functions such as your body temperature and heart rate
forward (v) send on

in the convenience of (phr) in a place that suits you
monitor (v) check, watch sth carefully for a period of time
rate (n) speed
detect (v) notice or discover sth
onset (n) start
blood vessel (n) tube that carries blood around the body
surface (n) top layer
absorb (v) take in
vein (n) tube that carries blood back to the heart
fraction (n) part
infrared (adj) rays of light which cannot be seen, but give off heat
clip (n) small object used to hold sth in place
gauge (n) instrument for measuring the size or amount of sth
convenient (adj) easy to use
conventional (adj) normal, usual, traditional
device (n) object or machine that does a particular job
flaw (n) imperfection
come on in leaps and bounds (expr) improve very quickly
assist (v) help
quantify (v) measure
cure (n) successful medical treatment
sophisticated (adj) complicated, complex
procedure (n) organised way of doing things
assign (v) decide that sth should be used for a particular purpose
calculation (n) adding, subtracting, multiplying or dividing mathematically

Reading and Use of English Part 6
resist (v) fight against
urge (n) strong desire
debt (n) money you owe to a person or a bank
outstanding (adj) owing, unpaid
balance (n) amount of money you have (or do not have) in a bank
signify (v) represent, mean
surplus (adj) extra
drastic (adj) serious and sudden
scenario (n) description of possible events
bankruptcy (n) the state of being unable to pay your debts
take something lightly (phr) do sth without serious thought
finances (n pl) money matters
credit rating (n) the assessment of how much a bank is willing to lend a person
creditor (n) person or organisation to whom you owe money

Reading and Use of English Part 7

beyond the reach of (phr) more than sb can afford to get
germ (n) small organism that causes disease
pill (n) small solid piece of medicine which you take by mouth
acne (n) skin disease, especially affecting teenagers
cleansing agent (n) chemical that is used to clean
tolerate (v) get used to
irritated (adj) painful and sore
mild (adj) weak
persistent (adj) continuing
prescription (n) written note from a doctor saying what medicine you need
affordable (adj) cheap enough to be bought
to a lesser degree (phr) not so much
side effect (n) unintended result
beyond the means of (phr) more than sb can afford to buy
topical (adj) local, limited to a certain area
derive from (phr v) come from
caution (n) the quality of not taking risks and avoiding danger
undergo (v) experience
over the counter (phr) available at the chemist's without the need for a doctor's prescription
oral (adj) taken by mouth
on the market (phr) available to buy
abrupt (adj) sudden

Listening Part 1

challenging (adj) difficult
pick somebody up (phr v) collect from a place
supper (n) last meal of the day
impressive (adj) sth that is impressive seems good, large, important, etc
postpone (v) change an event to a later time or date

Listening Part 2

shortly (adv) soon

Listening Part 4

snoring (n) making loud breathing noises while asleep
upset (adj) unhappy and worried
interfere with (phr v) prevent sth from happening in the way that was planned
embarrassed (adj) ashamed, nervous or uncomfortable in a social situation

Practice Test 7

Reading and Use of English Part 2

crown (v) make sb king or queen in a special ceremony
bury (v) put a body in the ground

Reading and Use of English Part 3

typical (adj) usual, showing characteristics that are normally expected
citizen (n) person who is a member of and has rights in a particular country
progressive (adj) forward thinking
coal (n) hard black substance found underground which can be burnt to produce heat or power
mine (v) make a hole by digging for metals, coal or other substances
institution (n) organisation, company
essential (adj) extremely important, vital

Reading and Use of English Part 5

definitely (adv) certainly, surely
serene (adj) peaceful and calm
chase away (phr v) run after sb to make them leave
promote (v) give sb in a company a more important job
relocate (v) go to live in a new place
van (n) medium-sized vehicle usually used for carrying things
removal man (n) person who moves things to sb's new home
in a daze (prep phr) in a confused state
significance (n) importance
blank (n) empty
take comfort from (phr) feel less anxious because of
interpret (v) consider events in a certain way
in the way (prep phr) blocking a place
numb (adj) not feeling anything
inconsiderate (adj) not caring about other people

Reading and Use of English Part 6

record (n) piece of written information
establish (v) start sth
amusement (n) feeling of being entertained or made to laugh
suffer (v) feel pain
cage (n) space surrounded on all sides by bars or wire in which animals are kept
public opinion (n) what people think
exhibitor (n) person or organisation that shows sth to the public
breeding programme (n) plan to get animals in zoos to have babies
in short (prep phr) in a few words
thrive (v) do well
conservation (n) protection of animals, plants, buildings, etc from the damaging effects of human activity
decline (v) go down, fall
in captivity (prep phr) not in a free, natural environment
on display (prep phr) on show to the public

Reading and Use of English Part 7

educational establishment (n) place of education such as a school or university

Glossary

self-supporting (adj) needing no help or money from outside
attraction (n) place that people want to visit
highlight (v) emphasise, pay special attention to
commitment (n) promise to follow a course of action
innovation (n) change, new idea or new way of doing things
illustrate (v) show with pictures, objects or details
inspiration (n) source of creativity and excitement
grounds (n pl) land around a building
holograph (n) image which looks as if it is real, not flat
largely (adv) mostly
admission (n) money you pay to go into a museum, gallery, etc
fund (v) pay for
embody (v) include as part of sth
on a regular basis (prep phr) regularly
mug (n) large cup
boast (v) be proud to have
vintage (adj) old and of high quality or value
supersonic (adj) able to travel faster than the speed of sound

Listening Part 1
broadcast (v) send out on TV or radio

Listening Part 2
dedication (n) complete giving of time or energy to sth
association (n) connection
aspect (n) part, area

Practice Test 8

Reading and Use of English Part 1
break up (phr v) finish a school or university at the end of term

Reading and Use of English Part 2
loss (n) death
renovate (v) fix and paint to make new again
struggling (adj) having financial difficulties
be somebody's cup of tea (expr) be to sb's taste

Reading and Use of English Part 3
gap year (n) the year off some students take between leaving school and starting university
pursuit (n) interest, hobby

Reading and Use of English Part 5
in the know (expr) having information about

brief (adj) short
in a nutshell (expr) in a few words, simply
initiative (n) action intended to start a larger movement
manufacture (v) make in large numbers
consume (v) eat
exploit (v) use (in a bad way)
mistreatment (n) way of treating sb badly
import (v) bring products into a country
profit (n) money you make in a business after costs
crop (n) plant which is grown for food
campaign (n) planned group of activities for a particular purpose
launch (v) start
foundation (n) organisation started to support a particular group of people in need
booth (n) small enclosed box-like space for selling sth or giving information
certify (v) officially say or write that sth is true or correct
ironic (adj) suggesting a different meaning from the words used

Reading and Use of English Part 6
slam (v) shut violently
mass (n) large amount of
hurtle (v) move at great speed and possibly out of control
loll (v) hang out
wag (v) move quickly from side to side
frenetically (adv) very excitedly
sloppy (adj) wet
lift your spirits (phr) make you feel happier
ecstatic (adj) very happy and excited
bark (n) loud noise a dog makes
contented (adj) satisfied and happy
purr (n) soft sound a cat makes
party (n) group
ancestor (n) relative from much earlier generation
breed (n) type of animal
team up (phr v) work together
ferocious (adj) dangerous and angry
loyal (adj) faithful
fierceness (n) ferocious anger
devotion (n) giving yourself to sth completely
domesticated (adj) not wild, made to live with people
feline (n) to do with cats
sacred (n) holy
mummified (adj) if a body is mummified, it is preserved using artificial means and can last for thousands of years

folklore (n) traditional stories and culture of a people

canine (n) to do with dogs

ailment (n) illness

ample (adj) plenty of

the aged (n pl) old people

litter box (n) container full of sand or grit provided for cats to go to the toilet

counterpart (n) person who has the same purpose as another in a different place or organisation

therapeutic (adj) causing sb to feel happier and healthier

household (n) group of people, usually a family, living together

vermin (n) small animals such as rats, mice or insects that can be harmful and difficult to control

dementia (n) mental illness usually affecting older people as a result of brain damage

autism (n) condition in which a person fails to develop social abilities and communication skills

addiction (n) inability to stop using, especially a drug

former (adj) first mentioned

latter (adj) last mentioned

Reading and Use of English Part 7

licensed (adj) given official permission to do sth

big top (n) circus tent

set eyes on (phr) see for the first time

inherit (v) get money or property from the death of a relative or friend

pool (v) share

buyout (n) take over a company by giving them money

keep something under your hat (expr) keep sth secret

pack up (phr v) put away

crystal ball (n) glass ball used to predict the future

pass away (phr v) die

observant (adj) able to pick up details

trapeze artist (n) circus performer who swings high above the ground

applause (n) show of enjoyment in the form of clapping

in awe of (prep phr) greatly respectful of

emigrate (v) leave one's country to live in another

first degree (adj) only affecting the surface of the skin

Listening Part 1

refreshments (n pl) drinks and snacks

Listening Part 2

temporarily (adv) for a short period of time

put up (phr v) give accommodation to

shelter (n) place to stay

hostel (n) cheap place to stay, especially for young people

herb (n) kind of plant used for cooking or medicines

Listening Part 4

the fifties (n) the period between 1950 and 1959

cover (v) report on a story in newspapers

in depth (prep phr) with details

Congress (n) elected group of politicians in the US

ban (v) officially stop

subliminal (adj) indirect, subconscious

Recording Script

Practice Test 1

This is the First Certificate in English for Schools Listening Test. Practice Test 1.

I'm going to give you instructions for this test. At the start of each piece you'll hear this sound.

You'll hear each piece twice. Now look at Part One.

PART ONE

You'll hear people talking in eight different situations. For questions 1 – 8, choose the best answer (A, B or C).

One **You hear two girls having a conversation.**

F1: Did you have a look at the timetable?

F2: Yes. It's better if we get the 42B because that takes us right into the centre where all the good shops are.

F1: Perfect! I want to look for some new trainers. So, what time does it leave?

F2: Every hour, on the hour. I don't want to go too late though because I have to be home by seven o'clock for dinner.

F1: That's fine. I have to visit my grandparents at half past six tonight, so maybe we can get the five o'clock bus home.

F2: Great! Let's catch the 42B into town at lunchtime. Then, we'll have all afternoon to look around the shops.

Two **You hear a boy talking about a pop concert.**

I was so excited about going to the concert with my older brother and his friends. We bought tickets weeks in advance and even though they were expensive, I knew it would be worth it. Well, when we got there we found that it was incredibly busy and we ended up standing right at the back. I was really upset, especially since I'd been looking forward to it so much. But actually, once the band came on and started playing, we all had an amazing time! It didn't matter that we couldn't really see because the music was just great! Even though I was annoyed at first, by the time we left I couldn't have been happier.

Three **You hear a woman leaving a voicemail message for her son.**

Hi, Mark, it's Mum. I've been on the phone to Mr Evans, your maths teacher, this afternoon. He's a little concerned that he hasn't received any homework from you this term. What's going on? He also told me that you didn't go to your lesson today. I just can't believe it! Especially since you know how I feel about you skipping school! Where were you, Mark? Look, you've got a maths exam on Thursday and you need to go to every lesson if you want to pass it, OK? Please come straight home after football practice. I really need to speak to you about this.

Four **You overhear a conversation between two friends.**

M: The barbecue was really good, except that it rained all day on Saturday, so by Sunday the garden was flooded.

F: Oh, that's a shame!

M: Yeah, we ended up eating inside. Never mind, I'm sure we'll be having loads of barbecues once the weather gets better. You should definitely come along to the next one.

F: I will, thanks. So, tell me more. Who went? What did you eat?

M: Well, everyone brought a dish. Jenny brought a salad, Pete brought homemade burgers and Ken made a cake for dessert. My dad did the cooking but he ended up burning the sausages. They were disgusting!

F: Oh no!

Five **You hear a woman speaking to a group of students.**

As you work your way around the museum please follow the arrows painted on the floor. This system allows you to look at the exhibits in chronological order. Please note that loud voices are not tolerated and you should on no occasion touch the paintings or exhibits. Please also bear in mind that the museum is open to all members of the public today, and not just your group, so please be sure not to disrupt other visitors. Finally, please stay as a group and remember that eating and drinking is only permitted in designated areas such as the café.

Six **You overhear two boys talking about a cinema.**

M1: What did you think of the new cinema complex?

M2: Well, I can't say that I was that impressed. There were only three screens.

M1: That's more than enough, isn't it? I mean you only see one film at a time. I love the fact they show 3D films there.

M2: I have to admit that is a great selling point. There's nowhere else round here that shows those kind of films, especially not with such amazing sound quality!

M1: I really liked that it was super-modern inside, too. Not like the old place down on Ride Street.

M2: OK, it's new so it should look modern, but I think the old cinema is great. It has a really traditional feel. Much more authentic!

Seven **You hear a girl and her brother talking.**

F: If you do the dishes and the ironing, I'll tell you the password for my computer.

M: No, I'm too busy with homework. Plus, I don't want to use your computer anymore. I'm not interested.

F: Look, I promised Natalie I'd go to her party tonight but Mum says I can't go if I haven't done my chores. Please, give me a hand.

M: I told you, no!

F: OK, I'll give you the answers to your homework if you just do some of the dishes for me. Deal?

M: Leave me alone, Sally.

F: Right, if you don't help me I'll tell Mum who smashed her favourite vase.

Eight **You hear a caller on a phone-in radio show talking about sport.**

Well of course things are so different now. When I was at school, we did rugby in the autumn, football in the spring and cricket in the summer. And that was it basically. Except for a bit of swimming and athletics and cross-country running. Which we all hated, by the way. My kids though get to try hang-gliding and bungee jumping and things like that, and some of the kids in my eldest's class are even doing a parachute jump for charity this weekend. I know some people worry that it's all a bit dangerous, but that's life, isn't it? I wish I'd had the chance to do those kinds of things when I was their age.

That is the end of Part One. Now turn to Part Two.

PART TWO

You'll hear a young fashion model called Monica Mansfield talking about shopping. For questions 9 – 18, complete the sentences with a word or short phrase. You now have forty-five seconds to look at Part Two.

F: When I posted on my fashion blog last week that I wanted to talk about shopping, I couldn't believe the response I got. People from all over the country sent in questions asking me about my shopping habits. I suppose because I'm a fashion model, people think I know a lot about what's in style and where the best places are to find the coolest clothes ... and, actually, I do know a lot about clothes and shopping! I have to really because of my job. I'm seventeen now and I've been modelling since I was thirteen. I got spotted at a school fashion show and I was asked if I'd ever considered modelling professionally. I guess I got the offer because, well, quite simply, I happen to be very tall and I suppose I just have the right look. I don't think I'll be doing it forever, but it's a good way to save up money to go to <u>university</u>.

So, anyway, about the questions that people posted on my blog. A girl named Katherine from Manchester asked me about the first time that I'd been clothes shopping and she wanted me to say what it'd been like. I told her that, strangely enough, the first time I'd been shopping hadn't really been very <u>enjoyable</u>. I must have been about five or six years old and I remember my mother took me shopping for my school uniform. The shops were really crowded and the whole experience was really boring!

Another girl, Rebecca from Liverpool, posted me a question asking whether I bought designer clothes or if I preferred to buy clothes from the high street. It was a good question because I usually just buy whatever suits me. I don't buy brand labels just because they happen to be trendy at the time. I did, however, tell Rebecca that there were two <u>designers</u> that I really liked and that I tended to buy their clothes more than others.

Then, Megan from London wanted to know if I ever bought things online. And, you know, I don't really. I'm not a fan of shopping online because if you don't like something when it gets delivered, it's difficult to <u>exchange</u> it. The same girl, Megan, also asked me what the most expensive item of clothing that I'd ever bought had been. I thought to myself, 'Oh, that's another good question!' I really had to think about it for a bit, then I told her that it was probably the <u>floor</u>-length dress that I'd worn to my brother's wedding. I've still got it. It's really lovely; a dark green colour with matching shoes.

Some of the people who posted on my blog asked me more general questions. For example, Jackie from Bristol asked if I could give her an idea of the kinds of things that I bought regularly. I said that I often shopped for jeans, T-shirts, the usual stuff, but that I probably bought T-shirts most often, especially ones with <u>writing</u> on them.

And then Nancy from London wanted to know if I usually shopped alone or if I liked going shopping with anyone in particular. The truth is, I shop by myself occasionally, but I definitely prefer to shop with others around. I told Nancy that I often shopped with Julia, my <u>best friend</u>, because we had the same taste in clothes.

One of the most often asked questions that people posted on my blog was about whether I had a favourite shop or an area where I particularly liked to shop. And my answer to that is that I haven't really got a favourite area to shop in, but my favourite shop is a small <u>second-hand clothes</u> shop near my home. You can find some great designer clothes there, plus normal streetwear, and it's much cheaper than buying them new!

Oh, and I had a rather unusual question ... someone asked me if I could only rescue one item of clothing from a fire, what would it be? Well, I thought about it and decided that it would have to be my jacket. It's made of <u>leather</u> and it's something I wear all the time. If I lost it, I think I'd feel like I'd lost a part of myself!

You know, all this talk about buying things reminds me that I actually do need to go shopping! I'm doing a photo shoot in Spain in two weeks, and I've got almost everything I need for the beach, such as a swimming costume, a towel and all of that. But what I'm still looking for is a really cool <u>pair of sunglasses</u>. I'll probably end up getting them at the airport!

Now you'll hear Part Two again.

That is the end of Part Two. Now turn to Part Three.

PART THREE

You'll hear five teenagers talking about summer camps. For questions 19 – 23, choose from the list (A – H) what each speaker says about it. Use the letters only once. There are three extra letters which you do not need to use. You now have thirty seconds to look at Part Three.

Speaker 1

This year, we had to leave early because it rained non-stop for a week! It was so bad at one point that we couldn't even leave the cabin. Fortunately, we'd already done everything before the storm started. The best day without a doubt was when we went hiking in the woods looking for a black bear or a deer. We followed Jack, our guide, and kept really quiet during the hike, but in the end we didn't see any. We did see lots of wild flowers and learnt a lot about other wild animals in the area though, which was really interesting. <u>After the hike, the little ones sang songs about animals and drew pictures of bears, but those activities are for younger children, so I didn't join in.</u> I spent the evening in the computer room with the older kids, looking at the photos I'd taken and uploading them onto Facebook!

Speaker 2

Last year, I failed an English exam and my mum was really worried because I'd always passed English and French with flying colours. So, my parents decided that it would be a good idea if I spent August in an English summer camp in Tarifa by the sea. At first I didn't like the idea at all. I thought it would be difficult to speak in English all the time. Plus, a friend of mine said it would be too hot and windy to do anything! But when the time came to go home I realised that it was the best experience I'd ever had. My English improved a lot because our teachers were British and American and they did all sorts of things with us like sailing and putting on plays. On the last day we went whale watching. <u>That was my favourite day because we saw lots of dolphins and a huge killer whale! It jumped in the air and I recorded it on video! Amazing!</u> I even tried to kite-surf, though I wasn't very good at it.

Speaker 3

My sister and I always go in the first week of September because that's when the weather's perfect: not too hot and not too cold. It's also the best time to go bird-watching or to go trekking looking for wild animals. If you're lucky you might see a deer or a fox. Sometimes they come close to the camp because they smell the food, but our leaders are quite strict and don't let us go near them. They're worried we might frighten them. This year, we were going to go rafting for the first time. We were so excited! We thought our parents wouldn't like the idea; they usually say that the sports we want to try are too dangerous, but this time they were all for it. <u>In the end, though, it was cancelled; the river had flooded because of heavy rain</u> so instead we helped our leaders teach the younger children how to fish. Oh, well. There's always next year!

Speaker 4

My friend Pete and I convinced our parents to let us go to an adventure camp in the Lake District. We were going to learn how to climb rocks, tie knots and read maps. Pete's parents were a bit worried because they thought we were too young to go rock climbing. We told them they could drive us there on Friday and meet the activity leaders. When we got there, Sarah, our group leader, showed us round and promised Pete's mum that she'd take good care of us. <u>The first thing we did on Saturday was a special survival workshop with Josh, who was the senior leader. He showed us what to do if we are hurt or injured and how to find our way if we got lost.</u> On Sunday, it looked like it was going to rain and it did a little bit. But then the sun came out and we managed to do all the activities that were planned for the day. I love rock climbing!

Speaker 5

My music teacher recommended the Summer Arts Camp because it's close to home and the camp leaders there are really friendly. The only problem was that most of the kids who went there were younger than me, but I didn't mind. I wanted to practise for my final piano exam in September, so I decided to go there for the summer. Of course, I didn't spend all day studying and playing the piano. There were other fun things to do like horse-riding, photography and drama. I could even choose to learn how to create a website or write a blog, but I'm not that keen on technology. I enjoyed playing tennis the most. My parents said I shouldn't because I might hurt my hands and spoil my chances for the music exam, but it all went well. I had a great time and actually made some good friends. I passed my piano exam last week, so we're celebrating this Friday!

Now you'll hear Part Three again.

That's the end of Part Three. Now turn to Part Four.

PART FOUR

You'll hear a radio interview with a man, Emmanuel Johnson, about how he began his career in the arts. For questions 24 – 30, choose the best answer (A, B or C). You now have one minute to look at Part Four.

F: Hello and welcome to the second episode in our new series, *My Early Life in Art*, in which we look at how some of the leading figures in the arts began their careers. Our guest this week is not an artist, but he is one of the most important people in the world of art today. Emmanuel Johnson, co-founder and director of the Goldstein Arts Centre in London, welcome to the programme.

M: Thank you, Alison. It's nice to be here.

F: Emmanuel, you didn't start out intending to work in the arts, did you?

M: No, that's right. My family have always been lawyers, and I studied law at the same university that my father, and his father before him, went to. According to tradition, I was supposed to follow them into the family law business and take it over one day.

F: But that didn't happen…?

M: No, not exactly. At university, you see, I met the love of my life, Lucasta. She was a ballerina, and I fell in love with her and the world of performing arts at the same moment. You might laugh, but I was just a young man, and I saw this beautiful creature on the stage one night in the university performance of *Swan Lake*. My life changed the moment I saw her. I had to meet her.

F: I should say at this point you've been married to Lucasta Reeno for the past thirty years!

M: Yes! Well, anyway, to cut a long story short, I volunteered to be a stagehand at the university theatre, you know, moving scenery and pulling ropes backstage, things like that – not on stage, because I am certainly *not* a performer – and we became engaged very soon after.

F: Had you been interested in working in the arts beforehand?

M: I suppose, like everyone, I knew the great works; paintings and operas and that sort of thing, but I didn't have a special feeling for anything in particular. At an early age, I discovered I have no creative talent at all. In fact, it's strange for someone who married a dancer, but I'm tone deaf, I have two left feet and absolutely no sense of rhythm!

F: After university, your career took some time to develop.

M: Yes. Of course, when I announced to my family my decision to become Lucasta's manager, they were very disappointed. I did actually start in the law firm to please them, but it was soon very clear it wasn't working, and thankfully, everyone agreed that I should follow my heart. I think I lasted three months in the office …

F: … and then it was the open road!

M: That's right. I went all round Europe with Lucasta and the London Ballet as the tour manager. That was our first professional engagement, and it was a wonderful time. In fact, we spent the next few years on the road, in many different countries, and only came back home after we were married. Lucasta's career was by far the most important in those days, but a dancer's life is short, and it was important to prepare for the day when she couldn't tour any more.

F: And when that day came …

M: Well, you see, on our travels, we met all sorts of fascinating people – artists, painters, musicians, all sorts – and I'd made many connections and friendships in the art world. When Lucasta reached the age when she had to retire from the stage I had a lot of offers of work from all over the world, and that's when the idea of the Arts Centre came up. David Goldstein was a rich art collector who was looking for a partner to open a gallery or establish an arts centre of some sort.

F: Yes, David Goldstein as in 'Goldstein Arts Centre', of course. What's your relationship with him?

M: Oh, we go back years together. We'd already formed a small company to work with children in the arts even before Lucasta's retirement, so I was no stranger to working with him. And socially, we've been very close since our wives met at a charity event in, er, oh, I can't remember when. I mean, I knew he was absolutely trustworthy, and his idea was very attractive. When we opened the Arts Centre, that's when my career really took off.

F: Yes, I see. And that's where we'll leave the story of your early life in art. Emmanuel Johnson, thank you very much.

M: Thank you again, Alison.

Now you'll hear Part Four again.

That's the end of Part Four. That's the end of the test. Please stop now.

Practice Test 2

This is the First Certificate in English for Schools Listening Test. Practice Test 2.
I'm going to give you instructions for this test. At the start of each piece you'll hear this sound.
You'll hear each piece twice. Now look at Part One.

PART ONE

You'll hear people talking in eight different situations. For questions 1 – 8, choose the best answer (A, B or C).

One **You hear a football coach talking to his players before the start of the new season.**

Get together, everyone. Now … I know we didn't do very well last season. And I know some people think it's because the referees weren't always very fair. And others say we didn't prepare well enough. But that's not why I've asked you to come here today. What I want to say is that I'm really glad I'm your coach. It's a privilege to be part of this team and nothing will change that. Win or lose, I'll always be proud of you! Don't worry about the next match yet. I know Newcastle is a strong team, but let's prepare for it on Saturday. Right, boys! Off you go!

Two **You overhear a conversation about a young woman called Beth.**

F1: Have you seen Beth since she came back from her holiday?

F2: Yes, I saw her yesterday at the gym. She looks really tanned.

F1: I know! She was so tanned that it looked like she'd spent weeks on a Caribbean island or something.

F2: Well, I do remember hearing her say that she was going to go on a cruise to Cuba, but in the end she decided to go to Paris for a month.

F1: Really? I thought she went to Madrid. So how did she get so tanned?

F2: Spain was last year, remember? No, she told me that after coming back from France she just went to the park to sunbathe.

F1: Oh, I see. She must get brown very quickly then. Lucky her!

Three You overhear a conversation at a hairdresser's.

M: So, what would you like, Madam? Just a haircut?

F: Well, how much does it cost to have it cut and dyed?

M: Let's see. For short hair, it's thirty-five pounds. But your hair is quite long, so it would be fifty.

F: That's not bad, actually. Does that also include blow-drying?

M: No. If you want a blow-dry as well, it would be fifty-five.

F: Ah, I see. And how much would it be if you just trimmed it?

M: That would be just twenty pounds.

F: Well, I've just been paid, so I guess I can have it all: haircut, dye and blow-dry.

M: Excellent! Come this way first for a wash. We've got this lovely new shampoo …

Four You hear an announcement at a supermarket.

Good morning, shoppers! Today, in addition to your favourite lemon, strawberry and kiwi yoghurts, you can also find the new summer fruit and orange flavours over in the dairy section, although the 'buy one get two free' offer has just finished. And if you were too late to stock up on Chocomad bars with last week's offer, remember that there's a discount starting today for the brand new Chocodark. You will find it in the 'sweets and crisps' section. Chocodark with nuts, raspberries or plain … 20% off, just for you! This offer is valid until April 25th, so buy Chocodark today!

Five You hear part of an interview with an actor who won an Oscar.

F: So, tell us, Bill. What's it like to win an Oscar after just a few years in the film industry?

M: Well, my family and friends are really proud. I mean, I've only made two films so far, so I'm quite lucky to have picked up an Oscar.

F: And how about yourself? Do you feel like the luckiest actor in the world?

M: Lucky, yes, but not because I won the Oscar. I feel lucky because I had a very good director and film crew. They were all incredibly professional. I don't think I would've won this award if it wasn't for them. So, I guess this experience has proved to me how important teamwork is. Of course, my fans are also important; I'd like to thank them for all their messages and support.

F: Great. Well, good luck with your next film!

Six You overhear a conversation between two sisters about a pair of trousers.

F1: Lizzie, have you seen my new trousers? You know, the ones you borrowed last Saturday when you went to the cinema.

F2: Erm … I think I saw them in your cupboard. Didn't you put them away when you were tidying up your room?

F1: Yes, but they're not there anymore. You didn't take them again, did you? I really wanted to wear them to the barbecue.

F2: Well, I don't think they're here, Maggie. Maybe Mum put them in the washing machine. Why don't you have a look in the bathroom?

F1: Hang on, they're here – under your coat! Oh, Lizzie!

F2: Well, at least you've found them! Enjoy the barbecue!

Seven You hear a presenter opening a music show.

Good evening, ladies and gentlemen! Welcome to what will be an unforgettable night! The one and only Rocking Chairs will be with you shortly. As you can see in the programme, in ten minutes' time our local singer Pete Williams will open tonight's show with his classic pop hits, including all our old favourites. And right after that, we've got your absolutely favourite rock band. So don't move! Please also note that at the end of the show, you can buy the latest CD by Rocking Chairs. There'll be a stand just outside the venue where you'll also find collections of Pete's hits. Let the show begin!

Eight You hear part of an interview with a young motorcyclist.

F: Thank you for your time, Johnny. You must be going through a rough time after having to drop out of the race. Your injury is quite serious, isn't it?

M: Well, it could've been worse, I can tell you. It was a very dangerous fall and I could've broken my leg.

F: So, you haven't?

M: Fortunately not. It's only my wrist that's broken.

F: So, how long will it take you to recover? When will we see you back on your bike?

M: The doctor said that my leg will heal quickly, so I could ride in the race in Malaysia in two months. But I don't want to risk it; I'd rather wait and strengthen my hand once they take the cast off. That'll take more than three months.

F: So, do you think we'll see you in the Hong Kong race in five months?

M: Oh, yes. If everything goes well, I'll be as good as new then! Although I am going to be commentating on the race in Malaysia for British television, so I might see you there, too!

That is the end of Part One. Now turn to Part Two.

PART TWO

You'll hear a young inventor called Sophie Williams talking about a competition. For questions 9 – 18, complete the sentences with a word or short phrase. You now have forty-five seconds to look at Part Two.

F: Good afternoon and thank you for inviting me to come in and speak in your technology class today. Firstly, my name is Sophie and I'm from Bath. I'm seventeen years old, so I'm actually only a few years older than most of you in here. Last month I came first in something called the Innovative Inventions competition; that's a competition which is organised in this country every two years. This afternoon, I'd like to tell you a little about my winning entry. So, my invention, something I call the Warm-mouse, is a mouse that gives off a small amount of heat whenever you hold it or click it while you're using your computer. Some people might think that it's not very useful, but it is! As some of you might know, when you spend most of the day working or playing on the computer, your 'mouse' hand gets cold and numb. With my invention this will no longer be a problem. It'll keep your hand warm even if the room's freezing cold! Imagine how nice that would be in the wintertime? But I've also made sure that you can use the Warm-mouse at other times of the year, too. When I was working on the mouse, I designed it so that there's the option of switching the heat function off. So, when it's on the 'off' mode, it's just like a normal mouse. What I mean is that if you select the 'off' mode, its <u>temperature</u> is the same as any other mouse. So you can use it all year round – even when it's a scorching day.

Warm-mouse can be connected to a laptop or netbook, as well as a normal PC. Actually this was something that caused me <u>trouble</u> when I first began designing the mouse. You see, it worked fine when I connected it to my PC, but when I plugged it into my <u>laptop</u>, it sometimes got stuck. It was so annoying! My brother and I did a couple of experiments to see if we could fix the problem; he was really helpful, but we couldn't find the solution. In the end, it was my <u>IT teacher</u> who suggested changing the cable. I did and it worked!

And that's when I decided to enter my mouse in the *Innovative Inventions* competition. As I mentioned, I won. It was brilliant and the award ceremony was amazing! It was held in a museum in London, so I went there by car with Mum and Dad, who were very excited and proud. I was really <u>nervous</u> even after it was all over. The room was full of people explaining their inventions. There were also reporters with cameras and important <u>scientists</u>.

The strange thing is that I never expected to win! I thought my invention was quite simple compared to others. So I was taken <u>by surprise</u> when I was announced as the winner! I simply couldn't believe it! The other two finalists seemed quite disappointed. I felt a bit bad for them afterwards, but I'm sure they won't give up inventing ... it's something that gets in your blood!

Even though I'm quite busy with school projects and exams at the moment, I still try to spend some time at the weekend on my next invention, which is something I call Cleverlights. They're lights for the <u>Christmas tree</u> that turn on only when people are in the room. I'm trying to find a way to add special sensors to the lights, but it's not as easy as it sounds. Inventing electronic devices is always challenging. And at times frustrating. But it's great when I manage to solve a technical problem. So, in the end, it's worth it. You should remember that when you're working on your gadgets and inventions ... never give up!

Now you'll hear Part Two again.

That is the end of Part Two. Now turn to Part Three.

PART THREE

You'll hear five people talking about natural disasters. For questions 19 – 23, choose from the list (A – H) which statement goes with each speaker's story. Use the letters only once. There are three extra letters which you do not need to use. You now have thirty seconds to look at Part Three.

Speaker 1
If you've ever been in an earthquake, you'll know how terrifying it is. It happens all of a sudden, without any warning at all. When an earthquake struck our town a few weeks ago, it was a Saturday so I was at home, studying in my room. The building started shaking and some of my stuff fell onto the floor. The first thing I wanted to do was run outside, but I know that's the worst thing you can do. A lot of people get injured trying to leave buildings because things like roof tiles can fall on them. Luckily, this last earthquake wasn't so bad. <u>Some buildings in the area had some broken windows, but our place was OK.</u>

Speaker 2
We're used to hurricanes where we live. We have one every three or four years. I'm not as scared of them as I used to be. I think that's because the first one I experienced was quite terrible. It caused really strong winds, and many homes were destroyed. Ours suffered quite a lot of damage, actually. And then there's the rain afterwards. There was a lot of flooding

in the area, and some people had to be rescued by boat. <u>Nowadays, when we hear of a hurricane coming our way, we drive up north to my aunt and uncle's house.</u> That's what we did three years ago, and I'm glad we did, because that last hurricane blew our roof off!

Speaker 3
Tsunamis are quite frightening. When we were on holiday last year, there was an undersea earthquake near our holiday flat. It was quite big, and a few minutes later I saw the sea pulling back away from the beach – and then it came rushing back in. We ran inside, but our flat was only on the first floor, and we soon had to find higher ground. <u>We raced up the stairs to the roof of the building, where we stayed for hours, safe</u> but worried. We didn't know how we'd get down. We heard there were boats coming to get people, but before they reached us, the waters started to go down, so we went back to our room to gather whatever we could.

Speaker 4
I'll never forget this one summer we had. The temperature was over 38 degrees every day for at least two weeks. Just going outside was awful, even as far as the shops. I'm just glad I didn't have to go to school every day. Luckily we have air-conditioning, so our house was cool. It was so hot that summer that there were often wildfires in the area. We live close to a forest, so we were quite worried. <u>The fire department had always told us to leave if fire ever came too close to our house.</u> One day a wildfire did get close, but the fire crew were able to put it out before it caused too much damage and <u>we were able to stay where we were.</u> The side of our house was burnt a bit, but not badly. Anyway, I hope it never happens again.

Speaker 5
Our area is at risk of flooding, as we live quite close to a river, and every spring we get quite a lot of rain. We didn't have a problem at all for many years. The river would rise, of course, but never so much that we would get trapped. Then one year it happened. The rain came and it lasted for several days – as usual, actually. But then it started to rain really heavily. We tried to leave by car but when we got to the bridge, it had collapsed. We went back home and soon our house was surrounded by water, and eventually we had to climb up onto our roof! Thankfully <u>the police</u> had received a lot of calls and <u>they sent a rescue team by water</u>. All our belongings were ruined, but at least we were safe.

Now you'll hear Part Three again.

That's the end of Part Three. Now turn to Part Four.

PART FOUR

You'll hear a radio interview with Dave Oliver, who is the organiser of *Medieval Norwich*, a festival held every year in Norwich. For questions 24 – 30, choose the best answer (A, B or C). You now have one minute to look at Part Four.

F: This year nearly 5,000 people visited the medieval festival in Norwich. Dave, you've been part of the festival from the very start. Why is *Medieval Norwich* becoming so popular these days?

M: Yes, this year *was* extremely successful, with many new visitors coming along. We did a survey to find out how people hear about our festival. Many said that it was through posters we put up at similar events in the area. But surprisingly, <u>this wasn't the main reason. Our Facebook and Twitter accounts have thousands of followers and that's how most people heard about the festival</u>. It's great because it's easy to update and it's free. Our personal website is quite expensive and not as popular, but we still think it's necessary for people who don't use networking sites. So that's why we use both.

F: And when did you first think of organising a medieval festival in Norwich?

M: I grew up in Norwich, which as you know was a very important city in the Middle Ages, and when I was at school, my friend Ben and I used to read a lot about knights, swords, castles and battles. Then, when I was a student at the University of Gloucestershire, I went every year to the medieval festival which they have there. <u>When I was working in the public library in the holidays,</u> I bumped into Ben again. We started talking about old times, and he mentioned a medieval festival he'd recently been to. I thought it was a shame Norwich didn't have one. <u>So that's when I got the idea.</u>

F: And was it hard to start the festival?

M: Anyone who's organised a big public event knows that the first problem is finding the money to fund it. But this wasn't the case with *Medieval Norwich*. My friends and family helped, so that wasn't a big problem for me, and neither was getting the actors and equipment. I had contacts at other festivals who were glad to participate. <u>Choosing the best site was tough.</u> We thought about having it near a lake, but it was quite humid. So we decided on the woods, but it was too hard for people to find. Now we use a park just outside town, which is easy to get to.

F: And what would you say is the best attraction for the visitors?

M: In the survey, we also asked people to vote for their favourite part of the festival. The three most popular elements were the market, <u>the medieval dress contest</u> and the *Medieval Fight* event.

F: I'm sure that the fighting event came first, didn't it?

M: Surprisingly, it didn't. There are many families with young children who prefer non-violent shows. And the market was very popular mainly because it had great food that people ate with their fingers or wooden forks and spoons. And everyone loved our souvenirs. <u>But it was the contest that came out top.</u> Anyone could take part, and most people came up with very <u>imaginative outfits</u>.

F: And what is your main responsibility during the weekend of the festival?

M: I'm usually behind the information desk answering questions and giving directions. I'm also responsible when there's a problem … like complaints about the food, the facilities and so on. <u>The hardest is when a little boy or girl gets lost. Parents get quite upset.</u> I used to help organise the camping area, but now I have someone else in charge of that.

F: So do you have any time to actually attend the different festival events?

M: Yes! I always watch the dancing show at the end of the festival. I don't find it that exciting, but my wife loves it! <u>What I really enjoy is acting in the play, although I'm not a very good actor.</u> I love wearing the armour and using the handmade swords. We have to rehearse quite a lot before the festival, but it's worth it.

F: And is there anything else you'd like to tell people who are thinking of going to the festival?

M: Well, if you'd like to camp, but you don't have a tent – don't worry. Next year we're going to have camping equipment to rent. We'll also be giving out blankets whenever it gets cold at night. We've been lucky so far and had lovely sunny days during our festival. But remember, this is the UK, and it can rain at any time even in the summer. <u>So I'd suggest bringing thick jumpers and good coats.</u> Some people also bring plates, forks and knives to eat with, but I wouldn't recommend that. Eating with your fingers in the medieval way is great!

F: Thank you, Dave. It's been interesting talking to you. See you in Norwich!

Now you'll hear Part Four again.

That's the end of Part Four. That's the end of the test. Please stop now.

Practice Test 3

This is the First Certificate in English for Schools Listening Test. Practice Test 3.
I'm going to give you instructions for this test. At the start of each piece you'll hear this sound.
You'll hear each piece twice. Now look at Part One.

PART ONE

You'll hear people talking in eight different situations. For questions 1 – 8, choose the best answer (A, B or C).

One **You hear a man talking on the radio about the weather.**

And now to the weather, which will unfortunately continue to be unsuitable for travellers. Temperatures will drop tonight, and the forecast is no better for tomorrow. <u>You're advised</u> to travel only if it's absolutely necessary. Airports have been closed, and most trains have been cancelled. Everything is being done to ensure that the roads stay clear, but <u>motorists should be aware that the continuing cold weather will cause heavy snow and freezing rain, so there will be icy roads all over the country.</u>

Two **You hear two people having a conversation while they are waiting for a bus.**

F: How long have we been waiting? I'm freezing!

M: It won't be long now, I'm sure. We just have to wait a bit longer.

F: What time is it supposed to arrive?

M: I don't know, really. I think the timetable said it comes at half past.

F: Well, what time is it now?

M: Nearly half past, according to my watch. <u>But I'm not sure it's right because I dropped it the other day and now I think it's a bit fast.</u>

F: <u>You mean it might be only quarter past?</u> Are we going to stand here for another fifteen minutes?

M: <u>Well, what time does *your* watch say?</u>

F: <u>I haven't *got* a watch!</u>

M: Well, that's no good, is it?

F: What are we going to do if the bus doesn't come?

M: I suppose we could walk …

F: Oh, here's the bus! Quick!

Three **You hear a voicemail message which a woman leaves for one of her colleagues at work.**

Hi, Jeff, it's Lucy from the office here. I know you told me to finish the report by Tuesday, but there's a problem, I'm afraid. I'm not sure it'll be done by then because, as I expected, the information the Belfast office promised me hasn't arrived. Most of the report is ready, but <u>I can't make any more progress without that information.</u> This always happens with the Belfast people. They say one thing and then they do something else. This time they said they were waiting for you to confirm. Could you telephone them and assure them that they don't need to wait? <u>I should have it finished on time if I get the information from them straightaway.</u> If not, I don't know what to tell you. I can't give you a definite date, but I don't think it'll be Tuesday. Thanks.

Four **You hear two schoolchildren discussing one of their teachers.**

M: What do you think of the new geography teacher, then?

F: I don't know. She seems OK but I've only had one lesson with her.

M: Well, at first I thought she was nice. Then she caught me talking in the test and now she says I've got to do it all over again. After school!

F: Really? Actually, I saw her in the playground yesterday watching everyone run around and suddenly she just started shouting at someone who was on the grass.

M: And Brian says she punished him unfairly because he hadn't brought all his books. She doesn't let you get away with anything! She's really hard on everyone!

Five **You hear two people talking about their friend.**

M: Did you hear what happened to Frankie?

F: Yes, it was terrible.

M: He could have been seriously hurt. I mean, you don't expect things like that to happen to you, do you? It's amazing, really, that he survived at all.

F: If he hadn't jumped out of the way at the last minute, the coach would have hit him. When you think about it, he was lucky just to hurt his arm.

M: The ambulance arrived very quickly, which was lucky, too. Somebody saw it happen and called them straight away, and they took him off to hospital. He wasn't in any pain, but they wanted to keep an eye on him anyway.

F: I hear he's out of hospital now?

M: Yes, he's better now. He only stayed in for a day or two. He's gone off coaches, though!

F: No wonder!

Six **You hear a travel agent talking about holidays.**

Here at the *Happy Holidays Travel Agency*, we want to find you the best holiday we can. At this time of year, a lot of people are thinking about where to go, and we are here to help you choose. These days there is so much to choose from, it's difficult to know what to decide, and that's where we come in. You can go skiing, swimming, sky-diving or just lie on a beach. You could see the sights of a modern city, walk along ancient roads or take a long cruise on a luxury ship. It's up to you. We will give you all the help you need to make your selection. You'll find the variety can be confusing, but with our expert assistance, you're bound to make the right choice!

Seven **You hear two teenagers talking.**

F: Hi, how's school?

M: Oh, fine, you know. We're not doing much now the exams are over.

F: Oh, lucky you! We're snowed under. Our university entrance exams are coming up next week, and everyone's really nervous about them. And I'm exhausted!

M: Have you just got exams or have you got other work to do as well?

F: We've got to do a big project as well. It's like a really long essay, and I haven't even started mine. I just haven't got the energy at the moment. But it's really interesting because you can choose your own subject, and I've chosen to write about celebrities.

M: When do you have to finish it?

F: This week. Then it's the exams. There's such a lot to get through!

M: Well, afterwards I suppose you can have a bit of a rest.

F: Not really. I've got a summer job, so I won't be going on holiday at all this year.

M: Well … good luck!

Eight **You hear a couple talking about a film they have just seen together.**

F: Well, I didn't expect it to finish like that! I thought they were going to just sail away on his boat and live happily ever after. But not this time. I didn't like the ending at all.

M: You can't always have a happy ending.

F: I know you can't stand films like that! You told me you would never go and see another film like the one we saw last time. You remember, the film with the sheep and the farmer and the farmer's wife?

M: Yes, I do remember. And yes, you're right, I like thrillers or police movies, not films about happy people. Especially happy people and animals.

F: But did you enjoy this one? It wasn't really happy, after all.

M: Yes, it was OK. But what an endless movie! I thought it would never finish!

F: Yes, it did go on longer than it should have. Do you fancy a pizza?

M: I'm really hungry actually, so yes. It seems like hours since we went in!

F: Come on, then.

That is the end of Part One. Now turn to Part Two.

PART TWO

You'll hear a radio programme about the problems facing young people today. For questions 9 – 18, complete the sentences with a word or short phrase. You now have forty-five seconds to look at Part Two.

F: I think that many of us would agree, at least partially, that life for young people was easier in the past than it is nowadays. There are many problems facing young people today, and the financial situation in the world is having a negative effect on everyone. When things go wrong with the economy, and nobody has any money, things can be very hard, especially for teenagers, who have to rely on their parents for money. Now everyone has less to spend, young people are finding it particularly difficult.

And while the teenage years have never been easy, it certainly seems to be worse than ever … especially if you look at the future for young people. When they leave school, some choose to continue their education. University is a great opportunity, but you need to think about it carefully. Most governments have reduced the amount of money they give to support students, and without that help, students have to pay more themselves, so it's more expensive than it was in the past, and some students can't afford it. For those students, the only real choice they have, aside from staying in education, is finding a job. Some people think starting work straight away is a good idea, because you begin earning money earlier. You miss the experience of university, but, on the other hand, you gain the experience of working and earning. But there can be problems with having a job, too, so the best thing to do is to consider your options carefully and ask for advice. Having a discussion with your parents about your intentions is always a good idea.

Of course there are problems which affect both people at university and people looking for a job. I mean, even if you go to university, sooner or later you'll be looking for work. But the situation isn't encouraging. The problem isn't only lack of money, but lack of jobs too. In difficult times, factories and other companies either close, or stop employing new workers. There are record numbers of unemployed people nearly everywhere, and finding work when you are an inexperienced youngster can be extremely challenging. However, although it doesn't sound very encouraging, there is some good news. If you compare the situation today with, say, that of seventy years ago, young people have more freedom and more opportunities than ever before. More than 55% of people in Europe between the ages of eighteen and twenty-one say they're optimistic about their future. That's the majority of young people. So there is hope ... at least in this country.

In other countries, in Africa, for example, young people are facing a very different situation. Apart from poverty – many of the countries in Africa have always been very poor – some young people have to deal with their country frequently being engaged in wars. There are often conflicts between different groups within a country, and some governments even force young people to join the army and fight even if they don't want to. These 'child soldiers' lose their freedom and sometimes lose their lives, which is terrible.

Then in other parts of the world, young children are forced to work in factories. They work long hours making things like shoes and bags to be sold in richer countries, but they aren't paid very much at all. Some people might think they are lucky to have a job, but again, the point is that they don't have any choice. Although child labour – children working – is against the law, this doesn't really protect them because they work illegally because they need the money. With no choice, the children are in a very difficult position. All I can say is that I hope these situations improve in the future, and that we find solutions to the problems facing our young people today.

Now you'll hear Part Two again.

That is the end of Part Two. Now turn to Part Three.

PART THREE

You'll hear five people talking about their favourite place. For questions 19 – 23, choose from the list (A – H) what each speaker says. Use the letters only once. There are three extra letters which you do not need to use. You now have thirty seconds to look at Part Three.

Speaker 1
I don't have one particular favourite spot because I just like the beach in general, and it isn't important *which* beach I choose. I love just sitting on the sand beside the sea and relaxing. It's the fact that I *can* choose that I like the most, so it could be a beach anywhere, really. I like being able to do exactly what I want, with nobody telling me what to do. I don't mind if I'm alone or if I go with friends. Sometimes I meet people I know or even make new friends at the beach. But that's not really what makes the beach so special for me. It's the feeling of independence I get, the feeling of being away from my responsibilities for a while.

Speaker 2
When I need some peace and quiet, I like to go up to my room, sit on my bed and look out of the window. My room is right at the top of the house. I don't put any music on, I turn my phone off and I just sit there on my own. It's very relaxing after a busy day at school, and I've got a big, loud family, too, so it's like a safe place away from all the noise for me. If I've had an argument with one of my friends or if I'm upset because I failed a test at school, I can shut the door behind me and calm down. It's a very special, private place for me.

Speaker 3
I love the wide streets, the tall buildings and the noise and traffic. It's so busy and colourful, and there's so much happening all around you. The first time I went there, I hardly slept for two days! I just wanted to see everything all at once. There are shops, museums, galleries, parks, there's music, theatre and the cinemas. Everything's so loud and fast, it takes your breath away. You can forget all your troubles among so many people. You're just another person in the city; you can lose yourself in the crowds. Nobody knows you and nobody cares what you do.

Speaker 4
Every Friday, I go to the local cinema, buy a ticket and sit in seat 27C. It's the best seat in the house, and it doesn't matter what film they're showing. I'll sit there in the dark with a drink and something to eat, usually ice cream or some popcorn, and watch anything at all. I like every film I've ever seen there just because I saw it there. The important thing is that it's my seat and my secret place, because I'm the only one who knows about my routine. I've never told my friends or my parents where I go every Friday and I always go on my own. 27C is where I go to get away from everyone, I suppose, but I'm doing it with everyone else watching the same film.

Speaker 5
I've got a favourite place in the park near my house. Well, it's a special place for me and for my friends. We all get together under the big tree on the hill, right in the middle of the park. It's our tree, and nobody else can go there – well, that's what we say, anyway. Of course, it's not our private property; we just hang out together and keep each other company there. We don't make any particular arrangements beforehand, we just go there when we want to find each other, and someone usually turns up after a while. It's not much fun being alone, is it? And having your friends around makes everything much more fun.

Now you'll hear Part Three again.

That's the end of Part Three. Now turn to Part Four.

PART FOUR

You'll hear a radio interview with Neil Stanton, a fiction writer from Blackpool. For questions 24 – 30, choose the best answer (A, B or C). You now have one minute to look at Part Four.

F: Neil Stanton's a local author who's been writing fiction for ten years now. His latest novel takes us on an historic journey through our very own Blackpool and examines the colourful life of a fortune teller who was living in the city when it became a fashionable tourist centre in the late 1800s. Neil, what an interesting story! Tell us, why do you write fiction?

M: Writing fiction has been a passion all my life. Ever since I was a young boy, I've been writing stories, though I never published anything. I really enjoy making things up, actually, because there's a sense that you can do anything. It's like magic, really. It's hard work, though, to write something good. It may sound glamorous to be a writer, but it's not always so great. I have to rewrite a lot of what I do, but the end result is personally rewarding.

F: Where do your ideas come from?

M: Sometimes I get them when I'm travelling abroad. I've written a novel set in Italy, since I've travelled there a few times. I also get ideas when I'm sitting in my house alone because the peace and quiet allows me to concentrate on a story idea. I'd say that having interesting conversations with friends produces the best results, though. For two of my best-selling novels, the ideas came from those occasions.

F: How do you organise a story?

M: Well, that has changed a lot over time. It used to be, after I'd decided on a setting, I would focus on writing a plot outline. That seemed like the most logical way of planning, from beginning to end. As I developed as a writer, I decided to begin writing detailed descriptions of the characters first. It's helpful to think about exactly who you want your characters to be. I find that a story often writes itself once I've done that.

F: What do you find most difficult about writing?

M: Well, that's an important question. Many people think writing comes easily to writers, but it doesn't. Some get stuck finding a good ending. I think for me, the middle part gets tricky, because the story has to stay exciting all the way through. The worst, though?

<u>Writing too much!</u> In the end, <u>I have to cut a lot of stuff out</u>. Knowing when to stop isn't easy.

F: Is there a type of character you favour most?

M: I like all my characters to some degree, but I write about characters I like. When I read other people's books, I notice that sometimes there are loud, abrasive characters, and I don't usually like that quality in a character. But when that character says something funny and clever, then I'm impressed! I'm not too fond of shy characters, but when they're hard working, I find that I like them more. <u>I think I'm most fond of characters who surprise you.</u> So, when a loud character keeps quiet at the right moment, <u>I find that special.</u>

F: What books do you like to read?

M: Well, I used to really love reading fiction, especially in my youth. I would go to the local library just a few blocks from here and spend hours reading at the weekend, after I finished reading for my degree, of course. I still read fiction now and again, but <u>I've become a bit of a history fan.</u> I think that's why my latest novel has an element of history in it.

F: What advice have you got for writers who are just getting started?

M: Many writers want their work to be perfect. They spend too much time making every word in every sentence just right. I admire their attention to detail, but sometimes you've just got to let your fingers run across the keyboard. <u>You know, relax, let your ideas come naturally and enjoy what you're doing.</u> You can always go back and fix your mistakes later.

F: Neil, thanks very much for your time. It's been a pleasure.

Now you'll hear Part Four again.

That's the end of Part Four. That's the end of the test. Please stop now.

Practice Test 4

This is the First Certificate in English for Schools Listening Test. Practice Test 4.

I'm going to give you instructions for this test. At the start of each piece you'll hear this sound.
You'll hear each piece twice. Now look at Part One.

PART ONE

You'll hear people talking in eight different situations. For questions 1 – 8, choose the best answer (A, B or C).

One You hear two teenagers talking about a misunderstanding.

M: So, I told her she couldn't have been more wrong. I mean, can you imagine? She thought I had taken – no stolen is the word – her tablet PC without asking first. All I did was congratulate her on it! It's a very practical gadget to have!

F: Mmm … why did she think that, though? I mean, what gave her the impression you took it?

M: I've no idea! Really! But <u>what am I supposed to do now?</u> She's asking me to give it back to her, but I haven't got it. Someone else must have taken it when she wasn't looking.

F: Have you tried to explain that to her?

M: Of course I have, but she won't listen! She says she'll go to the headmaster if I don't give it back. <u>Oh, what am I going to do?</u> My parents are going to be furious!

Two You hear a mother and her son talking about a concert.

F: You know, Ryan, I don't think it's such a good idea. <u>Wherever this band plays, there's trouble!</u> Who else is going to be there? What time does it start and end?

And how many people will be there? What about safety measures? And will there be any adults around? Just to keep an eye on things?

M: Come on, Mum, really! I'm not ten, you know! I can look after myself. I'm not a child any more! And don't worry, Darren's older brother Peter will be there, too. His dad said it's OK for Darren to go if Peter goes with us. And I won't do anything silly, I promise, even if the others go wild! And I'll have my mobile on me if it makes you feel better! Oh, come on, please! <u>I've been looking forward to this gig for ages! I can't miss it!</u>

F: <u>Your dad and I will discuss it, and I'll tell you tonight.</u>

Three You hear two people talking.

M: That film we were going to see isn't on this week! I forgot to look in the newspaper to check it was still showing. Sorry.

F: Never mind, we can get the DVD and watch it together at home sometime. Do you want to go out? We can go somewhere else. There's that nice looking new Chinese restaurant on the High Street.

M: It looks nice, yes. Nice and expensive! Can't we just order some food and stay at home and watch something on TV? Pizza? I love pizza!

F: On a Saturday night? Come on! We should make an effort and do something we can't do during the week. <u>What else is on at the cinema?</u>

M: That new Jim Crow thriller. You know, we've seen the first two in the series.

F: <u>Sounds fine to me.</u>

M: Ok, but we have to eat something afterwards!

Four You hear a man talking about his job to a class of students.

As a kid I was very much into mysterious old cultures and lost civilisations and I thought Indiana Jones was awesome! I had a very romantic view of what an archaeologist did, you see. Later though, I realised that real archaeologists don't go on adventures like his, but work very slowly, meticulously even, and with great respect for the place they're excavating. <u>It's a job that requires a lot of patience and it's much harder work than it looks – you have to stay bending down under the scorching sun for hours at a time, examining minute fragments of pots, or brushing the earth very gently to uncover what's lying there and making sure you don't damage anything that's stayed intact for centuries or even millennia!</u> But the joy you feel when you discover something new is amazing, believe me, and you know you've played your part in putting together the pieces of the puzzle that make up the history of humanity!

Five You overhear a boy leaving a voicemail message.

Hi Monica, it's Kevin here. I just wanted to make sure you know about next week. We're meeting up at Jessica's place to talk about the project and who's going to do what. Erm … <u>I'm trying to find out what time suits everyone, so when you get this, please give me a call.</u> We're thinking maybe around early evening some time on Monday or Wednesday if everyone's OK with that? I'll be at home for the next two hours and if I'm not there, my mum will be there, so you can leave a message with her. Oh, and can you please also text Samantha to ask her about the times that suit her? Thanks!

Six You hear a sister and a brother arguing about household chores.

F: That's not fair, Andrew, I'll tell Mum! You promised you would do it this time! <u>It's your turn to wash the dishes anyway! Why do I have to do it again?</u> And I've got loads of homework, too! I just don't have time!

M: <u>Come on, Jill, just this once!</u> I'm meeting my mates at the square in ten minutes, and Kate'll be there, too. I don't want to be late! You know how much I like her! Pleeeaaase! And I promise I'll do the washing-up all week after today, I promise!

F: All week, eh? Is that a promise? Can I have it in writing, then?

M: Oh, Jill, you're mean. OK, then. I'll sign anything you want.

Seven You overhear a boy talking on the phone.

Anyway, remember that cool game I love playing on the laptop? You know the one I'm talking about, the one where you get to fly those helicopters? Well, the latest version's just come out, and I have to have it, you know? And I was wondering, I'm a bit short of cash at the moment because I spent all my pocket money on that other game – the one you like playing, too, so I was wondering if you could help me out a bit until next Friday. I'll get my pocket money then and I promise I'll pay you back straight away. And you can come and try out the game on my laptop if you want, too. So … what do you say?

Eight You hear a conversation between two friends in a shop.

M: What do you think about this material? Do you think it'd suit Dave's room?

F: Oh, I'm not too sure. Isn't it a bit too pale? He's a teenager now, so he probably likes darker, bolder colours.

M: Hmm … perhaps you're right, but I'm afraid that a darker blue might be too dull. His room faces north and it doesn't get enough sunlight in the afternoons, which is when he's there. If the colour is too dark, he'll need to have the lights on all day.

F: Yes, you're right, of course. I hadn't thought of that. … What do you think about this one here? This colour isn't too dark, is it?

M: No, but he hates green, and to be honest, I think that shade is more suitable for a girl's room.

F: Oh, do you think so?

That is the end of Part One. Now turn to Part Two.

PART TWO

You'll hear a young sailor called Jasmine Schultz talking about sailing solo. For questions 9 – 18, complete the sentences with a word or short phrase. You now have forty-five seconds to look at Part Two.

F: Good morning, everyone. Thanks for coming today. As most of you know, my name is Jasmine Schultz and I was invited here to talk about my favourite pastime … sailing solo! I'm proud to be one of the youngest people to have sailed around the world solo. Lots of people ask me if it was difficult to make the decision to take on such a challenge. I always explain to these people that, no, for me, it wasn't. I've been sailing practically all my life, so it was something I've always wanted to do, but it was difficult for my parents to accept my decision and let me go at first. Fortunately, they did in the end. And, you know, my journey actually began a long time before I set off! About a year before, to be exact. My boat, the Blue Dolphin, had to be prepared and properly equipped for such a long journey, and I had to do a first-aid course to learn how to treat myself in case of an accident.

Then the real journey began! At first, after I had set sail, it took me some time to adjust to being alone all the time. It was a bit difficult. I missed my family and friends, of course, and it wasn't always possible to get in touch with them via the Internet, especially when I was far from land or when there was stormy weather. But it was all worth it because I got to see all these places around the world that most people only dream about, and I got to make amazing new friends! Also, sailing with dolphins and whales next to

me was pretty extraordinary. Oh, and I enjoyed scuba-diving whenever and wherever I could! And I saw some sharks, too! From a safe distance, though! But I'd be lying if I didn't say that what I enjoyed most was being alone in such a huge ocean. I think I'll miss that feeling most of all now I've come back home.

It was a wonderful experience. My voyage was quite a long one. It lasted three hundred and sixty six days and I travelled twenty-seven thousand nautical miles! That's really a lot! And I learnt so many things sailing around the world. I think the most important lesson I learnt was that if you set your mind to doing something and are really, really determined, you can do it in the end, no matter what. Also, I've learnt to rely on myself and my skills and never to give up, however difficult the situation is. I had to face a lot of problems and yet I came through a winner! That was the most valuable lesson for me.

People often ask me what's changed for me since I came back home and I tell them, well, everything and nothing, really! Nothing seems different, but I have a totally different mentality now. I know I can do things alone and I'm much more mature now. I consider myself very lucky that my parents and friends supported me throughout this. Because it hasn't been easy for them, you see. Not easy at all.

I think I'm almost out of time, so just let me tell you a little about my plans before I go. First of all, I want to rest a bit and enjoy my family's company and then I want to do some more sailing. I want to sail round Cape Horn and I'm also thinking of later following the same route as Magellan, you know, the explorer. But I've got other plans, too. At the moment, I'm working on a screenplay based on my circumnavigation of the world. A studio in Hollywood has already bought the rights to make the film, so hopefully in a year or two you'll be able to see everything I went through on the big screen!

Now you'll hear Part Two again.

That is the end of Part Two. Now turn to Part Three.

PART THREE

You'll hear five people talking about memorable experiences they have had. For questions 19 – 23, choose from the list (A – H) what each speaker considers was an important lesson that they learned. Use the letters only once. There are three extra letters which you do not need to use. You now have thirty seconds to look at Part Three.

Speaker 1
I remember that night so well. It had been my birthday the day before and I'd already been given presents. Well, that night my parents said there was something waiting for me in my room. I could see them giggling and I was puzzled because it wasn't like my parents to play pranks or anything like that. So I went into my room, and it was dark, so I couldn't see anything. When I turned on the light at first I didn't notice anything different. Then I saw this picture of a cute pony on the wall. I'd always wanted a pony, but I thought I could never have one because my family weren't well off – we just couldn't afford one. I thought my parents had put the photo up on the wall just because it was pretty, so I turned to go back into the living room and then I noticed that there were some riding trousers and a riding hat hanging behind the door. I still didn't get it for a moment, but then the penny dropped and I screamed and ran back to the living room and hugged them. I was so excited! And that was my first pony, Rusty. I'll never forget her!

Speaker 2
Oh, it was really awesome! We felt that we were truly alone: no parents, no teachers, no adults at all! We had a feeling of absolute freedom. It was an illusion, of course, but still, that camp was the best thing ever! I'll never forget it! It was like

an adventure, like Robinson Crusoe, my best buddies and me! There was everything kids our age could ever wish for in that camp! Water slides, water sports, tree-houses, you name it, it was there! There was even a dark cave, complete with bats and creepy crawlies! You know how boys go crazy about stuff like that! And in the late afternoon, when we were exhausted from all the exploring and the games and the climbing trees, we either went for a swim, or we played games on the beach. It wasn't all idyllic, of course. There were fights and difficulties, but looking after myself and being responsible for my actions for the first time was really invaluable.

Speaker 3

It was a stupid moment, really. I don't know what I was thinking – it's just that all the other girls in the class wore make-up, and I wanted so much to have some, too, but my mum said, 'No, you're way too young for stuff like that.' And so, I was there in the shop, looking around, and I picked up a lip gloss – the colour was so pretty – and I slipped it in my pocket. I didn't think twice, I didn't even look around to see who might've been watching! I just knew I had to have it! Bad luck! The shop security guard was watching me the whole time, and as soon as I walked out of the shop, he caught me and then called my parents and the police. I just wanted to disappear. I've never felt so bad in my entire life! And my parents … I let them down so badly. I don't go out much now. It's not only that I've been grounded, it's that I don't want to. I feel like people will stare and point at me now and I think all my friends will be gossiping about me, too. It's terrible. I'm so very, very sorry for what I did! I wish I hadn't, but it's too late now. Well, the only thing I can say is I've been cured for good from trying something like that ever again!

Speaker 4

I'll never forget the first time we climbed the cliff. It was my father, my older brother and me. My mum and my grandparents didn't want to let me go because they said I was too young, but I knew better. I'd been begging my dad to take me with them for so long I'd almost lost count of the times! Everybody said, 'Oh, you're too young to climb. You'll have to wait!' Well, I was sure I could do it and I was actually better than my older brother! I got to know something that day – you're never too young to do something if you really want it very, very much! The climb was exhilarating! It was difficult, yes, but my dad was there to help us and we got to the top of the cliff in no time. That was the first, unforgettable time and I haven't stopped climbing since – the sense of freedom and achievement is phenomenal and I wouldn't change it for anything in the world!

Speaker 5

Well, something that'll definitely always stay in my mind is the first day at my new school. I was rather shy and timid as a child and didn't have many friends – I preferred to stay with my family, and my older brother was my best friend. But then we moved to a new town and I had to go to a new school. I remember that my mum made sure I had everything I needed and that my school uniform was ready for my first day and she spent hours talking to me about how I needn't worry and that everything was going to turn out fine. But I spent night after night sleepless with worry, thinking about what it was going to be like and if the teacher would like me and whether the other kids in my class would be nice to me or not. So that week, before actually going to the new school, was an absolute nightmare for me. As it turned out, I needn't have worried. The school was fantastic. I made a lot of new friends and became very popular in the end! It's interesting really, how changing schools actually changed me as a person as well.

Now you'll hear Part Three again.

That's the end of Part Three. Now turn to Part Four.

PART FOUR

You'll hear a conversation between two people, Celia and Adam, who took part in an expedition to Mongolia, and a friend of theirs called Terry, who wants to know what it was like. For questions 24 – 30, choose the best answer (A, B or C). You now have one minute to look at Part Four.

M1: So, come on now Celia, tell all! What was it like?

F: Oh, Terry, it was fantastic! You can't even begin to imagine it!

M2: Yes, it was really amazing! All that open space, the wide blue skies, the steppe, I can't describe it!

M1: What did you do first of all? Where did you set off from?

F: We got on a train on the Trans-Mongolian railway in Beijing. The train isn't very comfortable if you aren't travelling first class, but we didn't mind. It was interesting to share a compartment with people from China and Mongolia and see how people from other cultures pass the time when travelling. And even this first part of the journey – before you even reach Mongolia – is unbelievable! The train goes through such extraordinary landscape – it goes past the Great Wall of China and then into Outer Mongolia and the Gobi Desert. The whole thing was breathtaking … just spectacular!

M2: When we arrived at the capital, Ulaanbaatar, we walked around the city for a while and then …

M1: What's Ulaanbaatar like? Is it interesting?

F: It's a very unusual place, you know. It's mostly flat! The horizon stretches for miles in every direction. And it's very cold!

M2: Yes, it's the coldest capital city in the world. I bet you didn't know that!

M1: Really?

F: Yes, really, and I'll tell you something else I bet you didn't know. You know how Genghis Khan is considered a bloodthirsty and fearsome conqueror, who invaded countries and killed thousands of people in wars in Asia and Eastern Europe, right? Well, when we visited the Museum of Mongolian History we learnt that there he's regarded as a great leader and a national hero. Well, after all, what he did was no mean feat.

M1: Oh? What did he do?

M2: He managed to unite most of Asia and parts of Europe into one empire – it stretched from Europe to the Pacific! It was huge!

F: Yes, well, and after we left Ulaanbaatar, we decided to go trekking into the Gobi Desert. And we didn't do it on horses! We went camel riding!

M2: Yes, and you know, their camels are Bactrian camels, with two humps – very funny! And we visited Gandan Monastery, one of the very few Buddhist monasteries that remain in the country. It's very important, and its architecture is very interesting. There's also an amazing statue of Megjid Janraisig there – he's referred to as the lord who looks in every direction. It's twenty five metres tall and covered in precious stones! Incredible, really!

M1: Wow! It sounds amazing! Oh, I'm so jealous! I really want to go to Mongolia now!

F: Well, you should. But if I were you, I'd avoid the winter – the weather can be really horrible! Did you know, even in summer it can vary from freezing rain, fog and storms to temperatures of thirty-nine degrees centigrade? But I guess that's the best time to go. It's crazy! Imagine what it's like the rest of the year!

M2: And if you do go, you must definitely visit the 'singing dunes' in the Gobi Desert.

M1: Singing dunes? What are they?

F: Oh, there are so many stories about them. We heard several different versions on the train and that's why we decided to visit them. They're sand dunes that make a funny noise when it's windy. We loved it, didn't we, Adam? It really sounds like they're singing in the wind!

M2: Yes, and we took lots of photos there. Do you want to see them?

M1: Sure, show me, but first, what else did you do?

F: We went trekking in the Altai mountain range. That was an adventure, and a very beautiful one. The landscape there is completely different, with high mountains, river gorges and lakes. There's even a glacier! Imagine that!

M2: Yes, and Celia, do you remember? We met some Kazakh people who were hunting with eagles, and one of them was training his new eagle! Awesome birds, actually.

M1: Hunting with eagles?

F: Well, in Europe people use dogs for hunting, but in Mongolia they train eagles!

M1: Imagine that!

F: Oh, and we also explored Karakorum!

M1: Karakorum? What's that?

M2 and F: It's the ...

F: No, you go ahead Adam, you'll explain it better. You're the history specialist.

M2: It was the ancient capital of Mongolia. There's very little left of it, but the ruins are spectacular! There's a statue of a huge stone turtle that's almost intact. And there are lots of other interesting artefacts to see, but most importantly, it was the city where Genghis Khan launched his first attacks from.

F: Although there isn't much left of the town, its ruins and history are very interesting! We really enjoyed that trip, didn't we, Adam?

M1: Wow! You've got me convinced it's a trip worth making.

M2: Oh, absolutely. It was the trip of a lifetime!

Now you'll hear Part Four again.

That's the end of Part Four. That's the end of the test. Please stop now.

Practice Test 5

This is the First Certificate in English for Schools Listening Test. Practice Test 5.
I'm going to give you instructions for this test. At the start of each piece you'll hear this sound.
You'll hear each piece twice. Now look at Part One.

PART ONE

You'll hear people talking in eight different situations. For questions 1 – 8, choose the best answer (A, B or C).

One   You hear part of an interview with a film director.

F: Thanks so much for agreeing to speak to our school newspaper, Mr Ryman. OK, first question. You've been working in the film industry since the 1980s. What's it been like to work in films all these years?

M: Well, I suppose it's changed a lot over time. The films I did when I was studying to be a director were the most fun to do, although I can't say they were my best. I really didn't know what I was doing, to be honest. But we were all so young: me, the actors, the crew. We were all friends, you know? It's different now. For example, take my last film. It was a greater piece of cinema than my earlier work, but the experience of making it was nowhere near as enjoyable as when I was younger.

Two   You overhear a woman leaving a voicemail message.

Hi Josh, it's Mum calling. Listen, I forgot to tell you this morning that we're going to Granny and Grandpa's house for dinner tonight, so be home at six this evening please, so we can be ready to leave. I don't want to stay long because your dad and I have got a

busy day tomorrow, but we haven't seen them in a while, and it'll be nice to spend some time with them. Oh, and let your sister know when you see her. She ran out of the door this morning without her phone, so I can't reach her. Will you do that? Thanks, see you later.

Three   You hear a brother and sister talking about a holiday.

F: Kyle, I am *not* spending every waking hour on the beach when we go on holiday!

M: Why not? That's where all the fun's at. You don't want to be stuck in a hotel room the whole time, do you? That's so boring!

F: No, of course not. What's the point of going on holiday if you're going to be stuck indoors? No, I just can't stand being in the sun all day. Why don't we spend half our time at the beach and the other half at the shopping centre?

M: You want to go shopping while we're on holiday? Hmm, I don't think I'll be joining you for that.

Four   You overhear two friends talking about a surprise party.

F: Are you going to Monica's surprise birthday party on Saturday, Martin?

M: Don't you mean 'birthday party' now, Jill? Haven't you heard? There's no 'surprise' about it.

F: What do you mean?

M: Well, we were all sitting in the canteen having lunch, and I suppose someone forgot to tell Rachel that the party was a surprise, so she started talking about it right in front of Monica. She did feel really bad about ruining the surprise.

F: No way! What a shame! So what are you going to do now? Is there still going to be a party?

M: Well, yes, and I'm sure it will be fun, just not as *much* fun.

Five   You overhear two friends talking about shopping.

F1: It's amazing how much people spend on clothes and accessories these days. Can you believe how much Jessica paid for her new boots?

F2: I know. That's a complete waste of money, in my opinion. For that amount of money you could buy three pairs of shoes at a normal shop.

F1: Yeah, I mean, I'm sure they'll last a long time and they're probably good quality and everything, but I think she paid for the brand name, really.

F2: Definitely. And how many times is she going to wear them? It'll be summer soon, and I doubt she'll wear them much then.

Six   You overhear two friends in the street.

F: Jason, can you wait a minute? I need to run into this shop for a second to pick up a few things for work.

M: No, Lisa, we're going to be late. We can't waste any more time.

F: What are you talking about? We have at least thirty minutes before the curtain goes up.

M: Yeah, but it drives me crazy to have to climb over a load of people just to sit down. Besides, we haven't even picked up our tickets yet.

F: Well, why don't you go ahead then and I'll catch up with you in a minute?

M: Fine, but I'm not waiting for you before I go in this time. The last time you were late we ended up missing the first half of the performance.

Seven   You hear a teacher give an important announcement to her class.

OK, class. Today we're going to have a safety drill. It's in case we need to leave quickly in an emergency situation such as a fire. So, as soon as you hear the bell, which will ring three times, I want each and every one of you to get up, walk calmly to the front of the class and leave through the classroom door. Once you're out of the classroom, I want you to walk to the end of the hallway, go down the stairs and out through the emergency exit door at the bottom of the stairs. Go outside and wait in the courtyard area. I'll be down there right after you. And remember ... no running!

Eight You hear a weather forecast on a television programme.

Today's temperatures are going to dive down into the single digits, with clouds forming late this afternoon and a forecast of light frost overnight. Tomorrow morning it'll be cloudy around sunrise with temperatures still in the low numbers. We'll see a break in the clouds sometime around ten and <u>we'll see some signs of relief from the cold around mid-afternoon</u>. Don't get too excited about it being warmer in the evening, though, as it's likely to be cold again tomorrow night, and we're looking at another night of frosty weather, especially in the central lowland areas.

That is the end of Part One. Now turn to Part Two.

PART TWO

You'll hear a head teacher called June Parnell talking about schools and education. For questions 9 – 18, complete the sentences with a word or short phrase. You now have forty-five seconds to look at Part Two.

F: Good morning. My name is June Parnell and, as most of you already know, I'm the head teacher at Moss Hill School. Today, I'd like to discuss some of the questions that I'm often asked by parents, teachers and students in regards to schools and education.

I suppose one of the most common questions that I get asked is how schools have changed since I was a student. First of all, the school curriculum offers a lot more subjects these days. Of course traditional subjects are still taught, but there's now a wider range of more <u>creative</u> subjects like drama for students to do. That kind of variety wasn't available to us when I was at school. But, I think it's obvious that studying a wider range of subjects is good for students. I think that it makes the whole experience of going to school a lot more interesting. Students can explore different subjects and also get a well-balanced education.

Despite that, I get students asking me why they still have to study 'boring' subjects like science and maths. Firstly, I think if subjects like those are taught well, then they're not boring at all! Secondly, subjects like maths, science and English teach students really important skills that they'll use throughout their life – things like reading and <u>spelling</u>, or sums that let them work out how much pocket money they need to save each week to buy a new pair of trainers. Or how many hours they need to do a certain amount of homework, which is the topic of another question I hear a lot. Students ask why they've got so much homework to do. If you teachers get asked that, then tell your students this: in order to get it all done, the most important thing to remember is not to panic. This actually makes it harder for them to <u>concentrate</u>. Then tell them that they should make a list of the homework they have and when they need to hand it in – it's all about careful planning.

Another thing students worry about is whether their exams will be more difficult than the previous year's, but normally this isn't true. In order to make sure that we test students to the same level each year, we have <u>national standards</u> in place for exams. And – of course – if part of an exam is actually a little bit harder, then all the students will find it more difficult, so they'll take that into account when they mark it. It's nothing to worry about.

Students worry a lot. I've got a nephew, named Harry, who's going to <u>secondary school</u> in September and will

be starting IT lessons there. He was worried that he might need a laptop or computer at home, but I told him that today's schools were fully-equipped with IT facilities that were available to students during and after school. In fact, one of the advantages of modern schools is that poorer families don't have to go to the <u>expense</u> of buying a computer for the home. But of course most households these days do have at least one computer of some description.

Another big concern of students these days is getting extra help if they need it. But most schools now run <u>extra tuition</u> sessions after school or at lunchtime. The main advantage of this is that students benefit a lot from knowing that support is available, whether it's with understanding a maths problem or getting some <u>revision tips</u> before a big exam. And that's just one way that education is more appealing to students these days. Most teachers nowadays believe that education should be fun and accessible to students. Lots of schools are now giving students the opportunity to take a more hands-on approach to learning. Take <u>school trips</u>, for instance. At our school, every class goes on at least one a term. They visit art galleries, museums and even demonstration days at science centres.

To sum up, I'd just like to say that schools have changed a lot since my day and they're going to change even more. We can already see the changes that <u>technology</u> has brought to schools, and I think that this will continue. Interactive software and the increase in lessons being taught through the use of IT and computers is the future of school education.

Now you'll hear Part Two again.

That is the end of Part Two. Now turn to Part Three.

PART THREE

You'll hear five people talking about their friends. For questions 19 – 23, choose from the list (A – H) how each speaker feels about friendship. Use the letters only once. There are three extra letters which you do not need to use. You now have thirty seconds to look at Part Three.

Speaker 1
Most of my friends are from my hockey team but they don't go to my school. Don't get me wrong, I have friends from school, but it's different with them. We just all got put into the same school because we live near each other. Me and my hockey friends are all really close because, well, <u>we all love hockey</u>! I'm actually glad that my best friends don't go to my school because, even though I have to travel a little way to see them, it means that when we see each other, it's a real event. <u>When we meet up we have loads to talk about,</u> like our upcoming matches and what happened at the last training session. It's brilliant!

Speaker 2
When I was young, we travelled around a lot because my dad was always changing jobs. It was actually OK, and the best thing is that I made lots of friends in loads of different places! The hard part is getting to see each other, which we don't really manage to do with homework and with exams coming up, plus <u>most of them live pretty far away. We all stay in touch, though</u>, and I'm always on my computer writing emails. My two best friends, Tom and Simon, even send me things in the post! It's funny, I don't feel like I haven't seen them for months, because we talk so often, and actually <u>I don't think that we could be closer as friends, even if we lived down the road from each other!</u>

Speaker 3
I've known my best friend for as long as I can remember. Our mums were friends when they were at university together, and now Sally and I are inseparable! It wasn't always like that, though. Sally and her mum used to live miles away, so I'd only

see her about once a month. We used to write each other letters in between seeing each other. I'm glad we did, though, because I don't think we would be such good friends now if we hadn't tried so hard to stay in touch. But we did, and now when Sally comes over, we read the letters and laugh about when we were younger. Actually, she comes over all the time now because she's my next-door neighbour! Her family moved to my town last summer, so I see her most days. I still call her and email her, though, because you have to work hard at having a really good friendship, even if that means just sending a text message and letting the person know you're thinking about them. It definitely works like that for me and Sally!

Speaker 4

My parents always nag me about spending time with my younger cousins. We used to play together when we were kids and we got on just fine – in fact, we had a lot of fun. But I'm older now, and they just seem really immature to me. I mean, they still like playing board games like we used to when we were all younger. It sounds terrible, but I have better things to do with my time now, especially with school and being part of the basketball team. Of course, I still see them at family occasions, but I prefer to spend my spare time with my school friends. At least we're the same age!

Speaker 5

My friends are my life. I really don't know what I'd do without them. I don't have any brothers or sisters, you see, so my mates are like my family. We all hang around together in a big group, and I know that I can always turn to them if I have a problem. The only difficulty is trying to get us all together to meet up. I swear I spend half my life on my mobile making arrangements! If I'm not texting my best friend, Sue, then I'm emailing my other friends. Sometimes I'll be online all evening just chatting. It's great really, though, because once we all meet up we have a lot of fun. There are always stories to be told and gossip to catch up on.

Now you'll hear Part Three again.

That's the end of Part Three. Now turn to Part Four.

PART FOUR

You'll hear an interview with a teenager called Kelly Turner, who recently returned from a trip abroad. For questions 24 – 30, choose the best answer (A, B or C). You now have one minute to look at Part Four.

M: European cities are becoming more and more popular as holiday destinations for people who want to get away from traditional beach holidays and experience other cultures. Kelly Turner, who has just returned from a long weekend in Paris, speaks to us about the French capital and all its charms. So, Kelly, what made you go to Paris?

F: Well, I'm studying French at school, and with the speaking exams coming up my mum and dad suggested we go, so that I could practise my French. My language teacher was thrilled when I told her, especially since I couldn't make it on the school trip over there last September.

M: How did you get there?

F: I wanted to fly, because I thought it would be quicker, and we would've had more time in the city, but we ended up taking the train, and it was really fast anyway. It was definitely much easier than driving and getting the ferry, as my auntie suggested. Plus, you don't really need a car when you get to Paris because public transport there is so convenient; it's really easy to get around the city. Anyway, we were happy enough on the train; it was very comfortable and not as pricey as flying. I would definitely recommend it!

M: What was the most memorable part of the trip?

F: Seeing the Eiffel Tower was pretty spectacular, especially at night when it was all lit up, but my favourite bit had to be something that happened before the boat cruise on the River Seine. I'll never forget my dad trying to buy tickets for it in French. He was gesturing and pointing at the river like a madman! When the ticket seller asked him what he wanted exactly – in perfect English – I couldn't stop laughing. It was hilarious!

M: What would you say is the one thing that all tourists should see or do in Paris?

F: A trip down to the catacombs is a must! They're a series of tunnels that run underneath the city. In 1786, human bones were transported down to this network of tunnels after the city's graveyards became completely full, and the Parisians had to decide where to bury the dead. For years, thousands of skulls and bones of all shapes and sizes have lined the walls in perfect rows. To be honest, it was a bit creepy seeing all those bones, but it was pretty amazing as well. All visitors should take the time to see the catacombs; it's really worth it.

M: What did you think of the French cuisine?

F: I'd heard lots of stories about how the French eat things like frogs' legs and snails, so I was a bit apprehensive about the food, but I needn't have been; it was amazing! We ate out both nights at restaurants. On the first night, I had duck with orange sauce, which is a typical French dish. I tried some different things like pâtés as well and found that I liked them, which is unusual because I'm quite a fussy eater.

M: What can you tell us about Parisian culture?

F: Where do I start? There's so much to say! I guess when people think of Paris they think of wonderful buildings, fabulous paintings and, of course, fashion. It's one of the big fashion capitals of the world and attracts thousands of designers every year. People also associate Paris with art, and there are some amazing galleries, like the Louvre, where Da Vinci's *Mona Lisa* is displayed. In fact, I think a lot of foreigners visit Paris for the art scene more than anything else. Not me, though! I think French cinema is the best part of the culture. France is often called 'the birthplace of cinema', and there are lots of old cinemas around the city that you can visit. Unfortunately, we just didn't have time.

M: So, did you get to practise your French?

F: Yes, a lot! It was really great to be able to speak in French wherever we went. I mean, when you're at school you have two hours of French lessons a week and that's it. You never really have a chance to practise speaking the language. Paris was great because everyone spoke to me in French, and even though a lot of people there speak English, especially the younger people, they were always keen to talk to us in their own language! I definitely feel like it was good practice for my exam.

M: Well, thanks, Kelly. It's been great talking to you about your trip.

Now you'll hear Part Four again.

That's the end of Part Four. That's the end of the test. Please stop now.

Practice Test 6

This is the First Certificate in English for Schools Listening Test. Practice Test 6.
I'm going to give you instructions for this test. At the start of each piece you'll hear this sound.
You'll hear each piece twice. Now look at Part One.

PART ONE

You'll hear people talking in eight different situations. For questions 1 – 8, choose the best answer (A, B or C).

One   You hear a reporter talking about travel.
        Tonight we've got an exciting programme for you

about travel in southern Europe. We visited the region during the spring when it's not quite so hot to check out some interesting locations. Our travels took us to the shores of Greece, to visit villages that have been there for hundreds of years alongside gorgeous beaches and clear blue seas. In nearby Italy we visited the world famous Mount Vesuvius in order to explore the ancient ruins of Pompeii. We also sought to get an idea of what life was like back then, and of course to see the kind of destruction a volcano can create. But we start our programme in Spain, with a visit to the amazing Prado Museum to see the paintings of some of Spain's most famous artists, and to enjoy cosmopolitan life in Madrid. Let's go!

Two   You overhear two friends talking about books.

F: Have you read any good books lately, Henry?

M: Yeah, Lindsay, I just finished a murder mystery that was set in the early 1960s. It was very well-written, and I liked reading about what life was like back then. The plot was full of suspense, too.

F: Hmm … that sounds interesting. Well, I've just started reading a book called *Silent Story*. It was written by a woman who couldn't read until the age of 25. After she learned how to read, she decided to write about her experiences when she was growing up.

M: Wow, Lindsay, that's quite an accomplishment!

F: I know, it's really inspirational. It's much better than the romance novel I was reading last month. I had to give up on that one!

Three   You hear part of an interview with a musician.

M: Thanks for coming to our show today, Mary. You've been a musician since you were fourteen years old, is that correct?

F: Actually, I learned how to play the violin at quite an early age. My mother plays the violin and I used to play with one of her old violins when I was a child. I picked it up quite easily actually, and my mother helped me with it for a while, in her spare time. We used to practise for hours together. It was quite good fun! Then my parents decided to hire a professional violinist, Maxwell Crawford, to train me. It was difficult in the beginning, because he taught me new ways of playing, but in the end, I found the hard work to be rewarding.

Four   You overhear two friends talking about shopping.

F1: Lisa, you're not seriously telling me you want to go shopping to Lindell's again, are you? I'm bored of going there.

F2: The thing is, they *do* have the best prices in town, and I really like their clothes. Don't you?

F1: I can't say I'm that keen on their clothes. At least not keen enough to go there twice in one week. But OK, they've got a lot of things at good prices, I can't argue with you on that.

F2: Hmm, well, I suppose we could try somewhere different if you like.

Five   You hear two friends in a study hall.

F: I'm not sure how much more studying I can do. My eyes are starting to hurt!

M: Do you want to take a break in half an hour? We can go to that new burger place in Long Street.

F: Oh, I think I've heard about that place. It's near my favourite music shop. We can go and have a snack, then go to the music shop before we come back to the study hall.

M: OK, that sounds like a good plan. So let's do a bit more here and then go.

Six   You hear a girl leaving a voicemail message.

Hi Mum, it's me. I'm calling because I'm going to be late home from basketball practice tonight. The coach

wants us to be prepared for the tournament this weekend, so he's really going to work us hard. I talked to Alicia about getting a lift with her mum, so anyway, I think I should be home around eight o'clock, in time for supper. Oh, and Mum … there's something I forgot to do … there's a programme on Channel 10 at seven o'clock. It's a basketball match that I really wanted to see. Would you mind setting the DVD recorder so I can watch it later? Thanks, Mum. See you at supper.

Seven   You hear a girl talking about a play she has just seen.

I wasn't sure what to think of the play in the beginning. I'll admit I actually considered leaving before the end of the first act. There didn't seem to be a lot of action going on, and it was difficult to hear the actors. True, I was sitting close to the back, but that shouldn't matter. An actor should deliver his or her lines so that everyone in the audience can hear. Anyway, the play got better as the evening went on, and in the end, I think the story was really quite interesting. I just think it would have been better with a bit more passion from the actors. The sets and costumes were gorgeous though, so I'd applaud the set designers rather than the actors!

Eight   You hear a woman talking to a class.

I wanted to pop into the class today to give you some important information about the reading club. Many of you have signed up for the club, and I'm really excited to see so many students interested in reading books and talking about them. We've got a great selection of books to discuss this term, so I think you're really going to enjoy it. We are, however, having a slight problem with our meeting place in the library. They're fixing the ceiling, as there appears to be a leak in the roof, so the room is quite a mess at the moment. So we're going to use room 315 instead, which is just down the hall. It will start at the same time, of course, at 5pm this Thursday, so I look forward to seeing you there!

That is the end of Part One. Now turn to Part Two.

PART TWO

You'll hear a young musician named Eric Moseley talking about himself and his band. For questions 9 – 18, complete the sentences with a word or short phrase. You now have forty-five seconds to look at Part Two.

M: My name is Eric Moseley and I'm the drummer in the band *Modern Idols*. Although lots of my fans don't know it, the drums weren't the first instrument I started to play. My dad used to play in a band when he was younger, and he played the guitar. I started playing around with it, and I enjoyed it. But my close friend Danny Wilson, our lead singer, had a drum set and when I first had a go on that, I fell in love with it. I think I love the drums so much because it's an instrument that takes a lot of energy to play. You also have to have a really good sense of rhythm because you have to hit each drum at exactly the right moment over and over again. And that takes a lot of practice. I'm actually still at university so if I've got a lot of studying to do, I only practise at the weekends. After my classes finish in June, I plan to practise something like 40 hours a week, which is quite a lot!

Fans ask me if there's a certain type of music that inspires me – I enjoy a lot of different types of music. Nearly every type of music has got a drum sound in it somewhere. Even classical music includes drums. That really impresses me, I must say, because they sound so grand in an orchestra. Of course, we play rock music, so we're never going to sound like that!

When I say 'we' I mean me and the other band members. They're all brilliant! Danny and I have been friends for years. We have another friend, George Carlson – he's our guitarist – and our fourth member, Frankie Carlson, is George's cousin, and he's our keyboard player. I hadn't met Frankie before we started the band, but he's a great keyboard player and I'm glad we have him.

We've been on two tours since we started. Our first tour was great fun, although it was stressful because we hadn't done anything like it before. On our second tour we went to many of the same places but I noticed that our audiences were larger. That was a great feeling because people were starting to notice us. And we like large audiences! It's strange, but when you're standing on stage, it looks like there might be millions of people out there! Actually, I think there were around a thousand people at our last show. It's quite a change from the first time we played when there were only about a hundred people in the crowd. I remember this one time at a show something really odd happened. Someone tossed a hamburger at us! I saw it fly over my head and land behind me. Don't ask me why that happened. I just kept playing!

The band is really happy at the moment because we're going into the recording studio to record our third album. We've been practising the new music for a while now, so it's time to record it. We've got two weeks recording time booked, and it's going to be a lot of work, but I'm really excited about it. And then, of course, we'll be giving more concerts. I really enjoy it when my family come to my concerts, like my sister and my mum and dad. But, you know, probably the one person I'd love to see in the audience — and don't laugh at me for saying this — is my grandma, because I love her very much, but she would never come to one of my concerts at all. She hates rock music! I'd love to play for her though.

Now you'll hear Part Two again.

That is the end of Part Two. Now turn to Part Three.

PART THREE

You'll hear five people talking about phobias. For questions 19 – 23, choose from the list (A – H) what each speaker's phobia is. Use the letters only once. There are three extra letters which you do not need to use. You now have thirty seconds to look at Part Three.

Speaker 1
There are some things I would probably be afraid of if I saw them, like big animals for example. I mean, if I was walking in a jungle and I came across a lion or a tiger, I'd probably be scared silly! But I've seen them in the zoo and they seem pretty quiet. So if I saw one in a jungle and it didn't seem like it was going to attack me, then maybe I wouldn't be afraid at all. But I'm definitely scared of at least one animal I've seen, namely this little mouse that lives in the wall of our living room. I've seen him run across the floor twice, and I screamed and jumped on the sofa both times.

Speaker 2
I have a fear that I don't like to talk about because it seems like such a silly thing to be afraid of. Maybe it's because I've watched too many scary films. At least that's what my dad tells me. Honestly, I'm not afraid of anything really – heights, bugs, flying – all the really scary stuff. Those things don't bother me at all. Really, it's only when it's late at night, the lights are off all over the house and it's really quiet that I get scared, especially if I hear a funny noise. It scares me so much, in fact, that I sometimes sleep with my lamp on.

Speaker 3
I enjoy travelling for many different reasons. I love planes because of the take-off. It's very exciting, really. The plane starts going very fast and it shakes a bit, then it's suddenly calm. I like trains too, because they're kind of relaxing, with the sound they make as they travel over the tracks. Even cars don't bother me. I can't wait to have one, one day. But I'll never forget one year when my family travelled to Jersey, an island south of England.

I'd never been so frightened in my life. All I kept thinking about was: what if we hit some rocks? How would we get back to land? Believe me, if my family had let me take the plane back home, I would have!

Speaker 4
There's a reason I've got my phobia, and it's because of something that happened to me as a child. When I was eight years old, I visited my aunt and uncle's ranch in Canada and we went horse riding. It was great fun. I went riding with my aunt through the wilderness around their house. It's quite exciting to ride on a horse. Sometimes they go really fast, and they're generally very nice and loving creatures. They're not, however, so gentle when they're threatened, as we were when we came across a pack of wolves in the forest. The horses my aunt and I were on started galloping, and we got away, but the whole experience was so terrifying that I decided I wouldn't get back on one ever again.

Speaker 5
I used to think I was just afraid of flying. I hate travelling by plane, and the two times I've done it have been two of the worst experiences of my life. Well, then my family went on a trip to London, and you know the famous London Eye, right? The giant wheel that takes you so many metres into the air, so you can see the whole city across the River Thames for miles and miles? Well, that's when I discovered my true fear. No, it isn't of amusement park rides! I love those, but only the ones that stay close to the ground. No, that's when I realised – planes, the London Eye, skyscrapers, or any other kind of tall building – that's where I feel my fear. I'm definitely staying away from those.

Now you'll hear Part Three again.

That's the end of Part Three. Now turn to Part Four.

PART FOUR

You'll hear two teenagers talking about funny things that have happened to them, their friends and other people after accidentally falling asleep. For questions 24 – 30, choose the best answer (A, B or C). You now have one minute to look at Part Four.

F: So, Greg, tell me what happened to you the other day in maths that you said I'd never believe.

M: Well, I suppose I had it coming, Carla. I'm always playing jokes on everyone in class. You know what I'm like. But I would never have imagined in a million years that the entire class would do this to me. You know I've been very busy lately, what with football practice and studying and everything. Well, I was so incredibly tired in the maths class the other day that I fell asleep. No big deal, right? But when I woke up, I was surrounded by completely different students!

F: Oh, my goodness! No way! That's hilarious! How did that happen?

M: When the bell rang, which I somehow didn't hear even though it's incredibly loud, Mr Briggs told the class to quietly get up and leave. Then he asked the other class to come in and sit down. When I finally woke up, I thought I was still sleeping! Actually I thought I was dreaming! Mr Biggs was teaching the class like normal. I looked over at the other kids and some of them were giggling a bit. It was then that I realised what had happened and everyone burst out laughing! It was really funny, actually. Like I said, Carla, I deserved it!

F: That's a very funny story, Greg! Well, talking of sleeping in strange places – something happened to me recently. It wasn't quite as funny as what happened to you, but anyway … I was at the cinema with Jessica the other day, and we were watching a romantic comedy. There were probably about twenty-five people in the cinema, so it wasn't packed. Anyway, in the row in front, a man and woman were sitting together, and the man had fallen asleep. You could tell because his head had fallen backwards and was tilted to the side. The woman was really upset, I guess because she thought it was rude.

M: Maybe they hadn't known each other long.

F: Yeah, who knows? Anyway, after about two minutes, she got up and left! Can you believe that? She didn't even wake him up. She just left him there. But then, after about five minutes, the guy started snoring really loudly. It was awful! You couldn't follow what was going on in the film at all. People started whispering to him to try to wake him up, but nothing worked. Some people even threw popcorn at him! Well, his snoring basically ruined the film for me, but I suppose the whole thing was funny in a way!

M: Actually, I think that *is* really funny. I hope I wasn't snoring in class!

F: Ha ha! I hope not! Well, another funny sleeping story happened to my friend Rebecca. She used to have this weird habit of falling asleep at night, like normal, and then sleepwalking. She's done lots of strange things, like woken up in the bathroom, or on the living room sofa. But apparently one time, she walked into the garage, climbed into the back of her brother's car, and slept there the whole night!

M: Oh, wow. That *is* strange!

F: Well, the funny thing was that her brother didn't notice her sleeping in the back of his car when he left for college in the morning. So there's Rebecca, sleeping in the back of her brother's car, in her pyjamas no less, and her brother's going to college. Rebecca still hadn't woken up by the time they arrived. Her brother got out of the car and slammed the door. She woke up and got a huge shock – she saw her brother walking off and started yelling at him to come back. Luckily he heard her, came back and took her back home!

M: That's unbelievable! I don't know if that's funny, or scary!

F: No, it's not really SO funny when you think about it, because she could have hurt herself. What if she walked out of the house and into the street? She visited a sleep therapist after that, though, and that's helped a lot. It still worries her a bit, but they joke about it now. She says she keeps a spare set of clothes in her brother's car, in case she wakes up in the back seat in her pyjamas again.

M: Well, that makes me feel better about falling asleep in class, anyway!

Now you'll hear Part Four again.

That's the end of Part Four. That's the end of the test. Please stop now.

Practice Test 7

This is the First Certificate in English for Schools Listening Test. Practice Test 7.
I'm going to give you instructions for this test. At the start of each piece you'll hear this sound.
You'll hear each piece twice. Now look at Part One.

PART ONE

You'll hear people talking in eight different situations. For questions 1 – 8, choose the best answer (A, B or C).

One   You hear an announcement on the radio.
This evening on Radio Nine, we have a change to the normal schedule. Tonight's episode of *The Secret Story*, our series featuring the fictional investigative reporter Frank McGinty, will now be broadcast tomorrow at the same time. This week, McGinty, played by Larry Shaw, uncovers a scandal involving a government minister and a national newspaper … an episode not to be missed. In place of *The Secret Story*, we present the first in a new series of interviews with famous figures from the world of journalism, *The World of the News*, in which some great writers share their fascinating stories.

Two   You hear a woman complaining on the telephone.

Hello, yes, this is Mrs Simons. I've called you twice already today and I still haven't received a satisfactory reply to my question. This is really quite unacceptable. I don't expect to be treated in such a manner, especially by an establishment of your reputation. I'm sick and tired of waiting for an answer! I will definitely not be staying with you again, and I intend to recommend that my friends find alternative accommodation if they visit your city. For the third time, I simply want to know if any of your staff found the watch I left in my room when I checked out.

Three You hear a teacher talking to a student's mother.

M: Hello, Mrs Asquith, please take a seat. Thank you for coming in for a chat.

F: Yes, hello, Mr Eden. No problem at all.

M: I'd like to talk to you about your son, Martin. He seems to be having a problem in the mornings. I've warned him, but he hasn't improved, I'm afraid. I don't really understand it because he's usually such a well-behaved boy.

F: Well, he's been having trouble waking up for school recently. But his schoolwork is fine, isn't it?

M: Oh, his marks are fine … always fine. He couldn't work any harder in class, but being late all the time means he misses part of the lesson and has to catch up, which sometimes disturbs the class.

F: I'll have a word with him, Mr Eden. And I can assure you that it won't happen again.

Four   You hear someone talking on the radio about his job.

F: Were you always attracted by the sea?

M: It has a deep meaning for me and my family. I was born in a town on the coast and my life has always been connected with the water. My father and my grandfather were both sailors, and my wife's relations were all fishermen. The sea is very familiar to me, and naturally it influences me when I express myself. It's almost as if I can't escape it. It's always there.

F: Most of your best work is indeed about the sea.

M: Yes, my painting seems to reflect the ocean. I can get that feeling into my art with very little effort, it seems. I need the sea to inspire me. I need what I know best. I have to paint, so I should paint what I know.

F: So really, painting chose you, and not the other way round?

M: I suppose that's true, yes.

Five   You hear part of an interview with a young writer.

M: Now, your new book has been a big success. You must be very pleased – but I imagine you were expecting it, weren't you?

F: Not that it would be as popular as it is, no! I mean, I brought out my first book two years ago and published it online, so it was a fairly cheap e-book that people could download. I couldn't believe how many people bought it and liked it, but with my new book – being published in the traditional way and being sold in bookshops – I really had no idea whether people would be willing to pay a much higher cover price. But it seems that they are!

Six   You hear an athlete talking about his training methods.
Well, it's not easy. If I'm getting ready for a competition, I'll step up my training. Usually I'm at the gym for three hours a day, and in the evenings I'll go running in the park for an hour or two. Before a big race, that will increase to four or five hours in the gym and a much longer run. I have to be careful not to get

too tired, but I also want to reach my peak just before I have to run against anyone else. The right balance is key. Too much training and I might injure myself or use up too much energy, and I won't recover in time for the race. Too little training, and, well, obviously I won't be fit enough to compete.

Seven You hear two children talking about their recent holidays.

M: We always go to the same place for our holiday … and I hate it. There's no beach and no town. There's nothing to do. My parents just want to relax and stay in the garden. The only thing to do is walk around the hills all day, and I don't like walking and walking. I get really tired.

F: You're lucky you can go walking. We went to the beach and that was it. We didn't do *anything*. For *weeks*. We just sat on the beach and looked at everyone else. When we got hot, we went into the sea.

M: Well, it rained the first three days when we were away, so we didn't even go into the garden. My dad read the paper and my mum watched TV all day.

F: I didn't like the food at our hotel, either. It was disgusting!

M: Oh, my mum does *all* the cooking when we're on holiday. At least she does something. But nothing else ever happens.

Eight You hear a man talking about travelling.

One thing you must remember when you decide to travel to an unfamiliar place is that you might not be able to find the things you need when you get there. What I mean is, you should take everything you need with you. Of course, this can create another problem, and that is taking too many items, but there's nothing worse than arriving in a place and realising that something essential is unavailable. So how do you avoid this? Well, do as much research as you can before you go. Read up on your destination and find out what's available and what isn't, so you know what to take and what to leave behind. And, of course, ask people who've been there before you. They'll be able to give you the best advice.

That is the end of Part One. Now turn to Part Two.

PART TWO

You'll hear a famous person called Gilbert Horne talking about his career in the world of sport. For questions 9 – 18, complete the sentences with a word or short phrase. You now have forty-five seconds to look at Part Two.

M: Hello, everyone! My name is Gilbert Horne. I was asked to come here today to talk to you about my career, which started more than thirty years ago, and some of my achievements as both a player and coach in the sports which I've been involved with.

I'd like to begin at the beginning and tell you about how I got into sport. Like many people, I began to play sport as a child. I played basketball as an eleven-year-old and I learnt all about competitive sport very quickly. I think it's important to start to learn at an early age, and school is obviously the best place. It's interesting that I didn't actually follow a career in my first sport, and I'll tell you why: I stopped growing! And, of course, you need to be very tall – or very, very good – to play basketball at a high level, and although I was quite a good player, I'm afraid I wasn't tall enough to compete with the best. I come from a family of pretty short people and I just didn't have the height. I changed to tennis, where this wasn't a problem. It's a sport for an all-round athlete, and it suited me well. I played tennis to national level, and eventually became the under-eighteen champion.

But then I decided to make a change again, and I had to make a choice. I was also playing football at a high level. If you want to be a successful professional, you have to dedicate yourself to just one sport. You can't divide your skills, your time or your effort. You have to give everything, all you've got, to one career, one sport. I wrote a lot about this in my autobiography.

So, anyway, I gave up tennis and decided to concentrate on football and only football. It wasn't long before I signed up with my first club. I love football and I think it's the – the playing in a group – you know. You play together, you win and lose together. The way you feel when you are part of a team is incredible. I think the most memorable moment for me was when we nearly won the Cup in my first year. We lost the final, but it drew us together as a team. The most vital thing for me when playing football is team spirit. Without it there's no hope of success, or enjoyment.

And I did have several near-misses with that club. We lost three finals altogether. But then I was transferred to my main club, Melchester, where I was very successful. I was lucky to play for such a good team. We won the Cup and we finished in my very first season as number one club, at the top of the league, champions! I already knew the team's style – the Melchester Way, as they called it – so I adapted very quickly to playing in that team. I fitted in right away. The Melchester Way, that famous Melchester style of football, established by Dave Grobbs, my manager at the time, really suited me.

And I've been at Melchester ever since. After playing for them for twelve years, I was asked if I wanted to stay on after my retirement, and of course I accepted. But before I could work in management, I had to get my qualifications in order. That took a couple of years. Then my predecessor, Dave Grobbs, made me assistant manager to start with, and when he moved on, I was asked if I would take the higher position, and I did. I took to management very quickly. That's probably because I learnt from the master. Dave Grobbs knew everything there was to know about the game, and he gave me a thorough education.

I've had many years of success, and I'm obviously very happy with my record, and I've always worked hard, whatever I've done. I'm extremely grateful to the people around me, players and managers, and all the non-playing staff. It's such an honour to represent this club and everything in it. I'm proud to be associated with them all.

Now you'll hear Part Two again.

That is the end of Part Two. Now turn to Part Three.

PART THREE

You'll hear five people talking about different types of transport. For questions 19 – 23, choose from the list (A – H) what each speaker talks about. Use the letters only once. There are three extra letters which you do not need to use. You now have thirty seconds to look at Part Three.

Speaker 1

There's nothing quite like moving with the wind in your face, the open road in front of you and the liberty to go wherever your journey takes you. The noise of the engine and the spinning wheels, it's just a great feeling. I work in an office, so it's great to get outside. It's like being released from prison! OK, sometimes the weather can make it difficult, especially if it's freezing cold or if it rains. It's no fun getting soaking wet, and it's really horrible in the snow and ice. And yes, some people say it's dangerous because cars can't see you so well, or because if you fall off you'll probably get hurt, even if you're wearing a helmet. There are disadvantages to everything, but there are so many advantages to riding that you shouldn't be put off. As long as you pay attention to the traffic around you, you'll be fine.

Speaker 2

There's never enough room, even for people as small as me, because the seats are so close together on these budget flights.

OK, the ticket costs a bit less, but then you have to pay for your luggage, and then they want you to pay to get on board first, then you don't get any free food like my dad says you used to get, and he gets angry because it costs so much to buy during the journey compared to the airport. I know it's much quicker than the coach or the train, and it's the only way to travel a really long distance, but it gets really boring just sitting there in your little seat with all that noise from the engines. I just think about where I'm going and try to sleep a bit.

Speaker 3

I take the number twenty-one every morning to go to college, and the same one brings me home in the afternoon. I often end up waiting ten minutes or more if there's a delay somewhere on the route, which is a nuisance, especially in bad weather. It's usually pretty full so I often don't find a seat, and sometimes when I do, an old lady or a woman with a young child will get on, and I get up and give them my seat. Then I have to stand the whole way, holding my bag, but you have to be polite, don't you? The drivers often go quite fast, especially round the corners, so if I'm standing up, I have to hold on to something to stop myself falling over. I'm taking driving lessons, so hopefully in six months' time I'll be speeding to college in my new motor, but until then I'll just have to grin and bear it.

Speaker 4

It's not the quickest way to travel, especially long distances, but in the summer, it's the best way of going from one island to another. It's so relaxing, sitting on the top deck in the sun and just enjoying the ride. When we go on holiday, we spend longer travelling than we do in a hotel! You can pay for a cabin if you want to travel in comfort, or even take a cruise for a week or two and make a holiday out of it. You don't have to step on dry land at all if you don't want to; everything you want is on board. That's my favourite part of the whole trip. Some people, though, don't like being on the water and get sea-sick, but not me. Life on the waves! What could be better?

Speaker 5

I didn't use to be a very confident traveler when I went everywhere by road, because I was always afraid of getting lost. But now … it's like … once you set off down the tracks, if you're on the right line, well, you can relax. It won't suddenly take a wrong turn and take you somewhere you weren't expecting to go. So you sit back in comfort, stretch out your legs, and watch the world go by. Occasionally, there can be a delay, if the signal is broken or something, but the weather won't stop you. Most of the time, you depart and arrive exactly on time, exactly according to the timetable.

Now you'll hear Part Three again.

That's the end of Part Three. Now turn to Part Four.

PART FOUR

You'll hear a radio interview with an animal expert called Daisy Neame. For questions 24 – 30, choose the best answer (A, B or C). You now have one minute to look at Part Four.

G: Hello, and welcome. This week on *Animal Lovers* we've got a very special guest indeed. Animal expert, Daisy Neame, has spent most of her life involved with various creatures one way or another, and she's here to tell us all about it. Isn't that right, Daisy?

D: Yes, that's right, George.

G: So, when did your experiences with animals really begin?

D: Well, I suppose like a lot of other people, I loved animals as a child. I used to spend hours in the garden, watching the birds or looking for insects. I'd take the neighbour's dog for a walk, and I loved playing with my friends' pets. Sadly, though, my parents didn't share my interest in animals, and I wasn't allowed to have one of my own. My mother used to say, 'No animals in my house!' My dad used to say 'Over my dead body!' He was joking, of course, but it wasn't funny to me – I couldn't even keep a rabbit in the garden.

G: So how did your interest survive?

D: I just became more and more determined. If I wasn't allowed to bring animals into the house, I decided I would go out to them! I got a Saturday job in the local pet shop. I helped clean the cages, feed the animals, and when the owner, Mr MacDonald, wasn't there, I used to pick up the animals and play with them. Apart from the fish, of course! I suppose this is when my relationship with animals of all kinds was established properly. I think that was when I decided to make animals my life.

G: How did that decision affect you at the time? I mean, how did you develop your relationship with the animal world?

D: At school, I chose related subjects, like biology and environmental studies, but they weren't really exactly what I wanted to study. There wasn't much choice at school, really, if you just want to study animals, zoology that is. You have to do maths and languages and things like that, so I had to do a lot of searching to find books on animals to read. I read all the books on animals and nature I could find in the local library. I subscribed to different magazines and watched every nature programme on TV.

G: But that all changed at university, surely?

D: Yes, of course; at university, the range of subjects is quite different and much wider. I spent a lot of time thinking about what I wanted to study, which course I wanted to apply for. I talked it over with my parents, and I actually had a hard time coming to a decision, but together we made the right choice.

G: What did you finally decide to study? Zoology?

D: Actually, by the time I was applying to university, my interest had taken a new direction. I'd become interested in helping animals, not just studying them. In the pet shop, some of my most vivid memories are of sick animals and how Mr MacDonald would call the vet and he would come and treat them and make them better. So I decided I wanted to be a vet, and I took a course in veterinary medicine. This is just like training to be a doctor for people; you learn all the same things, but about animals instead.

G: What did you do after you graduated?

D: Well, once I'd qualified as a vet, I took a position in a large nature reserve in Africa, a place which is protected by law, where animals can live in their natural habitat without any danger from humans. I lived there for two years and gained a lot of experience from my stay. I saw animals I'd never seen before, and I had to deal with some things I hadn't been taught at university. Luckily, there were other people already there who knew much more than me, who could show me what to do.

G: So what have you been doing since then?

D: I've been very lucky. You remember the shopkeeper I worked for, Mr MacDonald? Well, he called me and asked me to join the staff of a new zoo he was opening. It was so unexpected! He said he was expanding his business, and he had found a great place to establish a small zoo, not with lions and tigers, but, you know, more ordinary animals, like cows and sheep. It's called Old MacDonald's Farm Zoo, and we opened six months ago. We try to educate children about animals in a really practical way. I'm the Farm Zoo vet, and I'm loving it!

G: Well, we wish you the best of luck with that! Thank you for coming in, Daisy.

D: It was my pleasure, George.

Now you'll hear Part Four again.

That's the end of Part Four. That's the end of the test. Please stop now.

Practice Test 8

This is the First Certificate in English for Schools Listening Test. Practice Test 8.
I'm going to give you instructions for this test. At the start of each piece you'll hear this sound.
You'll hear each piece twice. Now look at Part One.

PART ONE

You'll hear people talking in eight different situations. For questions 1 – 8, choose the best answer (A, B or C).

One **You hear two friends talking about a match they've just watched.**

M: Wow! That was quite a match! The goalkeeper was fantastic!

F: Yes, but I think the referee needs to get his eyes checked. Some of his decisions were a bit off, don't you think?

M: Well, I thought Ferango's red card was a bit silly, but, to be fair, he did push Odega.

F: It was a football match. You should expect a bit of pushing – it's all part of the game, isn't it?

M: I suppose. But what about that deciding goal? That came out of nowhere! 6–5 for us; I still can't believe it!

F: Me neither. Like I said, the refereeing was terrible; that last goal should never have counted!

Two **You hear an announcement on a local radio station.**

Listen up, shopaholics … I've got news for you! It's time for shopping therapy because *Tiffany's* is coming to the high street! You heard me … *the* shop with *the* designer labels is coming! It all gets started on Friday at noon when *Tiffany's* opens with a bang! Pop diva, Dyna Myte, will be on hand to present her latest line in evening wear. Then bright and early the next day, you're invited for coffee and croissants in *Tiffany's Café*. And what's the best thing about that? There's no charge! In the afternoon … sales, sales, sales; everything from jeans to jackets – all at rock bottom prices!

Three **You hear a youth club leader talking to some teens about an excursion.**

Hey, everyone. Quieten down! Can I have your attention for a moment? Cheers. Now, as you all know, the club is having its yearly excursion to Lake Wilmot again next month and anyone who wants to go has to sign up by this Saturday. Don't look so surprised, you lot; the sign-up sheet's been up on the notice board for weeks! Now, I know I've already told you, but for those of you with really short memories, or short attention spans, you must have a signed permission note from one of your parents, or you are *not* getting on the bus. Got it? Great!

Four **You hear a girl talking about a book she's just read.**

I'm not what you'd call a bookworm. Reading takes up too much time. And some authors write these huge big novels and they don't really have anything to say. Or if they do, they could do it in a lot fewer words! You read and read and when you get to the last page you think, 'Well, that was a waste of time!' I've just read *Pulse* for my literature course. It's about disappointments in life. That writer can *write*! It was good … and short! I guess my only complaint is that I felt the book was somehow 'unfinished'. The last bit kind of left me hanging. I still can't figure out what happened to the main character.

Five **You overhear a girl talking on her mobile phone.**

Hey, Liddy, it's Joanna. You're going to have a fit, but I've got to tell you something: I'm really sorry but I can't drive us to the dance tonight. It's not my fault! My car's at the local garage … it broke down! You know how Dad's always going on and on about how I don't check the water level in the radiator often enough? Well, he was right. It was actually good sound advice, and now the car radiator has cracked. But I do have an idea! We could get a lift with Ollie. I'm sure he won't mind. What do you think? Should I give him a call? Let me know. Bye.

Six **You hear two friends talking about a concert they have just been to.**

F: That was fantastic! *Billy and the Liars* rocked! Absolutely amazing!

M: Calm down … they weren't all that great. And I think Billy had a head cold or something; his voice was kind of … off. Can you believe we paid £40 each to get in there?

F: Hmm, the concert did cost us an arm and a leg, didn't it? But our seats? Right up there by the stage!

M: Seats, what seats? I never got to sit down once. And I had a million people in front of me; I couldn't see a thing!

F: Stop exaggerating! The arena wasn't even half full. It could easily have held another thousand people!

Seven **You hear a boy leaving a voicemail message.**

Hey, Pete. Kyle here. Excited about your party tonight? I am; I can't wait! My sister says thanks for the invitation, but she won't be able to make it. She has to help her friend, Janine, with a history project or something. Anyway, the good thing is that she said she'd drive me to your place before she goes to Janine's. That'll be around eight. As your party doesn't start till ten, I can give you a hand setting up the sound system. If you need me to pick up anything on my way, just ask! See you!

Eight **You hear part of an interview with a young actress.**

M: The film's a box-office sensation! Jessica, you must be over the moon!

F: Yes! All our hard work really paid off. We travelled to five locations, and it was exhausting! But everything was fantastic; the sets, the costumes, even the make-up. Oh, the make-up! I didn't mind once it was on, but it took three hours to apply every morning! You know, the whole time I was playing the lead role of Princess Angeline, I thought about my dad, and the princesses in the fairy tales he used to tell me as a kid. Who'd have ever thought back then that one day I'd be a famous actress!

That is the end of Part One. Now turn to Part Two.

PART TWO

You'll hear a teenager named Jules talking about a charity called the Good Shepherd Centre. For questions 9 – 18, complete the sentences with a word or short phrase. You now have forty-five seconds to look at Part Two.

F: Hello, everyone. I'm Jules and I'd like to talk to you about an excellent local charity called the Good Shepherd Centre, which is located on Elm Street. There's so much I could tell you about the centre, but in a nutshell, it's a charity that helps young people, especially homeless young people who've lost their way for one reason or another. The charity's been around since 1969, and I read somewhere they've helped more than 72,000 young people over the years. Homeless people can end up on the streets for lots of reasons. And, you know, they aren't just those people you see sleeping on the streets or curled up in doorways. Homeless people are those who haven't got a permanent roof over their head; people who've made a temporary home in a hostel or in bed and breakfast accommodation. There are also people who spend a couple of nights on the sofa at one person's house and then move on and spend a few more nights at someone else's place. They're called <u>sofa surfers</u>. Imagine that! Sounds awful, doesn't it? And that's where the Good Shepherd Centre comes in. It tries to give young people a place to live. But homelessness affects more than <u>80,000</u> young people in the UK every year, so you can imagine what a challenge the Centre is facing. They've got different kinds of facilities for different kinds of young people.

Let me explain. The Centre has got night shelters where kids can get a bed for up to two nights, hostels for short stays, and then they've got <u>flats</u> for young people who need more permanent accommodation. Even that sounds pretty impressive, but that's not all they do! They also help young people with any health needs they might have. As you can imagine, sleeping rough can take its toll on someone's <u>mental and physical</u> health. The Centre has a programme where a health team teaches them about fitness, diet and exercise.

They also help homeless kids who don't go to school because, sadly, a lot of them are too busy trying to survive to get any kind of education. A lot of them have no qualifications at all. One of the Centre's goals is to help kids get the necessary skills to compete in the <u>job market</u>. Vocational training is a good way to do that.

The Centre does some really good work and I do volunteer work for them. If they didn't have volunteers and donations, they wouldn't be able to keep the charity up and running. This week, I'm working in the Elm Street garden. It's an amazing project! Last April, a group of volunteers got together and planted this big garden to grow <u>vegetables</u> and herbs. The produce from the garden is used in the centre's kitchen, where meals are prepared for the homeless teenagers.

Everybody can do something, and I've got a great idea to get you all started! On Thursday, 11th December, the centre is having what they call a *Night Out* to raise money. On that night, 650 people will find out exactly what it's like trying to sleep outside when all you've got is a <u>cardboard box</u> to keep you warm. To take part, there are a few things you have to do. First, you have to promise to raise at least <u>£350</u> through getting people to sponsor you – that's the amount if you register as an individual. If you register as part of a group of four, you only have to raise £250. Actually, if any of you are interested, you can join my group – we need another person. All you need to do is go online to the charity's website and <u>complete the form</u>. You don't have to call or write to anyone to get involved. That's how easy it is, so why not do your part?

Now you'll hear Part Two again.

That is the end of Part Two. Now turn to Part Three.

PART THREE

You'll hear five people talking about their eating habits. For questions 19 – 23, choose from the list (A – H) what each speaker says about their eating habits. Use the letters only once. There are three extra letters which you do not need to use. You now have thirty seconds to look at Part Three.

Speaker 1

My mother's one of those people that insists that the family sit down at least once a day and have a healthy home-cooked meal together. For me, that can be pretty tricky! I mean, what with being in the swimming team, in the drama club and on the school newspaper, I'm always on the move.

My mum's always advising me that I should eat better. It's not like I snack, I don't; <u>but on Tuesdays and Thursdays I can't eat lunch because of swimming practice, and on Wednesdays and Fridays I eat dinner late because of my acting and editing activities.</u> I always have a huge breakfast though … well … almost always!

Speaker 2

I used to be terrible for skipping meals; I was a travelling salesman, so you can imagine the kind of eating habits I had – I practically lived on packets of crisps and other healthy stuff like that! I recently retired and now <u>I go along with what my parents' and grandparents' generations used to say: 'In the morning, eat like a king; in the evening, eat like a poor man.'</u> Very wise words, don't you think? It makes total sense. Most of my friends have their main meal in the evening, say, around eight. But then they're in bed by half past ten or so. That doesn't allow time for digestion – it can't be good for them.

Speaker 3

I've never been a meat-eater. My mum says she gave up trying to get me to eat burgers and things like that when I was about five! I can't see that being a vegetarian has ever done me any harm. For lunch and dinner, mum usually makes me a nice veggie soup or stew, and then I snack on things like carrots, broccoli or fruit if I get peckish during the day. I used to absolutely adore peanuts … fantastic source of protein. But, unfortunately, a few months ago <u>I developed this horrible allergy to anything that even smells like a peanut! I get really ill!</u> <u>So, no more peanut butter</u> and banana sandwiches <u>for me!</u>

Speaker 4

I grew up on a farm; Dad raised pigs and cows. We were a family that ate bacon, ham and beef regularly! I never thought anything of it. I guess I never thought too much about the fact that the animals in the barn and the meat on my plate were one and the same thing! Then one day, I came home from school early. Dad had just butchered a pig – it was hanging in the barn. <u>I'm telling you, the look of it nearly made me sick. That's when it really hit me – where meat comes from. So now I'm a strict vegetarian</u>, but I don't criticise others for their eating habits. To each their own and, as they say, 'One man's meat is another man's poison.'

Speaker 5

<u>I'm what you might call a 'grazer'.</u> Yes, I have breakfast, lunch and dinner every day, but it's usually something very light like soup or a sandwich. I ate three square meals a day when the children were home, but now it's just me and, to tell the truth, I can't be bothered to cook a big meal. So, because I eat so little 'real food', <u>I tend to nibble all the time! And it's beginning to show! My doctor advised me to cut down on the snacks,</u> but it isn't easy, you know! Here, have one of these lovely biscuits!

Now you'll hear Part Three again.

That's the end of Part Three. Now turn to Part Four.

PART FOUR

You'll hear a conversation between two friends about a project they are doing on advertising. For questions 24 – 30, choose the best answer (A, B or C). You now have one minute to look at Part Four.

M: You know, Tanya, I'm a bit worried about this project. I mean, I don't know anything about advertising!

F: Don't panic, Joe. I've been working all weekend; <u>I've found loads of stuff. There's lots of information online. I couldn't believe how many sites there were</u> on the topic. Have you done anything … been to the library, talked to anyone who works in the industry, or anything like that? Or, let me guess – you've been too busy playing computer games!

M: Well, I was going to go to the, umm, go to the … so, what have you found?

F: Oh, honestly, Joe! Anyway! What I thought we'd do is focus on how advertising has worked over the years. Like, how have companies marketed their products? How have they got their products to sell? Back in the 50s, for example, there was lots of research being done on something called 'subliminal advertising'. That's advertising that works on a subconscious level. You see something, you want to buy it, but you're unaware of what it was that set off the desire for that specific product.

M: I'm afraid I'm not following you, Tanya. Give me an example.

F: OK – this is really cool! Back in 1957, there was this guy called James Vicary who was testing various marketing techniques and how effective they were. So, he goes into a cinema in Fort Lee, New Jersey with a tachistoscope – that's a device that can flash images onto a screen really quickly – and he flashes the messages 'Drink Coca-Cola' and 'Hungry? Eat popcorn' onto the film screen every five seconds while a bunch of cinema-goers are watching the film *Picnic*.

M: Didn't all those flashing messages bother the people watching the film?

F: No! Because they were subliminal messages! The messages were flashed so fast and were on the screen for so short a time – something like 1/3000th of a second – that no one watching the film saw them. Well, they saw them, but they didn't know they were seeing them! And this is the really brilliant part – Vicary claimed that during the film, soft drink sales went up by over 18% and popcorn sales jumped by a huge 57.8%!

M: What? That's kind of scary! I mean, it's kind of like brainwashing, or … hypnotism!

F: Well, yes, it would've been, except Vicary was lying! See, Vicary had planned to use those numbers to persuade big companies to give him money to increase sales of their products. But when Henry Link, the president of the Psychological Corporation, asked Vicary to do the test again, with expert witnesses this time, nobody in the cinema was jumping up and running to the canteen every five minutes to get a soft drink or some popcorn. Vicary had faked the results of his first experiment! Some people now say that he didn't even conduct the first experiment, and that he simply pulled the statistics out of his hat!

M: No! What a crook! Anyway, I never believed for a minute that …

F: Sure, Joe, whatever you say. But the crazy thing is that despite the fact that Vicary actually confessed the whole thing was a scam, a trick, to make money, the media didn't cover it! They just wrote story after story about how we, the consumers, were being made to buy products against our will. It got so bad that in 1958 and 1959, after people discovered that radio and TV stations were using subliminal advertisements, two bills were introduced in the American Congress to ban this kind of marketing! They never actually became laws, but it just goes to show how concerned people were.

M: But it had been proved that subliminal advertisements were not effective!

F: I know! But listen to this. In 1973, a man named Dr Wilson Key wrote a book that stirred up the whole mess yet again. In his book, he made this claim that subliminal adverts weren't only being used in films, and on radio and TV; he insisted they were being placed in newspaper and magazine advert photos too! For example, let's say in the magazine photo you had a glass of lemonade with ice in it. Key claimed that words were written on the ice cubes and that even though you weren't aware they were there, they caused you to immediately rush out and buy everything in sight! I mean, really? How silly!

M: Wow! This is really interesting stuff! In the end this was a great choice of topic for our …

Now you'll hear Part Four again.

That's the end of Part Four. That's the end of the test. Please stop now.